Learn to driv

Just a few fantastic reasons why…

– Train in an air-conditioned Vauxhall Corsa or Astra

– Get free Theory and Hazard Perception training

– Get access to the latest training technology, including the Mind Alertness Programme (MAP)

– Monitor your training progress with 'Track Record'

– Take a Mock Test with another instructor

For the best start, book today!

Simply call
08457 276 276
www.bsm.co.uk

British School of Motoring Limited (Company No. 291902). 8 Surrey Street, Norwich, Norfolk NR1 3NG. Calls may be monitored and recorded.

BSM
part of RaC

Theory Test Questions
for Car Drivers and Motorcyclists

All the questions and answers valid
for tests taken from 4 September 2006

Published by BSM
in association with
Virgin Books

First published in the UK in 2006 by
The British School of Motoring Ltd
8 Surrey Street
Norwich
Norfolk
NR1 3NG

First edition 2006

ISBN–13: 978-0-7535-1109-1
ISBN–10: 0-7535-1109-6

Design, typesetting and reprographics by Thalamus Publishing

Printed in Italy

Every effort has been made to ensure that the information contained in this publication
is accurate at the time of printing. BSM cannot be held responsible for any inaccuracies
or omissions.

Contents

About the Theory Test

All learner drivers and riders need to pass a Theory Test and Practical Test before they can obtain a full licence. The Theory Test comprises two separate elements:

❑ Multiple-Choice Questions
❑ Hazard Perception

You need to take the Test at a DSA (Driving Standards Agency) Test Centre. Each element of the Test has a separate pass mark (see below) and you need to pass both elements at the same sitting in order to pass the overall Theory Test.

About this book

This book contains all the official DSA questions from which those used in the Multiple-Choice element of the Test are taken – as well as the answers. The complete sets of questions for both learner drivers and riders are included.

Preparing for the Theory Test

Although you take the Theory Test separately from the Practical Test, it is important that you understand how the theory which you study relates to your practical driving skills. Simply learning the answers to questions without understanding the meaning will not improve your skills and is not the best way to pass your Theory Test. BSM recommend that you do not take the Theory Test until you have also undertaken some practical training. This makes it easier to relate your theoretical knowledge to your practical skills.

The best way to study

❑ The official source material for the Theory Test is in BSM's Highway Code and the DSA's Driving – the essential skills book.

Reading BSM's Pass Your Driving Theory Test book (the companion publication to this one) will also help you gain your basic knowledge. This publication is available through the online BSM store, which can be found at www.bsm.co.uk.

❑ Discuss what you have learned with your instructor and ask him or her to clarify any areas which you don't understand. As your driving lessons progress, try to relate your theoretical knowledge to real-life situations and understand why this knowledge is important. During your driving lessons, you will also tune your hazard awareness skills, which will be essential for the Hazard Perception element of the Theory Test.

❑ Test your knowledge by using this book or an interactive study solution, such as BSM's Theory Interactive CD-ROM. This computer-based learning aid is also particularly useful for practising your hazard perception skills and understanding how the Hazard Perception test is delivered and scored.

On the day

Get to the Test Centre in good time and ensure that you have all essential documentation with you. At the time of writing, this means:

❑ Your test appointment letter

❑ Your signed photo card licence and paper counterpart
or
❑ Your signed driving licence and other form of photo identification.

Because regulations change periodically, you should check what documentation you need to take to your Theory Test appointment by asking your instructor or the DSA.

Once you have registered with the Test Centre staff, you will be directed to the PC where you can take your Test.

Part one – Multiple-Choice Questions

You will be asked 35 multiple-choice questions. You need to provide the correct answers to at least 30 in order to pass this first element of the Theory Test. The questions appear on the computer screen and you select your answers by simply touching the screen. This touch-screen system has been carefully designed to make it easy to use. You are allowed up to 40 minutes to complete this element of the Test.

For advice about how to approach multiple-choice questions, please see page 8.

Part two – Hazard Perception

Once you have finished part one, you can have a break of up to three minutes before the second element, Hazard Perception. In this part of the Test, you are shown 14 video clips of real road situations and you are expected to quickly identify developing hazards. This part of the Test lasts about 20 minutes.

In order to pass the Hazard Perception element, you currently need to score 44 out of 75. Remember that you need to pass Hazard Perception at the same sitting as the multiple-choice element of the Test, otherwise you need to take the whole Test again.

For advice about how to approach the Hazard Perception element of the Test, please see page 9.

Once you have completed the Test, your results will be available from the Centre staff within a few minutes.

Answering multiple-choice questions

Most of the questions in the Test require you to select the one correct answer from four possible options. Some questions may ask for two or more correct answers and this is stated clearly next to the question.

When you are reading multiple-choice questions, try to avoid 'recognising' the question or the answer, because this often stops you from reading the whole question thoroughly. You should read the question carefully all the way through, together with each response.

Usually, there will be at least one response that is obviously not correct and so you can narrow the answers down. If you have no idea what the correct answer is, you should at least have a guess.

The following four examples illustrate the way in which you should look at each question and the possible answers. Some of these examples may seem like obvious points to make, but many people have got questions wrong by making basic mistakes such as these.

Example one

Which FOUR of these MUST be in good working order for your car to be roadworthy?
- ❑ a Speedometer
- ❑ b Oil warning light
- ❑ c Windscreen washers
- ❑ d Temperature gauge
- ❑ e Horn
- ❑ f Windscreen wipers

Here you are being asked to identify legal requirements which MUST be adhered to. Therefore MUST is the key word. In addition to this, you should notice that you are being asked for FOUR correct responses, and if you marked only one, you would not score a point for this question.

Example two

When should you NOT use your horn in a built-up area?
- ❑ a Between 8pm and 8am
- ❑ b Between 11.30pm and 7am
- ❑ c Between 9pm and dawn
- ❑ d Between dusk and 8pm

The key word here is NOT. If you missed it, you would be looking for the wrong answer.

Example three

You are driving on an icy road. How can you avoid wheel spin?
- ❑ a Drive at a slow speed in as high a gear as possible
- ❑ b Use the handbrake if the wheels start to slip
- ❑ c Brake gently and repeatedly
- ❑ d Drive in a low gear at all times

In this question, the key word is ICY. Noting the road condition affects your choice of answer.

Example four

Where may you overtake on a one-way street?
- ❑ a Only on the left-hand side
- ❑ b Overtaking is not allowed
- ❑ c Only on the right-hand side
- ❑ d Either on the right or the left

If you fail to note that the question is asking you about one-way streets, you may well choose 'c' as the correct answer, whereas it is actually 'd'.

Remember, when you actually sit the Theory Test you will have plenty of time to read the questions thoroughly. Make sure you understand what is being asked. Don't rush or panic; instead think carefully about each suggested answer. Invariably, if you have put the time and effort into studying, the correct answer or answers should be more than apparent.

Hazard Perception

Whereas the multiple-choice element of the Test assesses your knowledge and understanding, the Hazard Perception element tests your awareness and skills. Therefore, you need to prepare for this part of the Test in a different way.

You will see 14 video clips in total, each lasting about one minute. The clips show various types of hazards, such as vehicles, pedestrians and road conditions. Each developing hazard may require the driver/rider to take some form of action, such as changing speed or direction. You need to respond by pressing a mouse button as soon as you decide, from the clues in the clip, that this might happen. The earlier you do this for each developing hazard, the higher you score. Candidates can score up to five marks on each hazard and the Test contains 15 hazards. In order to pass this part of the Test, you need to score 44 out of 75.

BSM has several computer-based training aids which have been specially designed to help with your preparation for the Hazard Perception test; for details of these, visit www.bsm.co.uk or call us on 08457 276 276.

After the Theory Test

If you pass, ensure that you keep your Theory Test pass certificate safely – you will need it when you take your Practical Test. Once you have passed the Theory Test, you can apply to take the Practical Test as soon as you and your instructor agree that you are ready.

If you fail, don't worry. You can take the Test again after three days, but make sure you are properly prepared.

The important point about the Theory Test is that it is not an irrelevant exam. All parts of the Test are interconnected with the practical elements of your driver training and all contribute to making you a better, safer driver. Proper study and understanding of the subjects covered by both parts of the Theory Test will also be a great help in securing a pass on the Practical Test.

How to use this book

This book allows you to check your level of knowledge by presenting you with all the real examination questions. The questions are set out under topic headings, and as you work through each section you will prove to yourself that you not only understand what you have learnt, but can demonstrate this by answering the question correctly. In doing so, you will gradually boost your confidence and thereby recognise when you are ready to take and pass the Theory Test.

The book has been carefully laid out to allow both study and revision.

There are 14 sections, each containing the questions from one subject area of the Theory Test. Within each section, the first block of questions are those which are common to the Test both for learner drivers and riders. These

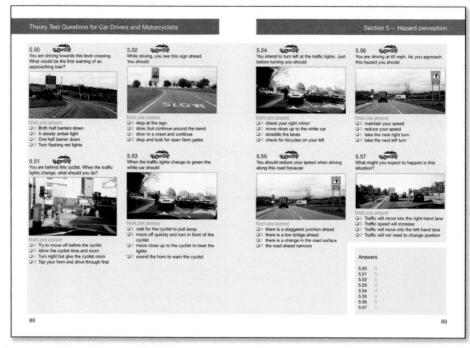

are indicated by both a car and motorbike symbol at the head of the question.

The second block of questions within each section covers those questions specific to drivers. These are indicated by a blue-coloured background and a car symbol at the head of the question.

The final block of questions within each section covers those questions specific to motorcyclists. These are indicated by a grey-coloured background and a bike symbol at the head of each question.

The answers to all the questions on a double page are given in a box at the bottom right of that double page. We have also included an explanation where we believe extra information about a particular answer is helpful. When you are testing your knowledge, you may find it useful to cover up this answer box.

And finally

Everyone at BSM wishes you good luck with your Theory Test. If you have any questions, or would like to find out why BSM offer the Best Start in Motoring, please give us a call on 08457 276 276 (calls may be recorded and monitored).

Theory Test Questions
for Car Drivers and Motorcyclists

Section 1 Alertness

1.1

Before you make a U-turn in the road, you should

Mark one answer

- ❑ a give an arm signal as well as using your indicators
- ❑ b signal so that other drivers can slow down for you
- ❑ c look over your shoulder for a final check
- ❑ d select a higher gear than normal

1.2

As you approach this bridge you should

Mark three answers

- ❑ a move into the middle of the road to get a better view
- ❑ b slow down
- ❑ c get over the bridge as quickly as possible
- ❑ d consider using your horn
- ❑ e find another route
- ❑ f beware of pedestrians

1.3

In which of these situations should you avoid overtaking?

Mark one answer

- ❑ a Just after a bend
- ❑ b In a one-way street
- ❑ c On a 30 mph road
- ❑ d Approaching a dip in the road

1.4

This road marking warns

Mark one answer

- ❑ a drivers to use the hard shoulder
- ❑ b overtaking drivers there is a bend to the left
- ❑ c overtaking drivers to move back to the left
- ❑ d drivers that it is safe to overtake

1.5

Your mobile phone rings while you are travelling. You should

Mark one answer

- ❑ a stop immediately
- ❑ b answer it immediately
- ❑ c pull up in a suitable place
- ❑ d pull up at the nearest kerb

1.6

Why are these yellow lines painted across the road?

Mark one answer

- ❑ a To help you choose the correct lane
- ❑ b To help you keep the correct separation distance
- ❑ c To make you aware of your speed
- ❑ d To tell you the distance to the roundabout

1.7

You are approaching traffic lights that have been on green for some time. You should

Mark one answer

- ☐ a accelerate hard
- ☐ b maintain your speed
- ☐ c be ready to stop
- ☐ d brake hard

1.8

When following a large vehicle you should keep well back because this

Mark one answer

- ☐ a allows you to corner more quickly
- ☐ b helps the large vehicle to stop more easily
- ☐ c allows the driver to see you in the mirrors
- ☐ d helps you to keep out of the wind

1.9

Which of the following should you do before stopping?

Mark one answer

- ☐ a Sound the horn
- ☐ b Use the mirrors
- ☐ c Select a higher gear
- ☐ d Flash your headlights

1.10

When you see a hazard ahead you should use the mirrors. Why is this?

Mark one answer

- ☐ a Because you will need to accelerate out of danger
- ☐ b To assess how your actions will affect following traffic
- ☐ c Because you will need to brake sharply to a stop
- ☐ d To check what is happening on the road ahead

1.11

You are waiting to turn right at the end of a road. Your view is obstructed by parked vehicles. What should you do?

Mark one answer

- ☐ a Stop and then move forward slowly and carefully for a proper view
- ☐ b Move quickly to where you can see so you only block traffic from one direction
- ☐ c Wait for a pedestrian to let you know when it is safe for you to emerge
- ☐ d Turn your vehicle around immediately and find another junction to use

Answers

1.1   c You should always check your blind spot just before moving off or starting a manoeuvre.

1.2   b, d, f

1.3   d

1.4   c

1.5   c Answering a hands-free mobile phone while driving might distract your attention. You should pull up first.

1.6   c

1.7   c Be ready to stop because the traffic lights may change colour before you pass them.

1.8   c

1.9   b

1.10   b

1.11   a Use clutch control to edge the car forwards. Keeping your speed right down will prevent you from being involved in a collision with any traffic you cannot see.

1.12

Objects hanging from your interior mirror may
Mark two answers

- ❏ a restrict your view
- ❏ b improve your driving
- ❏ c distract your attention
- ❏ d help your concentration

1.13

Which of the following may cause loss of concentration on a long journey?
Mark four answers

- ❏ a Loud music
- ❏ b Arguing with a passenger
- ❏ c Using a mobile phone
- ❏ d Putting in a cassette tape
- ❏ e Stopping regularly to rest
- ❏ f Pulling up to tune the radio

1.14

On a long motorway journey boredom can cause you to feel sleepy. You should
Mark two answers

- ❏ a leave the motorway and find a safe place to stop
- ❏ b keep looking around at the surrounding landscape
- ❏ c drive faster to complete your journey sooner
- ❏ d ensure a supply of fresh air into your vehicle
- ❏ e stop on the hard shoulder for a rest

1.15

You are driving at dusk. You should switch your lights on
Mark two answers

- ❏ a even when street lights are not lit
- ❏ b so others can see you
- ❏ c only when others have done so
- ❏ d only when street lights are lit

1.16

You are most likely to lose concentration when driving if you
Mark two answers

- ❏ a use a mobile phone
- ❏ b listen to very loud music
- ❏ c switch on the heated rear window
- ❏ d look at the door mirrors

1.17

Which FOUR are most likely to cause you to lose concentration while you are driving?
Mark four answers

- ❏ a Using a mobile phone
- ❏ b Talking into a microphone
- ❏ c Tuning your car radio
- ❏ d Looking at a map
- ❏ e Checking the mirrors
- ❏ f Using the demisters

1.18

You should ONLY use a mobile phone when
Mark one answer

- ❏ a receiving a call
- ❏ b suitably parked
- ❏ c driving at less than 30 mph
- ❏ d driving an automatic vehicle

1.19

Using a mobile phone while you are driving
Mark one answer

- ❏ a is acceptable in a vehicle with power steering
- ❏ b will reduce your field of vision
- ❏ c could distract your attention from the road
- ❏ d will affect your vehicle's electronic systems

1.20

You are driving on a wet road. You have to stop your vehicle in an emergency. You should
Mark one answer
- ❑ a apply the handbrake and footbrake together
- ❑ b keep both hands on the wheel
- ❑ c select reverse gear
- ❑ d give an arm signal

1.21

When you are moving off from behind a parked car you should
Mark three answers
- ❑ a look round before you move off
- ❑ b use all the mirrors on the vehicle
- ❑ c look round after moving off
- ❑ d use the exterior mirrors only
- ❑ e give a signal if necessary
- ❑ f give a signal after moving off

1.22

You are travelling along this narrow country road. When passing the cyclist you should go

Mark one answer
- ❑ a slowly, sounding the horn as you pass
- ❑ b quickly, leaving plenty of room
- ❑ c slowly, leaving plenty of room
- ❑ d quickly, sounding the horn as you pass

1.23

Your vehicle is fitted with a hand-held telephone. To use the telephone you should
Mark one answer
- ❑ a reduce your speed
- ❑ b find a safe place to stop
- ❑ c steer the vehicle with one hand
- ❑ d be particularly careful at junctions

1.24

To answer a call on your mobile phone while travelling you should
Mark one answer
- ❑ a reduce your speed wherever you are
- ❑ b stop in a proper and convenient place
- ❑ c keep the call time to a minimum
- ❑ d slow down and allow others to overtake

Answers

1.12 a, c
1.13 a, b, c, d
1.14 a, d
1.15 a, b
1.16 a, b
1.17 a, b, c, d
1.18 b
1.19 c
1.20 b This helps you maintain control of your car.
1.21 a, b, e
1.22 c
1.23 b You must not use a hand-held telephone while you are driving.
1.24 b If it's a hand-held phone you must pull up before answering. If it's hands-free it is still advisable to stop.

1.25

You lose your way on a busy road. What is the best action to take?

Mark one answer

- ☐ a Stop at traffic lights and ask pedestrians
- ☐ b Shout to other drivers to ask them the way
- ☐ c Turn into a side road, stop and check a map
- ☐ d Check a map, and keep going with the traffic flow

1.26

Windscreen pillars can obstruct your view. You should take particular care when

Mark one answer

- ☐ a driving on a motorway
- ☐ b driving on a dual carriageway
- ☐ c approaching a one-way street
- ☐ d approaching bends and junctions

1.27

You cannot see clearly behind when reversing. What should you do?

Mark one answer

- ☐ a Open your window to look behind
- ☐ b Open the door and look behind
- ☐ c Look in the nearside mirror
- ☐ d Ask someone to guide you

1.28

What does the term 'blind spot' mean for a driver?

Mark one answer

- ☐ a An area covered by your right-hand mirror
- ☐ b An area not covered by your headlights
- ☐ c An area covered by your left-hand mirror
- ☐ d An area not covered by your mirrors

1.29

You should not use a mobile phone while driving

Mark one answer

- ☐ a until you are satisfied that no other traffic is near
- ☐ b unless you are able to drive one-handed
- ☐ c because it might distract your attention from the road ahead
- ☐ d because reception is poor when the engine is running

1.30

Your vehicle is fitted with a hands-free phone system. Using this equipment while driving

Mark one answer

- ☐ a is quite safe as long as you slow down
- ☐ b could distract your attention from the road
- ☐ c is recommended by The Highway Code
- ☐ d could be very good for road safety

1.31

Using a hands-free phone is likely to

Mark one answer

- ☐ a improve your safety
- ☐ b increase your concentration
- ☐ c reduce your view
- ☐ d divert your attention

1.32

What is the safest way to use a mobile phone in your vehicle?

Mark one answer

- ☐ a Use hands-free equipment
- ☐ b Find a suitable place to stop
- ☐ c Drive slowly on a quiet road
- ☐ d Direct your call through the operator

1.33

Your mobile phone rings while you are on the motorway. Before answering you should
Mark one answer
- ❏ a reduce your speed to 30 mph
- ❏ b pull up on the hard shoulder
- ❏ c move into the left-hand lane
- ❏ d stop in a safe place

1.34

You are turning right onto a dual carriageway. What should you do before emerging?
Mark one answer
- ❏ a Stop, apply the handbrake and then select a low gear
- ❏ b Position your vehicle well to the left of the side road
- ❏ c Check that the central reservation is wide enough for your vehicle
- ❏ d Make sure that you leave enough room for a vehicle behind

1.35

You are waiting to emerge from a junction. The windscreen pillar is restricting your view. What should you be particularly aware of?

Mark one answer
- ❏ a Lorries
- ❏ b Buses
- ❏ c Motorcyclists
- ❏ d Coaches

1.36

When emerging from junctions, which is most likely to obstruct your view?
Mark one answer
- ❏ a Windscreen pillars
- ❏ b Steering wheel
- ❏ c Interior mirror
- ❏ d Windscreen wipers

Answers

1.25 c Because the road is busy it would be better to leave the road before stopping to check the map.
1.26 d
1.27 d If you cannot see properly, you need to get someone to help.
1.28 d
1.29 c
1.30 b
1.31 d You are not allowed to use a hand-held mobile phone whilst driving. Even a hands-free system can distract your attention from the road.
1.32 b
1.33 d
1.34 c This is because if there is no traffic coming from the right, but there is traffic coming from the left, you may wait in the central reservation provided that it's wide enough for your vehicle.
1.35 c Because they are small enough to be hidden by the pillar.
1.36 a

1.37

Your vehicle is fitted with a navigation system. How should you avoid letting this distract you while driving?

Mark one answer

- ❏ a Keep going and input your destination into the system
- ❏ b Keep going as the system will adjust to your route
- ❏ c Stop immediately to view and use the system
- ❏ d Stop in a safe place before using the system

1.38

Using a mobile phone when driving is illegal. The chance of you having an accident while using one is

Mark one answer

- ❏ a two times higher
- ❏ b four times higher
- ❏ c six times higher
- ❏ d ten times higher

1.39

You are driving on a motorway and want to use your mobile phone. What should you do?

Mark one answer

- ❏ a Try to find a safe place on the hard shoulder
- ❏ b Leave the motorway and stop in a safe place
- ❏ c Use the next exit and pull up on the slip road
- ❏ d Move to the left lane and reduce your speed

1.40

Using a mobile phone when driving is illegal. Your chances of having an accident increase by

Mark one answer

- ❏ a two times
- ❏ b four times
- ❏ c eight times
- ❏ d twelve times

1.41

Using a mobile phone when driving is illegal. If you do so your chances of having an accident increase by how many times?

Mark one answer

- ❏ a two
- ❏ b four
- ❏ c ten
- ❏ d twenty

1.42

You are about to turn right. What should you do just before you turn?

Mark one answer

- ❏ a Give the correct signal
- ❏ b Take a 'lifesaver' glance over your shoulder
- ❏ c Select the correct gear
- ❏ d Get in position ready for the turn

1.43

What is the 'lifesaver' when riding a motorcycle?

Mark one answer

- ❏ a A certificate every motorcyclist must have
- ❏ b A final, rearward glance before changing direction
- ❏ c A part of the motorcycle tool kit
- ❏ d A mirror fitted to check blind spots

1.44

You see road signs showing a sharp bend ahead. What should you do?

Mark one answer

- ❏ a Continue at the same speed
- ❏ b Slow down as you go around the bend
- ❏ c Slow down as you come out of the bend
- ❏ d Slow down before the bend

1.45

You are riding at night and are dazzled by the headlights of an oncoming car. You should

Mark one answer

- ❏ a slow down or stop
- ❏ b close your eyes
- ❏ c flash your headlight
- ❏ d turn your head away

1.46

When riding, your shoulders obstruct the view in your mirrors. To overcome this you should

Mark one answer

- ❏ a indicate earlier than normal
- ❏ b fit smaller mirrors
- ❏ c extend the mirror arms
- ❏ d brake earlier than normal

1.47

On a motorcycle you should only use a mobile telephone when you

Mark one answer

- ❏ a have a pillion passenger to help
- ❏ b have parked in a safe place
- ❏ c have a motorcycle with automatic gears
- ❏ d are travelling on a quiet road

1.48

You are riding along a motorway. You see an accident on the other side of the road. Your lane is clear. You should

Mark one answer

- ❏ a assist the emergency services
- ❏ b stop, and cross the road to help
- ❏ c concentrate on what is happening ahead
- ❏ d place a warning triangle in the road

Answers

1.37 d
1.38 b The question refers to hand held mobile phone usage while driving. Even hands free phone usage is likely to be distracting and should therefore be avoided while driving.
1.39 b
1.40 b
1.41 b
1.42 b
1.43 b
1.44 d
1.45 a
1.46 c Mirrors should be adjusted to give you the best view of the road behind. If your shoulders or elbows obstruct the view behind, you should fit alternative mirrors with longer stems.
1.47 b
1.48 c

1.49

You are riding at night. You have your headlight on main beam. Another vehicle is overtaking you. When should you dip your headlight?

Mark one answer

- ❏ a When the other vehicle signals to overtake
- ❏ b As soon as the other vehicle moves out to overtake
- ❏ c As soon as the other vehicle passes you
- ❏ d After the other vehicle pulls in front of you

1.50

To move off safely from a parked position you should

Mark one answer

- ❏ a signal if other drivers will need to slow down
- ❏ b leave your motorcycle on its stand until the road is clear
- ❏ c give an arm signal as well as using your indicators
- ❏ d look over your shoulder for a final check

1.51

Riding a motorcycle when you are cold could cause you to

Mark one answer

- ❏ a be more alert
- ❏ b be more relaxed
- ❏ c react more quickly
- ❏ d lose concentration

1.52

You are riding at night and are dazzled by the lights of an approaching vehicle. What should you do?

Mark one answer

- ❏ a Switch off your headlight
- ❏ b Switch to main beam
- ❏ c Slow down and stop
- ❏ d Flash your headlight

1.53

You should always check the 'blind areas' before

Mark one answer

- ❏ a moving off
- ❏ b slowing down
- ❏ c changing gear
- ❏ d giving a signal

1.54

The 'blind area' should be checked before

Mark one answer

- ❏ a giving a signal
- ❏ b applying the brakes
- ❏ c changing direction
- ❏ d giving an arm signal

1.55

It is vital to check the 'blind area' before

Mark one answer

- ❏ a changing gear
- ❏ b giving signals
- ❏ c slowing down
- ❏ d changing lanes

1.56

Why can it be helpful to have mirrors fitted on each side of your motorcycle?

Mark one answer

- ❏ a To judge the gap when filtering in traffic
- ❏ b To give protection when riding in poor weather
- ❏ c To make your motorcycle appear larger to other drivers
- ❏ d To give you the best view of the road behind

1.57

In motorcycling, the term 'lifesaver' refers to

Mark one answer

- ☐ a a final rearward glance
- ☐ b an approved safety helmet
- ☐ c a reflective jacket
- ☐ d the two-second rule

1.58

You are about to emerge from a junction. Your pillion passenger tells you it's clear. When should you rely on their judgement?

Mark one answer

- ☐ a Never, you should always look for yourself
- ☐ b When the roads are very busy
- ☐ c When the roads are very quiet
- ☐ d Only when they are a qualified rider

1.59

You are about to emerge from a junction. Your pillion passenger tells you it's safe to go. What should you do?

Mark one answer

- ☐ a Go, if you are sure they can see clearly
- ☐ b Check for yourself before pulling out
- ☐ c Take their advice and ride on
- ☐ d Ask them to check again before you go

1.60

What must you do before stopping normally?

Mark one answer

- ☐ a Put both feet down
- ☐ b Select first gear
- ☐ c Use your mirrors
- ☐ d Move into neutral

1.61

You want to change lanes in busy, moving traffic. Why could looking over your shoulder help?

Mark two answers

- ☐ a Mirrors may not cover blind spots
- ☐ b To avoid having to give a signal
- ☐ c So traffic ahead will make room for you
- ☐ d So your balance will not be affected
- ☐ e Drivers behind you would be warned

Answers

1.49 c
1.50 d
1.51 d
1.52 c
1.53 a Before moving off you should check over your right shoulder to make sure that no one is there who could not be seen in your mirrors.
1.54 c
1.55 d A motorcyclist or cyclist could be hidden in the blind area and not visible in your mirror. A quick sideways glance before changing lanes ensures that it is safe.
1.56 d
1.57 a
1.58 a A pillion rider will not have the same line of vision as you and should never be relied on to judge a road condition.
1.59 b
1.60 c
1.61 a, e If you have been stationary for some time there is a chance that another vehicle will have positioned themselves in your blind area.

1.62

You have been waiting for some time to make a right turn into a side road. What should you do just before you make the turn?

Mark one answer

❑ a Move close to the kerb
❑ b Select a higher gear
❑ c Make a 'lifesaver' check
❑ d Wave to the oncoming traffic

1.63

You are turning right onto a dual carriageway. What should you do before emerging?

Mark one answer

❑ a Stop, and then select a very low gear
❑ b Position in the left gutter of the side road
❑ c Check that the central reservation is wide enough
❑ d Check there is enough room for vehicles behind you

1.64

When riding a different motorcycle you should

Mark one answer

❑ a ask someone to ride with you for the first time
❑ b ride as soon as possible as all controls and switches are the same
❑ c leave your gloves behind so switches can be operated more easily
❑ d be sure you know where all controls and switches are

Answers

1.62 c
1.63 c A narrow central reservation could mean part of your motorcycle is obstructing the flow of traffic on the major road.
1.64 d

Theory Test Questions
for Car Drivers and Motorcyclists

Section 2 | Attitudes to other road users

2.1

At a pelican crossing the flashing amber light means you MUST

Mark one answer

- ❏ a stop and wait for the green light
- ❏ b stop and wait for the red light
- ❏ c give way to pedestrians waiting to cross
- ❏ d give way to pedestrians already on the crossing

2.2

You should never wave people across at pedestrian crossings because

Mark one answer

- ❏ a there may be another vehicle coming
- ❏ b they may not be looking
- ❏ c it is safer for you to carry on
- ❏ d they may not be ready to cross

2.3

'Tailgating' means

Mark one answer

- ❏ a using the rear door of a hatchback car
- ❏ b reversing into a parking space
- ❏ c following another vehicle too closely
- ❏ d driving with rear fog lights on

2.4

You are following a vehicle on a wet road. You should leave a time gap of at least

Mark one answer

- ❏ a one second
- ❏ b two seconds
- ❏ c three seconds
- ❏ d four seconds

2.5

Following this vehicle too closely is unwise because

Mark one answer

- ❏ a your brakes will overheat
- ❏ b your view ahead is increased
- ❏ c your engine will overheat
- ❏ d your view ahead is reduced

2.6

A long, heavily-laden lorry is taking a long time to overtake you. What should you do?

Mark one answer

- ❏ a Speed up
- ❏ b Slow down
- ❏ c Hold your speed
- ❏ d Change direction

2.7

Which of the following vehicles will use blue flashing beacons?

Mark three answers

- ❏ a Motorway maintenance
- ❏ b Bomb disposal
- ❏ c Blood transfusion
- ❏ d Police patrol
- ❏ e Breakdown recovery

2.8

Which THREE of these emergency services might have blue flashing beacons?
Mark three answers

- ☐ a Coastguard
- ☐ b Bomb disposal
- ☐ c Gritting lorries
- ☐ d Animal ambulances
- ☐ e Mountain rescue
- ☐ f Doctors' cars

2.9

When being followed by an ambulance showing a flashing blue beacon you should
Mark one answer

- ☐ a pull over as soon as safely possible to let it pass
- ☐ b accelerate hard to get away from it
- ☐ c maintain your speed and course
- ☐ d brake harshly and immediately stop in the road

2.10

A vehicle has a flashing green beacon. What does this mean?
Mark one answer

- ☐ a A doctor is answering an emergency call
- ☐ b The vehicle is slow-moving
- ☐ c It is a motorway police patrol vehicle
- ☐ d The vehicle is carrying hazardous chemicals

2.11

What type of emergency vehicle is fitted with a green flashing beacon?
Mark one answer

- ☐ a Fire engine
- ☐ b Road gritter
- ☐ c Ambulance
- ☐ d Doctor's car

2.12

A flashing green beacon on a vehicle means
Mark one answer

- ☐ a police on non-urgent duties
- ☐ b doctor on an emergency call
- ☐ c road safety patrol operating
- ☐ d gritting in progress

Answers

2.1 d
2.2 a
2.3 c
2.4 d In good conditions you should allow two seconds but on a wet road you should double this to four.
2.5 d If you hang back you will have a much better view of the road ahead.
2.6 b By slowing down, you allow the lorry to get past, which is the only safe option.
2.7 b, c, d
2.8 a, b, e
2.9 a
2.10 a
2.11 d Doctors on emergency call may display a flashing green beacon. Slow-moving vehicles have amber flashing beacons. Police, fire and ambulance service vehicles have blue flashing beacons.
2.12 b

25

2.13

Diamond-shaped signs give instructions to

Mark one answer

- ❑ a tram drivers
- ❑ b bus drivers
- ❑ c lorry drivers
- ❑ d taxi drivers

2.14

On a road where trams operate, which of these vehicles will be most at risk from the tram rails?

Mark one answer

- ❑ a Cars
- ❑ b Cycles
- ❑ c Buses
- ❑ d Lorries

2.15

What should you use your horn for?

Mark one answer

- ❑ a To alert others to your presence
- ❑ b To allow you right of way
- ❑ c To greet other road users
- ❑ d To signal your annoyance

2.16

You are in a one-way street and want to turn right. You should position yourself

Mark one answer

- ❑ a in the right-hand lane
- ❑ b in the left-hand lane
- ❑ c in either lane, depending on the traffic
- ❑ d just left of the centre line

2.17

You wish to turn right ahead. Why should you take up the correct position in good time?

Mark one answer

- ❑ a To allow other drivers to pull out in front of you
- ❑ b To give a better view into the road that you're joining
- ❑ c To help other road users know what you intend to do
- ❑ d To allow drivers to pass you on the right

2.18

At which type of crossing are cyclists allowed to ride across with pedestrians?

Mark one answer

- ❑ a Toucan
- ❑ b Puffin
- ❑ c Pelican
- ❑ d Zebra

2.19

You are travelling at the legal speed limit. A vehicle comes up quickly behind, flashing its headlights. You should

Mark one answer

- ❑ a accelerate to make a gap behind you
- ❑ b touch the brakes sharply to show your brake lights
- ❑ c maintain your speed to prevent the vehicle from overtaking
- ❑ d allow the vehicle to overtake

2.20

You should ONLY flash your headlights to other road users

Mark one answer

- ❑ a to show that you are giving way
- ❑ b to show that you are about to turn
- ❑ c to tell them that you have right of way
- ❑ d to let them know that you are there

2.21

You are approaching unmarked crossroads. How should you deal with this type of junction?

Mark one answer

- ❑ a Accelerate and keep to the middle
- ❑ b Slow down and keep to the right
- ❑ c Accelerate looking to the left
- ❑ d Slow down and look both ways

2.22

You are approaching a pelican crossing. The amber light is flashing. You must

Mark one answer

- ❑ a give way to pedestrians who are crossing
- ❑ b encourage pedestrians to cross
- ❑ c not move until the green light appears
- ❑ d stop even if the crossing is clear

2.23

The conditions are good and dry. You could use the 'two-second' rule,

Mark one answer

- ❑ a before restarting the engine after it has stalled
- ❑ b to keep a safe gap from the vehicle in front
- ❑ c before using the 'Mirror-Signal-Manoeuvre' routine
- ❑ d when emerging on wet roads

2.24

At a puffin crossing, which colour follows the green signal?

Mark one answer

- ❑ a Steady red
- ❑ b Flashing amber
- ❑ c Steady amber
- ❑ d Flashing green

2.25

You are in a line of traffic. The driver behind you is following very closely. What action should you take?

Mark one answer

- ❑ a Ignore the following driver and continue to travel within the speed limit
- ❑ b Slow down, gradually increasing the gap between you and the vehicle in front
- ❑ c Signal left and wave the following driver past
- ❑ d Move over to a position just left of the centre line of the road

Answers

2.13 a

2.14 b

2.15 a

2.16 a Remember you are in a one-way street. So to turn right you would normally position in the right-hand lane.

2.17 c The position of your car or motorcycle helps signal your intentions to other road users.

2.18 a

2.19 d This is your only safe option.

2.20 d This is the only correct and unambiguous meaning of this signal.

2.21 d Because no one has priority and caution is required.

2.22 a You must give way to pedestrians already on the crossing but may proceed if the crossing is clear.

2.23 b A two-second time gap from the vehicle in front provides a safe gap in good conditions.

2.24 c

2.25 b By increasing the gap between you and the vehicle in front, you give yourself and the driver behind more room to stop should you need it.

2.26

A bus has stopped at a bus stop ahead of you. Its right-hand indicator is flashing. You should

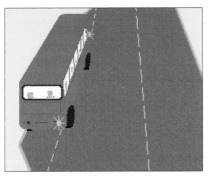

Mark one answer

❑ a flash your headlights and slow down
❑ b slow down and give way if it is safe to do so
❑ c sound your horn and keep going
❑ d slow down and then sound your horn

2.27

You are approaching a zebra crossing. Pedestrians are waiting to cross. You should

Mark one answer

❑ a give way to the elderly and infirm only
❑ b slow down and prepare to stop
❑ c use your headlights to indicate they can cross
❑ d wave at them to cross the road

2.28

A vehicle pulls out in front of you at a junction. What should you do?

Mark one answer

❑ a Swerve past it and sound your horn
❑ b Flash your headlights and drive up close behind
❑ c Slow down and be ready to stop
❑ d Accelerate past it immediately

2.29

You stop for pedestrians waiting to cross at a zebra crossing. They do not start to cross. What should you do?

Mark one answer

❑ a Be patient and wait
❑ b Sound your horn
❑ c Carry on
❑ d Wave them to cross

2.30

You are driving on a clear night. There is a steady stream of oncoming traffic. The national speed limit applies. Which lights should you use?

Mark one answer

❑ a Full beam headlights
❑ b Sidelights
❑ c Dipped headlights
❑ d Fog lights

2.31

You are driving behind a large goods vehicle. It signals left but steers to the right. You should

Mark one answer

❑ a slow down and let the vehicle turn
❑ b drive on, keeping to the left
❑ c overtake on the right of it
❑ d hold your speed and sound your horn

2.32

You are waiting in a traffic queue at night. To avoid dazzling following drivers you should

Mark one answer

❑ a apply the handbrake only
❑ b apply the footbrake only
❑ c switch off your headlights
❑ d use both the handbrake and footbrake

2.33

You are driving along this road. The red van cuts in close in front of you. What should you do?

Mark one answer
- ❏ a Accelerate to get closer to the red van
- ❏ b Give a long blast on the horn
- ❏ c Drop back to leave the correct separation distance
- ❏ d Flash your headlights several times

2.34

You are driving in traffic at the speed limit for the road. The driver behind is trying to overtake. You should

Mark one answer
- ❏ a move closer to the car ahead, so the driver behind has no room to overtake
- ❏ b wave the driver behind to overtake when it is safe
- ❏ c keep a steady course and allow the driver behind to overtake
- ❏ d accelerate to get away from the driver behind

2.35

A bus lane on your left shows no times of operation. This means it is

Mark one answer
- ❏ a not in operation at all
- ❏ b only in operation at peak times
- ❏ c in operation 24 hours a day
- ❏ d only in operation in daylight hours

Answers

2.26 b
2.27 b
2.28 c
2.29 a
2.30 c
2.31 a
2.32 a Using the footbrake would activate your brake lights and might dazzle following drivers.
2.33 c
2.34 c
2.35 c

2.36

You are driving along a country road. A horse and rider are approaching. What should you do?

Mark two answers

- ❑ a Increase your speed
- ❑ b Sound your horn
- ❑ c Flash your headlights
- ❑ d Drive slowly past
- ❑ e Give plenty of room
- ❑ f Rev your engine

2.37

A person herding sheep asks you to stop. You should

Mark one answer

- ❑ a ignore them as they have no authority
- ❑ b stop and switch off your engine
- ❑ c continue on but drive slowly
- ❑ d try and get past quickly

2.38

When overtaking a horse and rider you should

Mark one answer

- ❑ a sound your horn as a warning
- ❑ b go past as quickly as possible
- ❑ c flash your headlights as a warning
- ❑ d go past slowly and carefully

2.39

You are following this lorry. You should keep well back from it to

Mark one answer

- ❑ a give you a good view of the road ahead
- ❑ b stop following traffic from rushing through the junction
- ❑ c prevent traffic behind you from overtaking
- ❑ d allow you to hurry through the traffic lights if they change

2.40

You are approaching a red light at a puffin crossing. Pedestrians are on the crossing. The red light will stay on until

Mark one answer

- ❑ a you start to edge forward on to the crossing
- ❑ b the pedestrians have reached a safe position
- ❑ c the pedestrians are clear of the front of your vehicle
- ❑ d a driver from the opposite direction reaches the crossing

2.41

Which instrument panel warning light would show that headlights are on full beam?

Mark one answer

❑ a   ❑ b   ❑ c   ❑ d

2.42

At puffin crossings, which light will not show to a driver?

Mark one answer

❑ a Flashing amber
❑ b Red
❑ c Steady amber
❑ d Green

2.43

You should leave at least a two-second gap between your vehicle and the one in front when conditions are

Mark one answer

❑ a wet
❑ b good
❑ c damp
❑ d foggy

2.44

You are driving at night on an unlit road behind another vehicle. You should

Mark one answer

❑ a flash your headlights
❑ b use dipped beam headlights
❑ c switch off your headlights
❑ d use full beam headlights

2.45

You are driving a slow-moving vehicle on a narrow, winding road. You should

Mark one answer

❑ a keep well out to stop vehicles overtaking dangerously
❑ b wave following vehicles past you if you think they can overtake quickly
❑ c pull in safely when you can, to let following vehicles overtake
❑ d give a left signal when it is safe for vehicles to overtake you

2.46

You have a loose filler cap on your diesel fuel tank. This will

Mark two answers

❑ a waste fuel and money
❑ b make roads slippery for other road users
❑ c improve your vehicle's fuel consumption
❑ d increase the level of exhaust emissions

Answers

2.36 d, e
2.37 b
2.38 d
2.39 a
2.40 b
2.41 a
2.42 a
2.43 b
2.44 b
2.45 c 'a' and 'b' are dangerous and 'd' is confusing. Other drivers might think you are stopping or turning left.
2.46 a, b

2.47

To avoid spillage after refuelling, you should make sure that

Mark one answer

☐ a your tank is only three quarters full
☐ b you have used a locking filler cap
☐ c you check your fuel gauge is working
☐ d your filler cap is securely fastened

2.48

If your vehicle uses diesel fuel, take extra care when refuelling. Diesel fuel when spilt is

Mark one answer

☐ a sticky
☐ b odourless
☐ c clear
☐ d slippery

2.49

What style of driving causes increased risk to everyone?

Mark one answer

☐ a Considerate
☐ b Defensive
☐ c Competitive
☐ d Responsible

2.50

You are riding towards a zebra crossing. Pedestrians are waiting to cross. You should

Mark one answer

☐ a give way to the elderly and infirm only
☐ b slow down and prepare to stop
☐ c use your headlight to indicate they can cross
☐ d wave at them to cross the road

2.51

You are riding a motorcycle and following a large vehicle at 40 mph. You should position yourself

Mark one answer

☐ a close behind to make it easier to overtake the vehicle
☐ b to the left of the road to make it easier to be seen
☐ c close behind the vehicle to keep out of the wind
☐ d well back so that you can see past the vehicle

2.52

You are riding on a country road. Two horses with riders are in the distance. You should

Mark one answer

☐ a continue at your normal speed
☐ b change down the gears quickly
☐ c slow down and be ready to stop
☐ d flash your headlight to warn them

2.53

You are approaching a red light at a puffin crossing. Pedestrians are on the crossing. The red light will stay on until
Mark one answer

- ❑ a you start to edge forward on to the crossing
- ❑ b the pedestrians have reached a safe position
- ❑ c the pedestrians are clear of the front of your motorcycle
- ❑ d a driver from the opposite direction reaches the crossing

2.54

You are riding a slow-moving scooter on a narrow, winding road. You should
Mark one answer

- ❑ a keep well out to stop vehicles overtaking dangerously
- ❑ b wave vehicles behind you to pass, if you think they can overtake quickly
- ❑ c pull in safely when you can, to let vehicles behind you overtake
- ❑ d give a left signal when it is safe for vehicles to overtake you

2.55

When riding a motorcycle your normal road position should allow
Mark two answers

- ❑ a other vehicles to overtake on your left
- ❑ b the driver ahead to see you in their mirrors
- ❑ c you to prevent vehicles behind from overtaking
- ❑ d you to be seen by traffic that is emerging from junctions ahead
- ❑ e you to ride within half a metre (1 foot 8 ins) of the kerb

Answers

2.47 d
2.48 d
2.49 c Competitive driving puts you at greater risk of losing control of the vehicle and colliding with another road user, even a pedestrian.
2.50 b
2.51 d If you can see past the vehicle you can decide whether it is safe to overtake.
2.52 c Take extra care when there are horses around as they can easily be alarmed.
2.53 b
2.54 c
2.55 b, d

Theory Test Questions
for Car Drivers and Motorcyclists

Section 3 Vehicle defects, safety equipment and the environment

3.1

Before starting a journey it is wise to plan your route. How can you do this?

Mark one answer

- ❏ a Look at a map
- ❏ b Contact your local garage
- ❏ c Look in your vehicle handbook
- ❏ d Check your vehicle registration document

3.2

It can help to plan your route before starting a journey. You can do this by contacting

Mark one answer

- ❏ a your local filling station
- ❏ b a motoring organisation
- ❏ c the Driver Vehicle Licensing Agency
- ❏ d your vehicle manufacturer

3.3

How can you plan your route before starting a long journey?

Mark one answer

- ❏ a Check your vehicle's workshop manual
- ❏ b Ask your local garage
- ❏ c Use a route planner on the internet
- ❏ d Consult your travel agents

3.4

Planning your route before setting out can be helpful. How can you do this?

Mark one answer

- ❏ a Look in a motoring magazine
- ❏ b Only visit places you know
- ❏ c Try to travel at busy times
- ❏ d Print or write down the route

3.5

Why is it a good idea to plan your journey to avoid busy times?

Mark one answer

- ❏ a You will have an easier journey
- ❏ b You will have a more stressful journey
- ❏ c Your journey time will be longer
- ❏ d It will cause more traffic congestion

3.6

Planning your journey to avoid busy times has a number of advantages. One of these is

Mark one answer

- ❏ a your journey will take longer
- ❏ b you will have a more pleasant journey
- ❏ c you will cause more pollution
- ❏ d your stress level will be greater

3.7

It is a good idea to plan your journey to avoid busy times. This is because

Mark one answer

- ❏ a your vehicle will use more fuel
- ❏ b you will see less road works
- ❏ c it will help to ease congestion
- ❏ d you will travel a much shorter distance

3.8

By avoiding busy times when travelling

Mark one answer

- ❏ a you are more likely to be held up
- ❏ b your journey time will be longer
- ❏ c you will travel a much shorter distance
- ❏ d you are less likely to be delayed

3.9

It can help to plan your route before starting a journey. Why should you also plan an alternative route?

Mark one answer

- ❏ a Your original route may be blocked
- ❏ b Your maps may have different scales
- ❏ c You may find you have to pay a congestion charge
- ❏ d Because you may get held up by a tractor

3.10

As well as planning your route before starting a journey, you should also plan an alternative route. Why is this?

Mark one answer

❑ a To let another driver overtake
❑ b Your first route may be blocked
❑ c To avoid a railway level crossing
❑ d In case you have to avoid emergency vehicles

3.11

Who of these will not have to pay Congestion Charges in London?

Mark one answer

❑ a A van driver making deliveries
❑ b A rider of a two-wheeled vehicle
❑ c A car driver whose vehicle is more than 1000 cc
❑ d A driver who just wants to park in the area

3.12

You must NOT sound your horn

Mark one answer

❑ a between 10 pm and 6 am in a built-up area
❑ b at any time in a built-up area
❑ c between 11.30 pm and 7 am in a built-up area
❑ d between 11.30 pm and 6 am on any road

3.13

You are making an appointment and will have to travel a long distance. You should

Mark one answer

❑ a allow plenty of time for your journey
❑ b plan to go at busy times
❑ c avoid all national speed limit roads
❑ d prevent other drivers from overtaking

3.14

Rapid acceleration and heavy braking can lead to

Mark one answer

❑ a reduced pollution
❑ b increased fuel consumption
❑ c reduced exhaust emissions
❑ d increased road safety

Answers

3.1   a
3.2   b Planning your route before starting a journey saves time, fuel and stress. Motoring organisations such as the RAC are a great source of information.
3.3   c
3.4   d
3.5   a
3.6   b
3.7   c
3.8   d If you are able to avoid busy times there will be one less driver on the road which helps to ease congestion. Plan your route before you start the journey to save time, fuel and stress.
3.9   a
3.10 b
3.11 b Motorcycles, scooters, mopeds, etc., do not noticeably add to congestion, therefore they are exempt.
3.12 c The regulation applies in a built-up area only.
3.13 a
3.14 b Looking well ahead and planning your driving allows you to accelerate and brake smoothly, which will improve your fuel consumption as well as keeping you safer.

3.15

What percentage of all emissions does road transport account for?

Mark one answer

- ☐ a 10%
- ☐ b 20%
- ☐ c 30%
- ☐ d 40%

3.16

The pictured vehicle is 'environmentally friendly' because it

Mark three answers

- ☐ a reduces noise pollution
- ☐ b uses diesel fuel
- ☐ c uses electricity
- ☐ d uses unleaded fuel
- ☐ e reduces parking spaces
- ☐ f reduces town traffic

3.17

Supertrams or Light Rapid Transit (LRT) systems are environmentally friendly because

Mark one answer

- ☐ a they use diesel power
- ☐ b they use quieter roads
- ☐ c they use electric power
- ☐ d they do not operate during rush hour

3.18

'Red routes' in major cities have been introduced to

Mark one answer

- ☐ a raise the speed limits
- ☐ b help the traffic flow
- ☐ c provide better parking
- ☐ d allow lorries to load more freely

3.19

Motor vehicles can harm the environment. This has resulted in

Mark three answers

- ☐ a air pollution
- ☐ b damage to buildings
- ☐ c less risk to health
- ☐ d improved public transport
- ☐ e less use of electrical vehicles
- ☐ f using up of natural resources

3.20

Road humps, chicanes, and narrowings are

Mark one answer

- ☐ a always at major road works
- ☐ b used to increase traffic speed
- ☐ c at toll-bridge approaches only
- ☐ d traffic calming measures

3.21

The purpose of a catalytic converter is to reduce

Mark one answer

- ☐ a fuel consumption
- ☐ b the risk of fire
- ☐ c toxic exhaust gases
- ☐ d engine wear

3.22

Catalytic converters are fitted to make the

Mark one answer

- ☐ a engine produce more power
- ☐ b exhaust system easier to replace
- ☐ c engine run quietly
- ☐ d exhaust fumes cleaner

3.23

When should you NOT use your horn in a built-up area?

Mark one answer

- ☐ a Between 8 pm and 8 am
- ☐ b Between 9 pm and dawn
- ☐ c Between dusk and 8 am
- ☐ d Between 11.30 pm and 7 am

3.24

You will use more fuel if your tyres are

Mark one answer

- ❑ a under-inflated
- ❑ b of different makes
- ❑ c over-inflated
- ❑ d new and hardly used

3.25

How should you dispose of a used battery?

Mark two answers

- ❑ a Take it to a local authority site
- ❑ b Put it in the dustbin
- ❑ c Break it up into pieces
- ❑ d Leave it on waste land
- ❑ e Take it to a garage
- ❑ f Burn it on a fire

3.26

What is most likely to cause high fuel consumption?

Mark one answer

- ❑ a Poor steering control
- ❑ b Accelerating around bends
- ❑ c Staying in high gears
- ❑ d Harsh braking and accelerating

3.27

Which TWO are badly affected if the tyres are under-inflated?

Mark two answers

- ❑ a Braking
- ❑ b Steering
- ❑ c Changing gear
- ❑ d Parking

3.28

It is essential that tyre pressures are checked regularly. When should this be done?

Mark one answer

- ❑ a After any lengthy journey
- ❑ b After travelling at high speed
- ❑ c When tyres are hot
- ❑ d When tyres are cold

3.29

The fluid level in your battery is low. What should you top it up with?

Mark one answer

- ❑ a Battery acid
- ❑ b Distilled water
- ❑ c Engine oil
- ❑ d Engine coolant

3.30

You have too much oil in your engine. What could this cause?

Mark one answer

- ❑ a Low oil pressure
- ❑ b Engine overheating
- ❑ c Chain wear
- ❑ d Oil leaks

Answers

3.15 b Looking well ahead and planning your driving allows you to accelerate and brake smoothly, which will improve your fuel consumption and therefore reduce exhaust emissions.

3.16 a, c, f

3.17 c

3.18 b

3.19 a, b, f

3.20 d

3.21 c

3.22 d

3.23 d

3.24 a

3.25 a, e

3.26 d Harsh braking and accelerating is one of the major causes of high fuel consumption.

3.27 a, b

3.28 d

3.29 b

3.30 d

3.31

Which of these, if allowed to get low, could cause an accident?

Mark one answer

- ❑ a Anti-freeze level
- ❑ b Brake fluid level
- ❑ c Battery water level
- ❑ d Radiator coolant level

3.32

Excessive or uneven tyre wear can be caused by faults in which THREE of the following?

Mark three answers

- ❑ a The gearbox
- ❑ b The braking system
- ❑ c The accelerator
- ❑ d The exhaust system
- ❑ e Wheel alignment
- ❑ f The suspension

3.33

You need to top up your battery. What level should you fill to?

Mark one answer

- ❑ a The top of the battery
- ❑ b Half-way up the battery
- ❑ c Just below the cell plates
- ❑ d Just above the cell plates

3.34

You are parked on the road at night. Where must you use parking lights?

Mark one answer

- ❑ a Where there are continuous white lines in the middle of the road
- ❑ b Where the speed limit exceeds 30 mph
- ❑ c Where you are facing oncoming traffic
- ❑ d Where you are near a bus stop

3.35

You are parking on a two-way road at night. The speed limit is 40 mph. You should park on the

Mark one answer

- ❑ a left with parking lights on
- ❑ b left with no lights on
- ❑ c right with parking lights on
- ❑ d right with dipped headlights on

3.36

A roof rack fitted to your car will

Mark one answer

- ❑ a reduce fuel consumption
- ❑ b improve the road handling
- ❑ c make your car go faster
- ❑ d increase fuel consumption

3.37

New petrol-engined cars must be fitted with catalytic converters. The reason for this is to

Mark one answer

- ❑ a control exhaust noise levels
- ❑ b prolong the life of the exhaust system
- ❑ c allow the exhaust system to be recycled
- ❑ d reduce harmful exhaust emissions

3.38

When a roof rack is not in use it should be removed. Why is this?

Mark one answer

- ❑ a It will affect the suspension
- ❑ b It is illegal
- ❑ c It will affect your braking
- ❑ d It will waste fuel

3.39

How can you, as a driver, help the environment?

Mark three answers

- ❑ a By reducing your speed
- ❑ b By gentle acceleration
- ❑ c By using leaded fuel
- ❑ d By driving faster
- ❑ e By harsh acceleration
- ❑ f By servicing your vehicle properly

3.40

To help the environment, you can avoid wasting fuel by

Mark three answers

- ❑ a having your vehicle properly serviced
- ❑ b making sure your tyres are correctly inflated
- ❑ c not over-revving in the lower gears
- ❑ d driving at higher speeds where possible
- ❑ e keeping an empty roof rack properly fitted
- ❑ f servicing your vehicle less regularly

3.41

To reduce the volume of traffic on the roads you could

Mark three answers

- ❑ a use public transport more often
- ❑ b share a car when possible
- ❑ c walk or cycle on short journeys
- ❑ d travel by car at all times
- ❑ e use a car with a smaller engine
- ❑ f drive in a bus lane

3.42

Which THREE of the following are most likely to waste fuel?

Mark three answers

- ❑ a Reducing your speed
- ❑ b Carrying unnecessary weight
- ❑ c Using the wrong grade of fuel
- ❑ d Under-inflated tyres
- ❑ e Using different brands of fuel
- ❑ f A fitted, empty roof rack

3.43

Which THREE things can you, as a road user, do to help the environment?

Mark three answers

- ❑ a Cycle when possible
- ❑ b Drive on under-inflated tyres
- ❑ c Use the choke for as long as possible on a cold engine
- ❑ d Have your vehicle properly tuned and serviced
- ❑ e Watch the traffic and plan ahead
- ❑ f Brake as late as possible without skidding

3.44

To help protect the environment you should NOT

Mark one answer

- ❑ a remove your roof rack when unloaded
- ❑ b use your car for very short journeys
- ❑ c walk, cycle, or use public transport
- ❑ d empty the boot of unnecessary weight

Answers

3.31 b A low level of brake fluid may cause your brakes to fail.

3.32 b, e, f

3.33 d The 'topping up' level will normally be marked on the battery and is above the cell plates.

3.34 b

3.35 a

3.36 d

3.37 d This helps the car operate more efficiently and causes less air pollution. Only unleaded fuel may be used.

3.38 d

3.39 a, b, f

3.40 a, b, c

3.41 a, b, c

3.42 b, d, f

3.43 a, d, e

3.44 b

3.45
Driving at 70 mph uses more fuel than driving at 50 mph by up to
Mark one answer
- ❑ a 10%
- ❑ b 30%
- ❑ c 75%
- ❑ d 100%

3.46
Which TWO of the following will improve fuel consumption?
Mark two answers
- ❑ a Reducing your road speed
- ❑ b Planning well ahead
- ❑ c Late and harsh braking
- ❑ d Driving in lower gears
- ❑ e Short journeys with a cold engine
- ❑ f Rapid acceleration

3.47
You service your own vehicle. How should you get rid of the old engine oil?
Mark one answer
- ❑ a Take it to a local authority site
- ❑ b Pour it down a drain
- ❑ c Tip it into a hole in the ground
- ❑ d Put it into your dustbin

3.48
Why do MOT tests include a strict exhaust emission test?
Mark one answer
- ❑ a To recover the cost of expensive garage equipment
- ❑ b To help protect the environment against pollution
- ❑ c To discover which fuel supplier is used the most
- ❑ d To make sure diesel and petrol engines emit the same fumes

3.49
To reduce the damage your vehicle causes to the environment you should
Mark three answers
- ❑ a use narrow side streets
- ❑ b avoid harsh acceleration
- ❑ c brake in good time
- ❑ d anticipate well ahead
- ❑ e use busy routes

3.50
Your vehicle has a catalytic converter. Its purpose is to reduce
Mark one answer
- ❑ a exhaust noise
- ❑ b fuel consumption
- ❑ c exhaust emissions
- ❑ d engine noise

3.51
A properly serviced vehicle will give
Mark two answers
- ❑ a lower insurance premiums
- ❑ b you a refund on your road tax
- ❑ c better fuel economy
- ❑ d cleaner exhaust emissions

3.52
You enter a road where there are road humps. What should you do?

Mark one answer
- ❑ a Maintain a reduced speed throughout
- ❑ b Accelerate quickly between each one
- ❑ c Always keep to the maximum legal speed
- ❑ d Drive slowly at school times only

3.53

As a driver you can cause more damage to the environment by

Mark two answers

- ❑ a choosing a fuel-efficient vehicle
- ❑ b making a lot of short journeys
- ❑ c driving in as high a gear as possible
- ❑ d accelerating as quickly as possible
- ❑ e having your vehicle regularly serviced

3.54

As a driver, you can help reduce pollution levels in town centres by

Mark one answer

- ❑ a driving more quickly
- ❑ b over-revving in a low gear
- ❑ c walking or cycling
- ❑ d driving short journeys

3.55

On a vehicle, where would you find a catalytic converter?

Mark one answer

- ❑ a In the fuel tank
- ❑ b In the air filter
- ❑ c On the cooling system
- ❑ d On the exhaust system

3.56

You will find that driving smoothly can

Mark one answer

- ❑ a reduce journey times by about 15%
- ❑ b increase fuel consumption by about 15%
- ❑ c reduce fuel consumption by about 15%
- ❑ d increase journey times by about 15%

3.57

You can save fuel when conditions allow by

Mark one answer

- ❑ a using lower gears as often as possible
- ❑ b accelerating sharply in each gear
- ❑ c using each gear in turn
- ❑ d missing out some gears

3.58

Congestion Charges apply in the London area. Who of these will NOT have to pay?

Mark one answer

- ❑ a A person who lives in the area
- ❑ b A driver making deliveries
- ❑ c A person who is just driving through the area
- ❑ d A driver with no other passengers in the vehicle

Answers

3.45 b

3.46 a, b

3.47 a

3.48 b

3.49 b, c, d These make for smoother driving, which uses less fuel and so cuts down on pollution.

3.50 c

3.51 c, d

3.52 a Road humps are there to slow the traffic in residential areas.

3.53 b, d A lot of short journeys use up a lot of petrol and pollute the atmosphere with exhaust fumes.

3.54 c

3.55 d

3.56 c Gentle use of the major controls increases driver and passenger comfort, reduces wear and tear on the vehicle and decreases fuel consumption.

3.57 d It is not necessary to use all of the gears all of the time. Block changing is a fuel-efficient, relaxed and effective technique when used appropriately.

3.58 a A person living inside the zone will not be liable for the Congestion Charge. Some types of vehicle are also exempt, for example, two-wheeled vehicles, and vehicles adapted to use LPG.

3.59

How can driving in an Eco-safe manner help protect the environment?

Mark one answer

- a Through the legal enforcement of speed regulations
- b By increasing the number of cars on the road
- c Through increased fuel bills
- d By reducing exhaust emissions

3.60

What does Eco-safe driving achieve?

Mark one answer

- a Increased fuel consumption
- b Improved road safety
- c Damage to the environment
- d Increased exhaust emissions

3.61

How can missing out some gear changes save fuel?

Mark one answer

- a By reducing the amount of time you are accelerating
- b Because there is less need to use the footbrake
- c By controlling the amount of steering
- d Because coasting is kept to a minimum

3.62

Fuel consumption is at its highest when you are

Mark one answer

- a braking
- b coasting
- c accelerating
- d steering

3.63

Missing out some gears saves fuel by reducing the amount of time you spend

Mark one answer

- a braking
- b coasting
- c steering
- d accelerating

3.64

What can cause heavy steering?

Mark one answer

- a Driving on ice
- b Badly worn brakes
- c Over-inflated tyres
- d Under-inflated tyres

3.65

Driving with under-inflated tyres can affect

Mark two answers

- a engine temperature
- b fuel consumption
- c braking
- d oil pressure

3.66

Excessive or uneven tyre wear can be caused by faults in the

Mark two answers

- a gearbox
- b braking system
- c suspension
- d exhaust system

3.67

The main cause of brake fade is

Mark one answer

- a the brakes overheating
- b air in the brake fluid
- c oil on the brakes
- d the brakes out of adjustment

3.68
Your anti-lock brakes warning light stays on. You should
Mark one answer
- a check the brake fluid level
- b check the footbrake free play
- c check that the handbrake is released
- d have the brakes checked immediately

3.69
While driving, this warning light on your dashboard comes on. It means

Mark one answer
- a a fault in the braking system
- b the engine oil is low
- c a rear light has failed
- d your seat belt is not fastened

3.70
You are testing your suspension. You notice that your vehicle keeps bouncing when you press down on the front wing. What does this mean?
Mark one answer
- a Worn tyres
- b Tyres under-inflated
- c Steering wheel not located centrally
- d Worn shock absorbers

3.71
It is illegal to drive with tyres that
Mark one answer
- a have been bought second-hand
- b have a large deep cut in the side wall
- c are of different makes
- d are of different tread patterns

3.72
The legal minimum depth of tread for car tyres over three quarters of the breadth is
Mark one answer
- a 1 mm
- b 1.6 mm
- c 2.5 mm
- d 4 mm

3.73
Which THREE does the law require you to keep in good condition?
Mark three answers
- a Gears
- b Transmission
- c Headlights
- d Windscreen
- e Seat belts

Answers

3.59 d
3.60 b
3.61 a Every time you change up through the gears you come off the accelerator and then reapply it. This uses more fuel than maintaining a constant pressure on the accelerator. Missing out gears reduces the need to come off and back on the accelerator.
3.62 c
3.63 d
3.64 d
3.65 b, c
3.66 b, c
3.67 a
3.68 d
3.69 a
3.70 d
3.71 b
3.72 b
3.73 c, d, e

45

3.74

Your vehicle pulls to one side when braking. You should

Mark one answer

- ❏ a change the tyres around
- ❏ b consult your garage as soon as possible
- ❏ c pump the pedal when braking
- ❏ d use your handbrake at the same time

3.75

Unbalanced wheels on a car may cause

Mark one answer

- ❏ a the steering to pull to one side
- ❏ b the steering to vibrate
- ❏ c the brakes to fail
- ❏ d the tyres to deflate

3.76

Turning the steering wheel while your car is stationary can cause damage to the

Mark two answers

- ❏ a gearbox
- ❏ b engine
- ❏ c brakes
- ❏ d steering
- ❏ e tyres

3.77

Which FOUR of these must be in good working order for your car to be roadworthy?

Mark four answers

- ❏ a The temperature gauge
- ❏ b The speedometer
- ❏ c The windscreen washers
- ❏ d The windscreen wipers
- ❏ e The oil warning light
- ❏ f The horn

3.78

When should you especially check the engine oil level?

Mark one answer

- ❏ a Before a long journey
- ❏ b When the engine is hot
- ❏ c Early in the morning
- ❏ d Every 6000 miles

3.79

You are checking your trailer tyres. What is the legal minimum tread depth over the central three quarters of its breadth?

Mark one answer

- ❏ a 1 mm
- ❏ b 1.6 mm
- ❏ c 2 mm
- ❏ d 2.6 mm

3.80

It is important to wear suitable shoes when you are driving. Why is this?

Mark one answer

- ❏ a To prevent wear on the pedals
- ❏ b To maintain control of the pedals
- ❏ c To enable you to adjust your seat
- ❏ d To enable you to walk for assistance if you break down

3.81

What will reduce the risk of neck injury resulting from a collision?

Mark one answer

- ❏ a An air-sprung seat
- ❏ b Anti-lock brakes
- ❏ c A collapsible steering wheel
- ❏ d A properly adjusted head restraint

3.82

Car passengers MUST wear a seat belt if one is available, unless they are

Mark one answer

- ❏ a under 14 years old
- ❏ b under 1.5 metres (5 feet) in height
- ❏ c sitting in the rear seat
- ❏ d exempt for medical reasons

3.83

You are carrying two 13-year-old children and their parents in your car. Who is responsible for seeing that the children wear seat belts?

Mark one answer

- ❏ a The children's parents
- ❏ b You, the driver
- ❏ c The front-seat passenger
- ❏ d The children

3.84

The most important reason for having a properly-adjusted head restraint is to

Mark one answer

- ❏ a make you more comfortable
- ❏ b help you to avoid neck injury
- ❏ c help you to relax
- ❏ d help you to maintain your driving position

3.85

You are driving the children of a friend home from school. They are both under 14 years old. Who is responsible for making sure they wear a seat belt?

Mark one answer

- ❏ a An adult passenger
- ❏ b The children
- ❏ c You, the driver
- ❏ d Your friend

3.86

Rear-facing baby seats should NEVER be used on a seat protected with

Mark one answer

- ❏ a an airbag
- ❏ b seat belts
- ❏ c head restraints
- ❏ d seat covers

3.87

You have to leave valuables in your car. It would be safer to

Mark one answer

- ❏ a put them in a carrier bag
- ❏ b park near a school entrance
- ❏ c lock them out of sight
- ❏ d park near a bus stop

Answers

3.74 b
3.75 b
3.76 d, e
3.77 b, c, d, f These must, by law, be in good working order.
3.78 a
3.79 b Tyre regulations also cover tyres on your trailer or caravan.
3.80 b
3.81 d If you are involved in an accident, the head restraint helps protect your neck from whiplash.
3.82 d All passengers, front and rear, must were seat belts, if fitted, unless exempt for medical reasons.
3.83 b
3.84 b
3.85 c
3.86 a The impact of the airbag, released in an accident, could kill a baby in a rear-facing baby seat.
3.87 c

3.88

How could you deter theft from your car when leaving it unattended?

Mark one answer

- a Leave valuables in a carrier bag
- b Lock valuables out of sight
- c Put valuables on the seats
- d Leave valuables on the floor

3.89

Which of the following may help to deter a thief from stealing your car?

Mark one answer

- a Always keeping the headlights on
- b Fitting reflective glass windows
- c Always keeping the interior light on
- d Etching the car number on the windows

3.90

Which of the following should not be kept in your vehicle?

Mark one answer

- a A first aid kit
- b A road atlas
- c The tax disc
- d The vehicle documents

3.91

What should you do when leaving your vehicle?

Mark one answer

- a Put valuable documents under the seats
- b Remove all valuables
- c Cover valuables with a blanket
- d Leave the interior light on

3.92

Which of these is most likely to deter the theft of your vehicle?

Mark one answer

- a An immobiliser
- b Tinted windows
- c Locking wheel nuts
- d A sun screen

3.93

When parking and leaving your car you should

Mark one answer

- a park under a shady tree
- b remove the tax disc
- c park in a quiet road
- d engage the steering lock

3.94

When leaving your vehicle parked and unattended you should

Mark one answer

- a park near a busy junction
- b park in a housing estate
- c remove the key and lock it
- d leave the left indicator on

3.95

You are having difficulty finding a parking space in a busy town. You can see there is space on the zigzag lines of a zebra crossing. Can you park there?

Mark one answer

- a No, unless you stay with your car
- b Yes, in order to drop off a passenger
- c Yes, if you do not block people from crossing
- d No, not in any circumstances

3.96

When leaving your car unattended for a few minutes you should

Mark one answer

- a leave the engine running
- b switch the engine off but leave the key in
- c lock it and remove the key
- d park near a traffic warden

3.97

When parking and leaving your car for a few minutes you should

Mark one answer

- ❏ a leave it unlocked
- ❏ b lock it and remove the key
- ❏ c leave the hazard warning lights on
- ❏ d leave the interior light on

3.98

When leaving your vehicle, where should you park if possible?

Mark one answer

- ❏ a Opposite a traffic island
- ❏ b In a secure car park
- ❏ c On a bend
- ❏ d At or near a taxi rank

3.99

You are leaving your vehicle parked on a road. When may you leave the engine running?

Mark one answer

- ❏ a If you will be parking for less than five minutes
- ❏ b If the battery is flat
- ❏ c When in a 20 mph zone
- ❏ d Never on any occasion

3.100

In which THREE places would parking your vehicle cause danger or obstruction to other road users?

Mark three answers

- ❏ a In front of a property entrance
- ❏ b At or near a bus stop
- ❏ c On your driveway
- ❏ d In a marked parking space
- ❏ e On the approach to a level crossing

3.101

In which THREE places would parking cause an obstruction to others?

Mark three answers

- ❏ a Near the brow of a hill
- ❏ b In a lay-by
- ❏ c Where the kerb is raised
- ❏ d Where the kerb has been lowered for wheelchairs
- ❏ e At or near a bus stop

3.102

You are away from home and have to park your vehicle overnight. Where should you leave it?

Mark one answer

- ❏ a Opposite another parked vehicle
- ❏ b In a quiet road
- ❏ c Opposite a traffic island
- ❏ d In a secure car park

Answers

3.88 b
3.89 d Would-be thieves may well be able to steal any vehicle but the fact that the number is etched on the windows may deter them.
3.90 d
3.91 b
3.92 a An anti-theft device like an immobiliser makes it more difficult for a thief to steal your car.
3.93 d
3.94 c
3.95 d
3.96 c
3.97 b
3.98 b
3.99 d
3.100 a, b, e
3.101 a, d, e
3.102 d

3.103

How can you reduce the chances of your car being broken into when leaving it unattended?
Mark one answer

- ❑ a Take all valuables with you
- ❑ b Park near a taxi rank
- ❑ c Place any valuables on the floor
- ❑ d Park near a fire station

3.104

How can you help to prevent your car radio being stolen?
Mark one answer

- ❑ a Park in an unlit area
- ❑ b Hide the radio with a blanket
- ❑ c Park near a busy junction
- ❑ d Install a security-coded radio

3.105

You are parking your car. You have some valuables which you are unable to take with you. What should you do?
Mark one answer

- ❑ a Park near a police station
- ❑ b Put them under the driver's seat
- ❑ c Lock them out of sight
- ❑ d Park in an unlit side road

3.106

Wherever possible, which one of the following should you do when parking at night?
Mark one answer

- ❑ a Park in a quiet car park
- ❑ b Park in a well-lit area
- ❑ c Park facing against the flow of traffic
- ❑ d Park next to a busy junction

3.107

How can you lessen the risk of your vehicle being broken into at night?
Mark one answer

- ❑ a Leave it in a well-lit area
- ❑ b Park in a quiet side road
- ❑ c Don't engage the steering lock
- ❑ d Park in a poorly-lit area

3.108

To help keep your car secure you could join a
Mark one answer

- ❑ a vehicle breakdown organisation
- ❑ b vehicle watch scheme
- ❑ c advanced driver's scheme
- ❑ d car maintenance class

3.109

When leaving your car to help keep it secure you should
Mark one answer

- ❑ a leave the hazard warning lights on
- ❑ b lock it and remove the key
- ❑ c park on a one-way street
- ❑ d park in a residential area

3.110

A motorcycle engine that is properly maintained will

Mark one answer

- ❏ a use much more fuel
- ❏ b have lower exhaust emissions
- ❏ c increase your insurance premiums
- ❏ d not need to have an MOT

3.111

After warming up the engine you leave the choke ON. What will this do?

Mark one answer

- ❏ a Discharge the battery
- ❏ b Use more fuel
- ❏ c Improve handling
- ❏ d Use less fuel

3.112

Your motorcycle has a catalytic converter. Its purpose is to reduce

Mark one answer

- ❏ a exhaust noise
- ❏ b fuel consumption
- ❏ c exhaust emissions
- ❏ d engine noise

3.113

You enter a road where there are road humps. What should you do?

Mark one answer

- ❏ a Maintain a reduced speed throughout
- ❏ b Accelerate quickly between each one
- ❏ c Always keep to the maximum legal speed
- ❏ d Ride slowly at school times only

3.114

You service your own motorcycle. How should you get rid of the old engine oil?

Mark one answer

- ❏ a Take it to a local authority site
- ❏ b Pour it down a drain
- ❏ c Tip it into a hole in the ground
- ❏ d Put it into your dustbin

3.115

A properly serviced motorcycle will give

Mark two answers

- ❏ a lower insurance premiums
- ❏ b a refund on your road tax
- ❏ c better fuel economy
- ❏ d cleaner exhaust emissions

Answers

3.103 a Your car is more likely to be broken into if valuables are visible through the windows.

3.104 d Having a security-coded radio makes your vehicle less desirable to a thief.

3.105 c

3.106 b

3.107 a Avoid leaving your car unattended in poorly lit areas, especially if they are known to be high risk.

3.108 b

3.109 b

3.110 b

3.111 b

3.112 c

3.113 a Road humps are there to slow the traffic in residential areas.

3.114 a

3.115 c, d

3.116

Refitting which of the following will disturb
your wheel alignment?

Mark one answer

- ❑ a front wheel
- ❑ b front brakes
- ❑ c rear brakes
- ❑ d rear wheel

3.117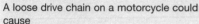

A loose drive chain on a motorcycle could
cause

Mark one answer

- ❑ a the front wheel to wobble
- ❑ b the ignition to cut out
- ❑ c the brakes to fail
- ❑ d the rear wheel to lock

3.118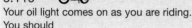

Riding your motorcycle with a slack or worn
drive chain may cause

Mark one answer

- ❑ a an engine misfire
- ❑ b early tyre wear
- ❑ c increased emissions
- ❑ d a locked wheel

3.119

Your oil light comes on as you are riding.
You should

Mark one answer

- ❑ a go to a dealer for an oil change
- ❑ b go to the nearest garage for their advice
- ❑ c ride slowly for a few miles to see if the
  light goes out
- ❑ d stop as quickly as possible and try to find
  the cause

3.120

After refitting your rear wheel what should
you check?

Mark one answer

- ❑ a Your steering damper
- ❑ b Your side stand
- ❑ c Your wheel alignment
- ❑ d Your suspension preload

3.121

After adjusting the final drive chain what
should you check?

Mark one answer

- ❑ a The rear wheel alignment
- ❑ b The suspension adjustment
- ❑ c The rear shock absorber
- ❑ d The front suspension forks

3.122

You have adjusted your drive chain. If this is
not done properly, what problem could it
cause?

Mark one answer

- ❑ a Inaccurate speedometer reading
- ❑ b Loss of braking power
- ❑ c Incorrect rear wheel alignment
- ❑ d Excessive fuel consumption

3.123

You have adjusted your drive chain. Why is it
also important to check rear wheel alignment?

Mark one answer

- ❑ a Your tyre may be more likely to puncture
- ❑ b Fuel consumption could be greatly
  increased
- ❑ c You may not be able to reach top speed
- ❑ d Your motorcycle could be unstable on
  bends

3.124

An engine cut-out switch should be used to

- ❏ a reduce speed in an emergency
- ❏ b prevent the motorcycle being stolen
- ❏ c stop the engine normally
- ❏ d stop the engine in an emergency

3.125

When should you especially check the engine oil level?

- ❏ a Before a long journey
- ❏ b When the engine is hot
- ❏ c Early in the morning
- ❏ d Every 6000 miles

3.126

When adusting your chain it is important for the wheels to be aligned accurately. Incorrect wheel alignment can cause

- ❏ a a serious loss of power
- ❏ b reduced braking performance
- ❏ c increased tyre wear
- ❏ d reduced ground clearance

3.127

What problem can incorrectly aligned wheels cause?

- ❏ a Faulty headlight adjustment
- ❏ b Reduced braking performance
- ❏ c Better ground clearance
- ❏ d Instability when cornering

3.128

What is most likely to be affected by incorrect wheel alignment?

- ❏ a Braking performance
- ❏ b Stability
- ❏ c Acceleration
- ❏ d Suspension preload

3.129

You should use the engine cut-out switch on your motorcycle to

- ❏ a save wear and tear on the battery
- ❏ b stop the engine for a short time
- ❏ c stop the engine in an emergency
- ❏ d save wear and tear on the ignition

Answers

3.116 d

3.117 d Drive chains require frequent adjustment and lubrication. If the chain is loose it can jump off the sprocket and lock the rear wheel.

3.118 d

3.119 d

3.120 c

3.121 a

3.122 c

3.123 d

3.124 d This switch only isolates the engine. Lights, if in use, will remain on.

3.125 a

3.126 c

3.127 d

3.128 b

3.129 c

3.130

You have adjusted the tension on your drive chain. You should check the

Mark one answer

- ❏ a rear wheel alignment
- ❏ b tyre pressures
- ❏ c valve clearances
- ❏ d sidelights

3.131

A loosely adjusted drive chain could

Mark one answer

- ❏ a lock the rear wheel
- ❏ b make wheels wobble
- ❏ c cause a braking fault
- ❏ d affect your headlight beam

3.132

What is the most important reason why you should keep your motorcycle regularly maintained?

Mark one answer

- ❏ a To accelerate faster than other traffic
- ❏ b So the motorcycle can carry panniers
- ❏ c To keep the machine roadworthy
- ❏ d So the motorcycle can carry a passenger

3.133

Your motorcycle has tubed tyres fitted as standard. When replacing a tyre you should

Mark one answer

- ❏ a replace the tube if it is 6 months old
- ❏ b replace the tube if it has covered 6,000 miles
- ❏ c replace the tube only if replacing the rear tyre
- ❏ d replace the tube with each change of tyre

3.134

How should you ride a motorcycle when NEW tyres have just been fitted?

Mark one answer

- ❏ a Carefully, until the shiny surface is worn off
- ❏ b By braking hard especially into bends
- ❏ c Through normal riding with higher air pressures
- ❏ d By riding at faster than normal speeds

3.135

The legal minimum depth of tread for motorcycle tyres is

Mark one answer

- ❏ a 1 mm
- ❏ b 1.6 mm
- ❏ c 2.5 mm
- ❏ d 4 mm

3.136

Motorcycle tyres MUST

Mark two answers

- ❏ a have the same tread pattern
- ❏ b be correctly inflated
- ❏ c be the same size, front and rear
- ❏ d both be the same make
- ❏ e have sufficient tread depth

3.137

You forget to switch the choke off after the engine warms up. This could

Mark one answer
- ❏ a flatten the battery
- ❏ b reduce braking distances
- ❏ c use less fuel
- ❏ d cause much more engine wear

3.138

When riding your motorcycle a tyre bursts. What should you do?
Mark one answer
- ❏ a Slow gently to a stop
- ❏ b Brake firmly to a stop
- ❏ c Change to a high gear
- ❏ d Lower the side stand

3.139

You are checking your direction indicators. How often per second must they flash?
Mark one answer
- ❏ a Between 1 and 2 times
- ❏ b Between 3 and 4 times
- ❏ c Between 5 and 6 times
- ❏ d Between 7 and 8 times

3.140

Your steering feels wobbly. Which of these is a likely cause?
Mark one answer
- ❏ a Tyre pressure is too high
- ❏ b Incorrectly adjusted brakes
- ❏ c Worn steering head bearings
- ❏ d A broken clutch cable

3.141

You see oil on your front forks. Should you be concerned about this?
Mark one answer
- ❏ a No, unless the amount of oil increases
- ❏ b No, lubrication here is perfectly normal
- ❏ c Yes, it is illegal to ride with an oil leak
- ❏ d Yes, oil could drip onto your tyre

Answers

3.130 a
3.131 a
3.132 c
3.133 d A punctured tyre should be properly repaired or replaced, and if you have tubed tyres this means replacing the inner tyre as well.
3.134 a New tyres have a shiny surface which can reduce the grip. You need to ride carefully until the shiny surface is worn off. This could take up to 100 miles.
3.135 a
3.136 b, e
3.137 d As soon as the engine warms up remember to push in the manual choke, otherwise the engine could be damaged and petrol wasted.
3.138 a With emergencies of this nature avoid sudden braking or changes of direction.
3.139 a
3.140 c
3.141 d

3.142

You have a faulty oil seal on a shock absorber. Why is this a serious problem?

Mark one answer

- ❑ a It will cause excessive chain wear
- ❑ b Dripping oil could reduce the grip of your tyre
- ❑ c Your motorcycle will be harder to ride uphill
- ❑ d Your motorcycle will not accelerate so quickly

3.143

Oil is leaking from your forks. Why should you NOT ride a motorcycle in this condition?

Mark one answer

- ❑ a Your brakes could be affected by dripping oil
- ❑ b Your steering is likely to seize up
- ❑ c The forks will quickly begin to rust
- ❑ d The motorcycle will become too noisy

3.144

There is a cut in the sidewall of one of your tyres. What should you do about this?

Mark one answer

- ❑ a Replace the tyre before riding the motorcycle
- ❑ b Check regularly to see if it gets any worse
- ❑ c Repair the puncture before riding the motorcycle
- ❑ d Reduce pressure in the tyre before you ride

3.145

You need to put air into your tyres. How would you find out the correct pressure to use?

Mark one answer

- ❑ a It will be shown on the tyre wall
- ❑ b It will be stamped on the wheel
- ❑ c By checking the vehicle owner's manual
- ❑ d By checking the registration document

3.146

You can prevent a cable-operated clutch from becoming stiff by keeping the cable

Mark one answer

- ❑ a tight
- ❑ b dry
- ❑ c slack
- ❑ d oiled

3.147

What safeguard could you take against fire risk to your motorcycle?

Mark one answer

- ❑ a Keep water levels above maximum
- ❑ b Check out any strong smell of petrol
- ❑ c Avoid riding with a full tank of petrol
- ❑ d Use unleaded petrol

3.148

When may you have to increase the tyre pressures on your motorcycle?

Mark three answers

- ❑ a When carrying a passenger
- ❑ b After a long journey
- ❑ c When carrying a load
- ❑ d When riding at high speeds
- ❑ e When riding in hot weather

3.149

You are riding a motorcycle of more than 50 cc. Which FOUR would make a tyre illegal?

Mark four answers

- ❑ a Tread less than 1.6 mm deep
- ❑ b Tread less than 1 mm deep
- ❑ c A large bulge in the wall
- ❑ d A recut tread
- ❑ e Exposed ply or cord
- ❑ f A stone wedged in the tread

3.150

You should maintain cable operated brakes

Mark two answers

- ❑ a by regular adjustment when necessary
- ❑ b at normal service times only
- ❑ c yearly, before taking the motorcycle for its MOT
- ❑ d by oiling cables and pivots regularly

3.151

Tyre pressures should usually be increased on your motorcycle when

Mark one answer

- ❑ a riding on a wet road
- ❑ b carrying a pillion passenger
- ❑ c travelling on an uneven surface
- ❑ d riding on twisty roads

3.152

When riding and wearing brightly coloured clothing you will

Mark one answer

- ❑ a dazzle other motorists on the road
- ❑ b be seen more easily by other motorists
- ❑ c create a hazard by distracting other drivers
- ❑ d be able to ride on unlit roads at night with sidelights

3.153

Why should you wear fluorescent clothing when riding in daylight?

Mark one answer

- ❑ a It reduces wind resistance
- ❑ b It prevents injury if you come off the machine
- ❑ c It helps other road users to see you
- ❑ d It keeps you cool in hot weather

3.154

Why should riders wear reflective clothing?

Mark one answer

- ❑ a To protect them from the cold
- ❑ b To protect them from direct sunlight
- ❑ c To be seen better in daylight
- ❑ d To be seen better at night

3.155

Which of the following makes it easier for motorcyclists to be seen?

Mark three answers

- ❑ a Using a dipped headlight
- ❑ b Wearing a fluorescent jacket
- ❑ c Wearing a white helmet
- ❑ d Wearing a grey helmet
- ❑ e Wearing black leathers
- ❑ f Using a tinted visor

Answers

3.142 b
3.143 a
3.144 a
3.145 c
3.146 d
3.147 b
3.148 a, c, d
3.149 b, c, d, e
3.150 a, d
3.151 b Inflate the tyres according to the maker's instruction.
3.152 b
3.153 c
3.154 d
3.155 a, b, c

3.156

You want to ride your motorcycle in the dark. What could you wear to be seen more easily?

Mark two answers

- ❑ a A black leather jacket
- ❑ b Reflective clothing
- ❑ c A white helmet
- ❑ d A red helmet

3.157

Which of the following would NOT make you more visible in daylight?

Mark one answer

- ❑ a Wearing a black helmet
- ❑ b Wearing a white helmet
- ❑ c Switching on your dipped headlight
- ❑ d Wearing a fluorescent jacket

3.158

Which TWO of these items on a motorcycle MUST be kept clean?

Mark two answers

- ❑ a Number plate
- ❑ b Wheels
- ❑ c Engine
- ❑ d Fairing
- ❑ e Headlight

3.159

Your motorcycle is NOT fitted with daytime running lights. When MUST you use a dipped headlight during the day?

Mark one answer

- ❑ a On country roads
- ❑ b In poor visibility
- ❑ c Along narrow streets
- ❑ d When parking

3.160

You are riding a motorcycle in very hot weather. You should

Mark one answer

- ❑ a ride with your visor fully open
- ❑ b continue to wear protective clothing
- ❑ c wear trainers instead of boots
- ❑ d slacken your helmet strap

3.161

Which of the following fairings would give you the best weather protection?

Mark one answer

- ❑ a Handlebar
- ❑ b Sports
- ❑ c Touring
- ❑ d Windscreen

3.162

Your visor becomes badly scratched. You should

Mark one answer

- ❑ a polish it with a fine abrasive
- ❑ b replace it
- ❑ c wash it in soapy water
- ❑ d clean it with petrol

3.163

What should you clean visors and goggles with?

Mark one answer

- ❑ a Petrol
- ❑ b White spirit
- ❑ c Antifreeze
- ❑ d Soapy water

3.164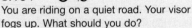

You are riding on a quiet road. Your visor fogs up. What should you do?

Mark one answer

- ❏ a Continue at a reduced speed
- ❏ b Stop as soon as possible and wipe it
- ❏ c Build up speed to increase air flow
- ❏ d Close the helmet air vents

3.165

You are riding in hot weather. What is the safest type of footwear?

Mark one answer

- ❏ a Sandals
- ❏ b Trainers
- ❏ c Shoes
- ❏ d Boots

3.166

Which of the following should not be used to fasten your safety helmet?

Mark one answer

- ❏ a Double D ring fastening
- ❏ b Velcro tab
- ❏ c Quick release fastening
- ❏ d Bar and buckle

3.167

Why should you wear specialist motorcycle clothing when riding?

Mark one answer

- ❏ a Because the law requires you to do so
- ❏ b Because it looks better than ordinary clothing
- ❏ c Because it gives best protection from the weather
- ❏ d Because it will reduce your insurance

3.168

It would be illegal to ride with a helmet on when

Mark one answer

- ❏ a the helmet is not fastened correctly
- ❏ b the helmet is more than four years old
- ❏ c you have borrowed someone else's helmet
- ❏ d the helmet does not have chin protection

Answers

3.156 b, c
3.157 a
3.158 a, e
3.159 b Motorbike riders are small and difficult to see in comparison to a car, so in poor visibility it is important that you make yourself as visible as possible by switching on your dipped headlight.
3.160 b Protective clothing offers some kind of protection against injury in the event of an accident.
3.161 c
3.162 b A badly scratched visor can distort your vision, causing dazzle from oncoming headlights at night and glare from a low winter sun.
3.163 d Most other cleaning agents may have a solvent content, which will damage the visor.
3.164 b
3.165 d Whatever the weather conditions, full safety clothing should always be worn.
3.166 b Velcro is only designed to tidy up more secure fastenings and would not be safe in an accident.
3.167 c
3.168 a

3.169

A friend offers you a second-hand safety helmet for you to use. Why may this be a bad idea?

Mark one answer
- ❑ a It may be damaged
- ❑ b You will be breaking the law
- ❑ c You will affect your insurance cover
- ❑ d It may be a full-face type

3.170

When leaving your motorcycle parked, you should always

Mark one answer
- ❑ a remove the battery lead
- ❑ b pull it onto the kerb
- ❑ c use the steering lock
- ❑ d leave the parking light on

3.171

You are parking your motorcycle. Chaining it to an immovable object will

Mark one answer
- ❑ a be against the law
- ❑ b give extra security
- ❑ c be likely to cause damage
- ❑ d leave the motorcycle unstable

3.172

You are parking your motorcycle and sidecar on a hill. What is the best way to stop it rolling away?

Mark one answer
- ❑ a Leave it in neutral
- ❑ b Put the rear wheel on the pavement
- ❑ c Leave it in a low gear
- ❑ d Park very close to another vehicle

3.173

You are leaving your motorcycle parked on a road. When may you leave the engine running?

Mark one answer
- ❑ a If you will be parked for less than five minutes
- ❑ b If the battery is flat
- ❑ c When in a 20 mph zone
- ❑ d Not on any occasion

Answers

3.169 a
3.170 c
3.171 b
3.172 c
3.173 d

Theory Test Questions
for Car Drivers and Motorcyclists

Section 4 — Safety margins

4.1

Braking distances on ice can be

Mark one answer

- ❑ a twice the normal distance
- ❑ b five times the normal distance
- ❑ c seven times the normal distance
- ❑ d ten times the normal distance

4.2

Freezing conditions will affect the distance it takes you to come to a stop. You should expect stopping distances to increase by up to

Mark one answer

- ❑ a two times
- ❑ b three times
- ❑ c five times
- ❑ d ten times

4.3

In windy conditions you need to take extra care when

Mark one answer

- ❑ a using the brakes
- ❑ b making a hill start
- ❑ c turning into a narrow road
- ❑ d passing pedal cyclists

4.4

When approaching a right-hand bend you should keep well to the left. Why is this?

Mark one answer

- ❑ a To improve your view of the road
- ❑ b To overcome the effect of the road's slope
- ❑ c To let faster traffic from behind overtake
- ❑ d To be positioned safely if you skid

4.5

You should not overtake when

Mark three answers

- ❑ a intending to turn left shortly afterwards
- ❑ b in a one-way street
- ❑ c approaching a junction
- ❑ d going up a long hill
- ❑ e the view ahead is blocked

4.6

You have just gone through deep water. To dry off the brakes you should

Mark one answer

- ❑ a accelerate and keep to a high speed for a short time
- ❑ b go slowly while gently applying the brakes
- ❑ c avoid using the brakes at all for a few miles
- ❑ d stop for at least an hour to allow them time to dry

4.7

In very hot weather the road surface can become soft. Which TWO of the following will be most affected?

Mark two answers

- ❑ a The suspension
- ❑ b The grip of the tyres
- ❑ c The braking
- ❑ d The exhaust

4.8

Where are you most likely to be affected by a side wind?

Mark one answer

- ❑ a On a narrow country lane
- ❑ b On an open stretch of road
- ❑ c On a busy stretch of road
- ❑ d On a long, straight road

4.9

In good conditions, what is the typical stopping distance at 70 mph?

Mark one answer

- ❑ a 53 metres (175 feet)
- ❑ b 60 metres (197 feet)
- ❑ c 73 metres (240 feet)
- ❑ d 96 metres (315 feet)

4.10

What is the shortest overall stopping distance on a dry road at 60 mph?

Mark one answer

- ❑ a 53 metres (175 feet)
- ❑ b 58 metres (190 feet)
- ❑ c 73 metres (240 feet)
- ❑ d 96 metres (315 feet)

4.11

You are following a vehicle at a safe distance on a wet road. Another driver overtakes you and pulls into the gap you have left. What should you do?

Mark one answer

- ❑ a Flash your headlights as a warning
- ❑ b Try to overtake safely as soon as you can
- ❑ c Drop back to regain a safe distance
- ❑ d Stay close to the other vehicle until it moves on

4.12

What is the most common cause of skidding?

Mark one answer

- ❑ a Worn tyres
- ❑ b Driver error
- ❑ c Other vehicles
- ❑ d Pedestrians

4.13

You are driving on an icy road. How can you avoid wheelspin?

Mark one answer

- ❑ a Drive at a slow speed in as high a gear as possible
- ❑ b Use the handbrake if the wheels start to slip
- ❑ c Brake gently and repeatedly
- ❑ d Drive in a low gear at all times

4.14

Skidding is mainly caused by

Mark one answer

- ❑ a the weather
- ❑ b the driver
- ❑ c the vehicle
- ❑ d the road

Answers

4.1   d
4.2   d
4.3   d In windy conditions cyclists are all too easily blown about and may wobble or steer off course.
4.4   a You can see further round the bend earlier if you keep to the left.
4.5   a, c, e
4.6   b
4.7   b, c
4.8   b
4.9   d
4.10 c
4.11 c
4.12 b
4.13 a
4.14 b Skidding is usually caused by harsh braking, harsh acceleration or harsh steering – all actions of the driver. You are, however, more likely to cause a skid in a poorly maintained car, in bad weather or on a poor road surface.

4.15

You are driving in freezing conditions. What should you do when approaching a sharp bend?

Mark two answers

- a Slow down before you reach the bend
- b Gently apply your handbrake
- c Firmly use your footbrake
- d Coast into the bend
- e Avoid sudden steering movements

4.16

You are turning left on a slippery road. The back of your vehicle slides to the right. You should

Mark one answer

- a brake firmly and not turn the steering wheel
- b steer carefully to the left
- c steer carefully to the right
- d brake firmly and steer to the left

4.17

Before starting a journey in freezing weather you should clear ice and snow from your vehicle's

Mark four answers

- a aerial
- b windows
- c bumper
- d lights
- e mirrors
- f number plates

4.18

You are trying to move off on snow. You should use

Mark one answer

- a the lowest gear you can
- b the highest gear you can
- c a high engine speed
- d the handbrake and footbrake together

4.19

When driving in falling snow you should

Mark one answer

- a brake firmly and quickly
- b be ready to steer sharply
- c use sidelights only
- d brake gently in plenty of time

4.20

The MAIN benefit of having four-wheel drive is to improve

Mark one answer

- a road holding
- b fuel consumption
- c stopping distances
- d passenger comfort

4.21

You are about to go down a steep hill. To control the speed of your vehicle you should

Mark one answer

- a select a high gear and use the brakes carefully
- b select a high gear and use the brakes firmly
- c select a low gear and use the brakes carefully
- d select a low gear and avoid using the brakes

4.22

You wish to park facing DOWNHILL. Which TWO of the following should you do?

Mark two answers

- a Turn the steering wheel towards the kerb
- b Park close to the bumper of another car
- c Park with two wheels on the kerb
- d Put the handbrake on firmly
- e Turn the steering wheel away from the kerb

4.23

You are driving in a built-up area. You approach a speed hump. You should

Mark one answer

- ❑ a move across to the left-hand side of the road
- ❑ b wait for any pedestrians to cross
- ❑ c slow your vehicle right down
- ❑ d stop and check both pavements

4.24

You are on a long, downhill slope. What should you do to help control the speed of your vehicle?

Mark one answer

- ❑ a Select neutral
- ❑ b Select a lower gear
- ❑ c Grip the handbrake firmly
- ❑ d Apply the parking brake gently

4.25

Anti-lock brakes prevent wheels from locking. This means the tyres are less likely to

Mark one answer

- ❑ a aquaplane
- ❑ b skid
- ❑ c puncture
- ❑ d wear

4.26

Anti-lock brakes reduce the chances of a skid occurring particularly when

Mark one answer

- ❑ a driving down steep hills
- ❑ b braking during normal driving
- ❑ c braking in an emergency
- ❑ d driving on good road surfaces

Answers

4.15   a, e Braking on an icy bend is extremely dangerous. It could cause your vehicle to spin.

4.16   c

4.17   b, d ,e, f

4.18   b

4.19   d

4.20   a

4.21   c A low gear will help control your speed, but on a steep hill you will also need your brakes.

4.22   a, d If the handbrake should fail, the car will roll into the kerb and not down the road.

4.23   c

4.24   b You should ideally have selected the lower gear before starting down the slope. Doing 'a' would be likely to make your car go faster as you would no longer be in any gear at all.

4.25   b

4.26   c You should brake rapidly and firmly.

4.27

Vehicles fitted with anti-lock brakes
Mark one answer

- ❑ a are impossible to skid
- ❑ b can be steered while you are braking
- ❑ c accelerate much faster
- ❑ d are not fitted with a handbrake

4.28

Anti-lock brakes may not work as effectively
if the road surface is
Mark two answers

- ❑ a dry
- ❑ b loose
- ❑ c wet
- ❑ d good
- ❑ e firm

4.29

Anti-lock brakes are of most use when you are
Mark one answer

- ❑ a braking gently
- ❑ b driving on worn tyres
- ❑ c braking excessively
- ❑ d driving normally

4.30

Driving a vehicle fitted with anti-lock brakes
allows you to
Mark one answer

- ❑ a brake harder because it is impossible to
    skid
- ❑ b drive at higher speeds
- ❑ c steer and brake at the same time
- ❑ d pay less attention to the road ahead

4.31

Anti-lock brakes can greatly assist with
Mark one answer

- ❑ a a higher cruising speed
- ❑ b steering control when braking
- ❑ c control when accelerating
- ❑ d motorway driving

4.32

You are driving a vehicle fitted with anti-lock
brakes. You need to stop in an emergency.
You should apply the footbrake
Mark one answer

- ❑ a slowly and gently
- ❑ b slowly but firmly
- ❑ c rapidly and gently
- ❑ d rapidly and firmly

4.33

Your vehicle has anti-lock brakes, but they
may not always prevent skidding. This is most
likely to happen when driving
Mark two answers

- ❑ a in foggy conditions
- ❑ b on surface water
- ❑ c on loose road surfaces
- ❑ d on dry tarmac
- ❑ e at night on unlit roads

4.34

You are driving along a country road. You see
this sign. AFTER dealing safely with the hazard
you should always

Mark one answer

- ❑ a check your tyre pressures
- ❑ b switch on your hazard warning lights
- ❑ c accelerate briskly
- ❑ d test your brakes

4.35

When driving in fog, which of the following are correct?

Mark three answers

- ❑ a Use dipped headlights
- ❑ b Use headlights on full beam
- ❑ c Allow more time for your journey
- ❑ d Keep close to the car in front
- ❑ e Slow down
- ❑ f Use side lights only

4.36

You are driving in heavy rain. Your steering suddenly becomes very light. You should

Mark one answer

- ❑ a steer towards the side of the road
- ❑ b apply gentle acceleration
- ❑ c brake firmly to reduce speed
- ❑ d ease off the accelerator

4.37

The roads are icy. You should drive slowly

Mark one answer

- ❑ a in the highest gear possible
- ❑ b in the lowest gear possible
- ❑ c with the handbrake partly on
- ❑ d with your left foot on the brake

4.38

You are driving along a wet road. How can you tell if your vehicle is aquaplaning?

Mark one answer

- ❑ a The engine will stall
- ❑ b The engine noise will increase
- ❑ c The steering will feel very heavy
- ❑ d The steering will feel very light

4.39

How can you tell if you are driving on ice?

Mark two answers

- ❑ a The tyres make a rumbling noise
- ❑ b The tyres make hardly any noise
- ❑ c The steering becomes heavier
- ❑ d The steering becomes lighter

Answers

4.27 b A vehicle fitted with anti-lock brakes is very difficult, but not impossible, to skid. Take care if the road surface is loose or wet.

4.28 b, c

4.29 c

4.30 c

4.31 b

4.32 d

4.33 b, c

4.34 d Drive slowly forwards with your left foot gently on the footbrake. This helps dry out the brakes.

4.35 a, c, e

4.36 d

4.37 a

4.38 d

4.39 b, d

4.40

You are driving along a wet road. How can you tell if your vehicle's tyres are losing their grip on the surface?

Mark one answer

- ❑ a The engine will stall
- ❑ b The steering will feel very heavy
- ❑ c The engine noise will increase
- ❑ d The steering will feel very light

4.41

You are travelling at 50 mph on a good, dry road. What is your shortest overall stopping distance?

Mark one answer

- ❑ a 36 metres (120 feet)
- ❑ b 53 metres (175 feet)
- ❑ c 75 metres (245 feet)
- ❑ d 96 metres (315 feet)

4.42

Your overall stopping distance will be much longer when driving

Mark one answer

- ❑ a in the rain
- ❑ b in fog
- ❑ c at night
- ❑ d in strong winds

4.43

You have driven through a flood. What is the first thing you should do?

Mark one answer

- ❑ a Stop and check the tyres
- ❑ b Stop and dry the brakes
- ❑ c Check your exhaust
- ❑ d Test your brakes

4.44

You are on a good, dry road surface. Your vehicle has good brakes and tyres. What is the BRAKING distance at 50 mph?

Mark one answer

- ❑ a 38 metres (125 feet)
- ❑ b 14 metres (46 feet)
- ❑ c 24 metres (79 feet)
- ❑ d 55 metres (180 feet)

4.45

You are on a good, dry, road surface and your vehicle has good brakes and tyres. What is the typical overall stopping distance at 40 mph?

Mark one answer

- ❑ a 23 metres (75 feet)
- ❑ b 36 metres (120 feet)
- ❑ c 53 metres (175 feet)
- ❑ d 96 metres (315 feet)

4.46

You are on a fast, open road in good conditions. For safety, the distance between you and the vehicle in front should be

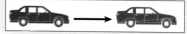

Mark one answer

- ❑ a a two-second time gap
- ❑ b one car length
- ❑ c 2 metres (6 feet 6 inches)
- ❑ d two car lengths

4.47

You are braking on a wet road. Your vehicle begins to skid. It does not have anti-lock brakes. What is the FIRST thing you should do?

Mark one answer

- ❑ a Quickly pull up the handbrake
- ❑ b Release the footbrake fully
- ❑ c Push harder on the brake pedal
- ❑ d Gently use the accelerator

4.48

How can you use your vehicle's engine as a brake?

Mark one answer

- ❑ a By changing to a lower gear
- ❑ b By selecting reverse gear
- ❑ c By changing to a higher gear
- ❑ d By selecting neutral gear

4.49

Anti-lock brakes are most effective when you

Mark one answer

- ❑ a keep pumping the foot brake to prevent skidding
- ❑ b brake normally, but grip the steering wheel tightly
- ❑ c brake promptly and firmly until you have slowed down
- ❑ d apply the handbrake to reduce the stopping distance

4.50

Your car is fitted with anti-lock brakes. You need to stop in an emergency. You should

Mark one answer

- ❑ a brake normally and avoid turning the steering wheel
- ❑ b press the brake pedal promptly and firmly until you have stopped
- ❑ c keep pushing and releasing the foot brake quickly to prevent skidding
- ❑ d apply the handbrake to reduce the stopping distance

4.51

When would an anti-lock braking system start to work?

Mark one answer

- ❑ a After the parking brake has been applied
- ❑ b Whenever pressure on the brake pedal is applied
- ❑ c Just as the wheels are about to lock
- ❑ d When the normal braking system fails to operate

4.52

Anti-lock brakes will take effect when

Mark one answer

- ❑ a you do not brake quickly enough
- ❑ b maximum brake pressure has been applied
- ❑ c you have not seen a hazard ahead
- ❑ d speeding on slippery road surfaces

Answers

4.40 d This problem is sometimes called aquaplaning. Your tyres build up a thin film of water between them and the road and lose all grip. The steering suddenly feels light and uncontrollable. The solution is to ease off the accelerator until you feel the tyres grip the road again.

4.41 b

4.42 a

4.43 d Your brakes may be wet. The first thing you should do is check them and then dry them.

4.44 a Note this is the braking distance. The overall stopping distance is further because you have to add 'thinking' distance.

4.45 b

4.46 a

4.47 b Note that the question asks for the first thing you should do, which is always to remove the cause of the skid – in this case braking. You would next need to re-apply the brakes more gently. Answer 'c' is wrong because braking harder would increase the skid.

4.48 a

4.49 c

4.50 b

4.51 c

4.52 b

4.53

You are on a wet motorway with surface spray. You should use

Mark one answer

- ❑ a hazard flashers
- ❑ b dipped headlights
- ❑ c rear fog lights
- ❑ d sidelights

4.54

Your vehicle is fitted with anti-lock brakes. To stop quickly in an emergency you should

Mark one answer

- ❑ a brake firmly and pump the brake pedal on and off
- ❑ b brake rapidly and firmly without releasing the brake pedal
- ❑ c brake gently and pump the brake pedal on and off
- ❑ d brake rapidly once, and immediately release the brake pedal

4.55

Travelling for long distances in neutral (known as coasting)

Mark one answer

- ❑ a improves the driver's control
- ❑ b makes steering easier
- ❑ c reduces the driver's control
- ❑ d uses more fuel

4.56

How can you tell when you are driving over black ice?

Mark one answer

- ❑ a It is easier to brake
- ❑ b The noise from your tyres sounds louder
- ❑ c You will see tyre tracks on the road
- ❑ d Your steering feels light

4.57

Your overall stopping distance will be longer when riding

Mark one answer

- ❑ a at night
- ❑ b in the fog
- ❑ c with a passenger
- ❑ d up a hill

4.58

On a wet road what is the safest way to stop?

Mark one answer

- ❑ a Change gear without braking
- ❑ b Use the back brake only
- ❑ c Use the front brake only
- ❑ d Use both brakes

4.59

You are riding in heavy rain when your rear wheel skids as you accelerate. To get control again you must

Mark one answer

- ❑ a change down to a lower gear
- ❑ b ease off the throttle
- ❑ c brake to reduce speed
- ❑ d put your feet down

4.60

It is snowing. Before starting your journey you should

Mark one answer

- ❑ a think if you need to ride at all
- ❑ b try to avoid taking a passenger
- ❑ c plan a route avoiding towns
- ❑ d take a hot drink before setting out

4.61

Why should you ride with a dipped headlight on in the daytime?

Mark one answer

- ❏ a It helps other road users to see you
- ❏ b It means that you can ride faster
- ❏ c Other vehicles will get out of the way
- ❏ d So that it is already on when it gets dark

4.62

Motorcyclists are only allowed to use high-intensity rear fog lights when

Mark one answer

- ❏ a a pillion passenger is being carried
- ❏ b they ride a large touring machine
- ❏ c visibility is 100 metres (328 feet) or less
- ❏ d they are riding on the road for the first time

4.63

When riding at night you should

Mark two answers

- ❏ a ride with your headlight on dipped beam
- ❏ b wear reflective clothing
- ❏ c wear a tinted visor
- ❏ d ride in the centre of the road
- ❏ e give arm signals

4.64

You MUST use your headlight

Mark three answers

- ❏ a when riding in a group
- ❏ b at night when street lighting is poor
- ❏ c when carrying a passenger
- ❏ d on motorways during darkness
- ❏ e at times of poor visibility
- ❏ f when parked on an unlit road

4.65

You are riding in town at night. The roads are wet after rain. The reflections from wet surfaces will

Mark one answer

- ❏ a affect your stopping distance
- ❏ b affect your road holding
- ❏ c make it easy to see unlit objects
- ❏ d make it hard to see unlit objects

Answers

4.53 b
4.54 b
4.55 c When you travel in neutral (because you are out of gear or have the clutch down) the engine is disengaged from the wheels and there is no effect from engine braking.
4.56 d Black ice is normally invisible when you are driving. The tyres will lose grip with the road which will make the steering feel light.
4.57 c Remember, therefore, to allow a bigger gap when following another vehicle.
4.58 d
4.59 b
4.60 a
4.61 a Motorcycles are small and difficult to see. Anything that increases your chances of being seen by other road users is a good thing.
4.62 c
4.63 a, b
4.64 b, d, e
4.65 d

4.66

You are riding through a flood. Which TWO should you do?

Mark two answers

- ❏ a Keep in a high gear and stand up on the footrests
- ❏ b Keep the engine running fast to keep water out of the exhaust
- ❏ c Ride slowly and test your brakes when you are out of the water
- ❏ d Turn your headlight off to avoid any electrical damage

4.67

You have just ridden through a flood. When clear of the water you should test your

Mark one answer

- ❏ a starter motor
- ❏ b headlight
- ❏ c steering
- ❏ d brakes

4.68

When going through flood water you should ride

Mark one answer

- ❏ a quickly in a high gear
- ❏ b slowly in a high gear
- ❏ c quickly in a low gear
- ❏ d slowly in a low gear

4.69

When riding at night you should NOT

Mark one answer

- ❏ a switch on full beam headlights
- ❏ b overtake slower vehicles in front
- ❏ c use dipped beam headlights
- ❏ d use tinted glasses, lenses or visors

4.70

Which of the following should you do when riding in fog?

Mark two answers

- ❏ a Keep close to the vehicle in front
- ❏ b Use your dipped headlight
- ❏ c Ride close to the centre of the road
- ❏ d Keep your visor or goggles clear
- ❏ e Keep the vehicle in front in view

4.71

You are riding in heavy rain. Why should you try to avoid this marked area?

Mark one answer

- ❏ a It is illegal to ride over bus stops
- ❏ b The painted lines may be slippery
- ❏ c Cyclists may be using the bus stop
- ❏ d Only emergency vehicles may drive over bus stops

4.72

When riding at night you should

Mark one answer

- ❏ a wear reflective clothing
- ❏ b wear a tinted visor
- ❏ c ride in the middle of the road
- ❏ d always give arm signals

4.73

When riding in extremely cold conditions what can you do to keep warm?

Mark one answer

- ❏ a Stay close to the vehicles in front
- ❏ b Wear suitable clothing
- ❏ c Lie flat on the tank
- ❏ d Put one hand on the exhaust pipe

4.74

You are riding at night. To be seen more easily you should

Mark two answers

- ❏ a ride with your headlight on dipped beam
- ❏ b wear reflective clothing
- ❏ c keep the motorcycle clean
- ❏ d stay well out to the right
- ❏ e wear waterproof clothing

4.75

Your overall stopping distance will be much longer when riding

Mark one answer

- ❏ a in the rain
- ❏ b in fog
- ❏ c at night
- ❏ d in strong winds

4.76

The road surface is very important to motorcyclists. Which FOUR of these are more likely to reduce the stability of your motorcycle?

Mark four answers

- ❏ a Potholes
- ❏ b Drain covers
- ❏ c Concrete
- ❏ d Oil patches
- ❏ e Tarmac
- ❏ f Loose gravel

4.77

You are riding in very hot weather. What are TWO effects that melting tar has on the control of your motorcycle?

Mark two answers

- ❏ a It can make the surface slippery
- ❏ b It can reduce tyre grip
- ❏ c It can reduce stopping distances
- ❏ d It can improve braking efficiency

4.78

You are riding past queuing traffic.
Why should you be more cautious when approaching this road marking?

Mark one answer

- ❏ a Lorries will be unloading here
- ❏ b Schoolchildren will be crossing here
- ❏ c Pedestrians will be standing in the road
- ❏ d Traffic could be emerging and may not see you

Answers

4.66	b, c
4.67	d
4.68	d
4.69	d
4.70	b, d
4.71	b
4.72	a
4.73	b
4.74	a, b
4.75	a
4.76	a, b, d, f
4.77	a, b
4.78	d

4.79

What can cause your tyres to skid and lose their grip on the road surface?

Mark one answer

- ❑ a Giving hand signals
- ❑ b Riding one handed
- ❑ c Looking over your shoulder
- ❑ d Heavy braking

4.80

It has rained after a long dry spell. You should be very careful because the road surface will be unusually

Mark one answer

- ❑ a loose
- ❑ b dry
- ❑ c sticky
- ❑ d slippery

4.81

When riding in heavy rain a film of water can build up between your tyres and the road surface. This may result in loss of control. What can you do to avoid this happening?

Mark one answer

- ❑ a Keep your speed down
- ❑ b Increase your tyre pressures
- ❑ c Decrease your tyre pressures
- ❑ d Keep trying your brakes

4.82

When riding in heavy rain a film of water can build up between your tyres and the road. This is known as aquaplaning. What should you do to keep control?

Mark one answer

- ❑ a Use your rear brakes gently
- ❑ b Steer to the crown of the road
- ❑ c Ease off the throttle smoothly
- ❑ d Change up into a higher gear

4.83

You are on a good, dry road surface and your motorcycle has good brakes and tyres. What is the typical overall stopping distance at 40 mph?

Mark one answer

- ❑ a 23 metres (75 feet)
- ❑ b 36 metres (120 feet)
- ❑ c 53 metres (175 feet)
- ❑ d 96 metres (315 feet)

4.84

You have to ride in foggy weather. You should

Mark two answers

- ❑ a stay close to the centre of the road
- ❑ b switch only your sidelights on
- ❑ c switch on your dipped headlights
- ❑ d be aware of others not using their headlights
- ❑ e always ride in the gutter to see the kerb

4.85

After riding through deep water you notice your scooter brakes do not work properly. What would be the best way to dry them out?

Mark one answer

- ❑ a Ride slowly, braking lightly
- ❑ b Ride quickly, braking harshly
- ❑ c Stop and dry them with a cloth
- ❑ d Stop and wait for a few minutes

4.86

Only a fool breaks the two-second rule refers to

Mark one answer

- ❑ a the time recommended when using the choke
- ❑ b the separation distance when riding in good conditions
- ❑ c restarting a stalled engine in busy traffic
- ❑ d the time you should keep your foot down at a junction

4.87

At a mini roundabout it is important that a motorcyclist should avoid

Mark one answer

- ❏ a turning right
- ❏ b using signals
- ❏ c taking 'lifesavers'
- ❏ d the painted area

4.88

You are riding on a motorway in a crosswind. You should take extra care when

Mark two answers

- ❏ a approaching service areas
- ❏ b overtaking a large vehicle
- ❏ c riding in slow-moving traffic
- ❏ d approaching an exit
- ❏ e riding in exposed places

4.89

Why should you try to avoid riding over this marked area?

Mark one answer

- ❏ a It is illegal to ride over bus stops
- ❏ b It will alter your machine's centre of gravity
- ❏ c Pedestrians may be waiting at the bus stop
- ❏ d A bus may have left patches of oil

4.90

Your overall stopping distance comprises thinking and braking distance. You are on a good, dry road surface with good brakes and tyres. What is the typical BRAKING distance at 50 mph?

Mark one answer

- ❏ a 14 metres (46 feet)
- ❏ b 24 metres (79 feet)
- ❏ c 38 metres (125 feet)
- ❏ d 55 metres (180 feet)

4.91

You are riding at speed through surface water. A thin film of water has built up between your tyres and the road surface. To keep control what should you do?

Mark one answer

- ❏ a Turn the steering quickly
- ❏ b Use the rear brake gently
- ❏ c Use both brakes gently
- ❏ d Ease off the throttle

Answers

4.79 d
4.80 d Rain after a long, dry spell will cause any oil or diesel to float to the surface.
4.81 a
4.82 c
4.83 b
4.84 c, d
4.85 a
4.86 b
4.87 d
4.88 b, e
4.89 d
4.90 c
4.91 d

Theory Test Questions
for Car Drivers and Motorcyclists

Section 5 Hazard perception

5.1

Where would you expect to see these markers?

Mark two answers

❑ a On a motorway sign
❑ b At the entrance to a narrow bridge
❑ c On a large goods vehicle
❑ d On a builder's skip placed on the road

5.2

What is the main hazard shown in this picture?

Mark one answer

❑ a Vehicles turning right
❑ b Vehicles doing U-turns
❑ c The cyclist crossing the road
❑ d Parked cars around the corner

5.3

Which road user has caused a hazard?

Mark one answer

❑ a The parked car (arrowed A)
❑ b The pedestrian waiting to cross (arrowed B)
❑ c The moving car (arrowed C)
❑ d The car turning (arrowed D)

5.4

What should the driver of the car approaching the crossing do?

Mark one answer

❑ a Continue at the same speed
❑ b Sound the horn
❑ c Drive through quickly
❑ d Slow down and get ready to stop

5.5

What THREE things should the driver of the grey car (arrowed) be especially aware of?

Mark three answers
- ❏ a Pedestrians stepping out between cars
- ❏ b Other cars behind the grey car
- ❏ c Doors opening on parked cars
- ❏ d The bumpy road surface
- ❏ e Cars leaving parking spaces
- ❏ f Empty parking spaces

5.6

In heavy motorway traffic you are being followed closely by the vehicle behind. How can you lower the risk of an accident?

Mark one answer
- ❏ a Increase your distance from the vehicle in front
- ❏ b Tap your foot on the brake pedal sharply
- ❏ c Switch on your hazard lights
- ❏ d Move onto the hard shoulder and stop

5.7

You see this sign ahead. You should expect the road to

Mark one answer
- ❏ a go steeply uphill
- ❏ b go steeply downhill
- ❏ c bend sharply to the left
- ❏ d bend sharply to the right

5.8

You are approaching this cyclist. You should

Mark one answer
- ❏ a overtake before the cyclist gets to the junction
- ❏ b flash your headlights at the cyclist
- ❏ c slow down and allow the cyclist to turn
- ❏ d overtake the cyclist on the left-hand side

Answers	
5.1	c, d
5.2	c
5.3	a
5.4	d
5.5	a, c, e
5.6	a
5.7	c
5.8	c

5.9

Why must you take extra care when turning right at this junction?

Mark one answer

- ❏ a Road surface is poor
- ❏ b Footpaths are narrow
- ❏ c Road markings are faint
- ❏ d There is reduced visibility

5.10

When approaching this bridge you should give way to

Mark one answer

- ❏ a bicycles
- ❏ b buses
- ❏ c motorcycles
- ❏ d cars

5.11

What type of vehicle could you expect to meet in the middle of the road?

Mark one answer

- ❏ a Lorry
- ❏ b Bicycle
- ❏ c Car
- ❏ d Motorcycle

5.12

At this blind junction you must stop

Mark one answer

- ❏ a behind the line, then edge forward to see clearly
- ❏ b beyond the line at a point where you can see clearly
- ❏ c only if there is traffic on the main road
- ❏ d only if you are turning to the right

5.13

You have just passed these warning lights. What hazard would you expect to see next?

- ❏ a A level crossing with no barrier
- ❏ b An ambulance station
- ❏ c A school crossing patrol
- ❏ d An opening bridge

5.14

The red lights are flashing. What should you do when approaching this level crossing?

- ❏ a Go through quickly
- ❏ b Go through carefully
- ❏ c Stop before the barrier
- ❏ d Switch on hazard warning lights

5.15

You are approaching crossroads. The traffic lights have failed. What should you do?
- ❏ a Brake and stop only for large vehicles
- ❏ b Brake sharply to a stop before looking
- ❏ c Be prepared to brake sharply to a stop
- ❏ d Be prepared to stop for any traffic

5.16

What should the driver of the red car (arrowed) do?

- ❏ a Wave the pedestrians who are waiting to cross
- ❏ b Wait for the pedestrian in the road to cross
- ❏ c Quickly drive behind the pedestrian in the road
- ❏ d Tell the pedestrian in the road she should not have crossed

Answers

5.9	d
5.10	b
5.11	a
5.12	a
5.13	c
5.14	c
5.15	d
5.16	b

5.17

You are following a slower-moving vehicle on a narrow country road. There is a junction just ahead on the right. What should you do?

Mark one answer

- ❑ a Overtake after checking your mirrors and signalling
- ❑ b Stay behind until you are past the junction
- ❑ c Accelerate quickly to pass before the junction
- ❑ d Slow down and prepare to overtake on the left

5.18

What should you do as you approach this overhead bridge?

Mark one answer

- ❑ a Move out to the centre of the road before going through
- ❑ b Find another route, this is only for high vehicles
- ❑ c Be prepared to give way to large vehicles in the middle of the road
- ❑ d Move across to the right hand side before going through

5.19

Why are mirrors often slightly curved (convex)?

Mark one answer

- ❑ a They give a wider field of vision
- ❑ b They totally cover blind spots
- ❑ c They make it easier to judge the speed of following traffic
- ❑ d They make following traffic look bigger

5.20

You see this sign on the rear of a slow-moving lorry that you want to pass. It is travelling in the middle lane of a three-lane motorway. You should

Mark one answer

- ❑ a cautiously approach the lorry then pass on either side
- ❑ b follow the lorry until you can leave the motorway
- ❑ c wait on the hard shoulder until the lorry has stopped
- ❑ d approach with care and keep to the left of the lorry

5.21

You think the driver of the vehicle in front has forgotten to cancel their right indicator. You should

Mark one answer

- ❑ a flash your lights to alert the driver
- ❑ b sound your horn before overtaking
- ❑ c overtake on the left if there is room
- ❑ d stay behind and not overtake

5.22

This yellow sign on a vehicle indicates this is

Mark one answer

- ❑ a a broken-down vehicle
- ❑ b a school bus
- ❑ c an ice cream van
- ❑ d a private ambulance

5.23

What is the main hazard the driver of the red car (arrowed) should be aware of?

Mark one answer

- ❑ a Glare from the sun may affect the driver's vision
- ❑ b The black car may stop suddenly
- ❑ c The bus may move out into the road
- ❑ d Oncoming vehicles will assume the driver is turning right

5.24

What TWO main hazards should you be aware of when going along this street?

Mark two answers

- ❑ a Glare from the sun
- ❑ b Car doors opening suddenly
- ❑ c Lack of road markings
- ❑ d The headlights on parked cars being switched on
- ❑ e Large goods vehicles
- ❑ f Children running out from between vehicles

5.25

What is the main hazard you should be aware of when following this cyclist?

Mark one answer

- ❑ a The cyclist may move to the left and dismount
- ❑ b The cyclist may swerve out into the road
- ❑ c The contents of the cyclist's carrier may fall onto the road
- ❑ d The cyclist may wish to turn right at the end of the road

Answers

5.17	b
5.18	c
5.19	a
5.20	d
5.21	d
5.22	b
5.23	c
5.24	b, f
5.25	b

5.26

When approaching this hazard why should you slow down?

Mark two answers
- ❑ a Because of the bend
- ❑ b Because it's hard to see to the right
- ❑ c Because of approaching traffic
- ❑ d Because of animals crossing
- ❑ e Because of the level crossing

5.27

Why are place names painted on the road surface?

Mark one answer
- ❑ a To restrict the flow of traffic
- ❑ b To warn you of oncoming traffic
- ❑ c To enable you to change lanes early
- ❑ d To prevent you changing lanes

5.28

Some two-way roads are divided into three lanes. Why are these particularly dangerous?

Mark one answer
- ❑ a Traffic in both directions can use the middle lane to overtake
- ❑ b Traffic can travel faster in poor weather conditions
- ❑ c Traffic can overtake on the left
- ❑ d Traffic uses the middle lane for emergencies only

5.29

To avoid an accident when entering a contraflow system, you should

Mark three answers
- ❑ a reduce speed in good time
- ❑ b switch lanes any time to make progress
- ❑ c choose an appropriate lane early
- ❑ d keep the correct separation distance
- ❑ e increase speed to pass through quickly
- ❑ f follow other motorists closely to avoid long queues

5.30

You are on a dual carriageway. Ahead you see a vehicle with an amber flashing light. What could this be?

Mark one answer
- ❑ a An ambulance
- ❑ b A fire engine
- ❑ c A doctor on call
- ❑ d A disabled person's vehicle

5.31

What does this signal from a police officer mean to oncoming traffic?

Mark one answer
- ❑ a Go ahead
- ❑ b Stop
- ❑ c Turn left
- ❑ d Turn right

5.32

Why should you be especially cautious when going past this stationary bus?

Mark two answers

- ❏ a There is traffic approaching in the distance
- ❏ b The driver may open the door
- ❏ c It may suddenly move off
- ❏ d People may cross the road in front of it
- ❏ e There are bicycles parked on the pavement

5.33

A driver pulls out of a side road in front of you. You have to brake hard. You should

Mark one answer

- ❏ a ignore the error and stay calm
- ❏ b flash your lights to show your annoyance
- ❏ c sound your horn to show your annoyance
- ❏ d overtake as soon as possible

5.34

An elderly person's driving ability could be affected because they may be unable to

Mark one answer

- ❏ a obtain car insurance
- ❏ b understand road signs
- ❏ c react very quickly
- ❏ d give signals correctly

5.35

You are planning a long journey. Do you need to plan rest stops?

Mark one answer

- ❏ a Yes, you should plan to stop every half an hour
- ❏ b Yes, regular stops help concentration
- ❏ c No, you will be less tired if you get there as soon as possible
- ❏ d No, only fuel stops will be needed

5.36

A driver does something that upsets you. You should

Mark one answer

- ❏ a try not to react
- ❏ b let them know how you feel
- ❏ c flash your headlights several times
- ❏ d sound your horn

5.37

A driver's behaviour has upset you. It may help if you

Mark one answer

- ❏ a stop and take a break
- ❏ b shout abusive language
- ❏ c gesture to them with your hand
- ❏ d follow their car, flashing your headlights

Answers	
5.26	a, e
5.27	c
5.28	a
5.29	a, c, d
5.30	d
5.31	b
5.32	c, d
5.33	a
5.34	c
5.35	b
5.36	a
5.37	a

5.38

In areas where there are 'traffic calming' measures you should

Mark one answer

- ❑ a travel at a reduced speed
- ❑ b always travel at the speed limit
- ❑ c position in the centre of the road
- ❑ d only slow down if pedestrians are near

5.39

You are driving on this dual carriageway. Why may you need to slow down?

Mark one answer

- ❑ a There is a broken white line in the centre
- ❑ b There are solid white lines either side
- ❑ c There are roadworks ahead of you
- ❑ d There are no footpaths

5.40

Which of the following types of glasses should NOT be worn when driving at night?

Mark one answer

- ❑ a Half-moon
- ❑ b Round
- ❑ c Bi-focal
- ❑ d Tinted

5.41

When should you use hazard warning lights?

Mark one answer

- ❑ a When you are double-parked on a two-way road
- ❑ b When your direction indicators are not working
- ❑ c When warning oncoming traffic that you intend to stop
- ❑ d When your vehicle has broken down and is causing an obstruction

5.42

You want to turn left at this junction. The view of the main road is restricted. What should you do?

Mark one answer

- ❑ a Stay well back and wait to see if something comes
- ❑ b Build up your speed so that you can emerge quickly
- ❑ c Stop and apply the handbrake even if the road is clear
- ❑ d Approach slowly and edge out until you can see more clearly

5.43

When may you use hazard warning lights?

Mark one answer

- ❑ a To park alongside another car
- ❑ b To park on double yellow lines
- ❑ c When you are being towed
- ❑ d When you have broken down

5.44

Hazard warning lights should be used when vehicles are

- a broken down and causing an obstruction
- b faulty and moving slowly
- c being towed along a road
- d reversing into a side road

5.45

When driving a car fitted with automatic transmission what would you use 'kick down' for?

- a Cruise control
- b Quick acceleration
- c Slow braking
- d Fuel economy

5.46

For which of these may you use hazard warning lights?

- a When driving on a motorway to warn traffic behind of a hazard ahead
- b When you are double-parked on a two-way road
- c When your direction indicators are not working
- d When warning oncoming traffic that you intend to stop

5.47

You are driving on a motorway. The traffic ahead is braking sharply because of an accident. How could you warn traffic behind you?

- a Briefly use the hazard warning lights
- b Switch on the hazard warning lights continuously
- c Briefly use the rear fog lights
- d Switch on the headlights continuously

5.48

You are waiting to emerge at a junction. Your view is restricted by parked vehicles. What can help you to see traffic on the road you are joining?

- a Looking for traffic behind you
- b Reflections of traffic in shop windows
- c Making eye contact with other road users
- d Checking for traffic in your interior mirror

5.49

What does the solid white line at the side of the road indicate?

- a Traffic lights ahead
- b Edge of the carriageway
- c Footpath on the left
- d Cycle path

Answers

5.38   a Road humps and rumble strips are examples of traffic calming measures. They are often found in residential areas and have been introduced to reduce the overall speed of traffic.

5.39   c
5.40   d
5.41   d
5.42   d
5.43   d
5.44   a
5.45   b
5.46   a
5.47   a
5.48   b
5.49   b

5.50

You are driving towards this level crossing. What would be the first warning of an approaching train?

Mark one answer

- ❑ a Both half barriers down
- ❑ b A steady amber light
- ❑ c One half barrier down
- ❑ d Twin flashing red lights

5.51

You are behind this cyclist. When the traffic lights change, what should you do?

Mark one answer

- ❑ a Try to move off before the cyclist
- ❑ b Allow the cyclist time and room
- ❑ c Turn right but give the cyclist room
- ❑ d Tap your horn and drive through first

5.52

While driving, you see this sign ahead. You should

Mark one answer

- ❑ a stop at the sign
- ❑ b slow, but continue around the bend
- ❑ c slow to a crawl and continue
- ❑ d stop and look for open farm gates

5.53

When the traffic lights change to green the white car should

Mark one answer

- ❑ a wait for the cyclist to pull away
- ❑ b move off quickly and turn in front of the cyclist
- ❑ c move close up to the cyclist to beat the lights
- ❑ d sound the horn to warn the cyclist

5.54

You intend to turn left at the traffic lights. Just before turning you should

Mark one answer
- ❑ a check your right mirror
- ❑ b move close up to the white car
- ❑ c straddle the lanes
- ❑ d check for bicycles on your left

5.55

You should reduce your speed when driving along this road because

Mark one answer
- ❑ a there is a staggered junction ahead
- ❑ b there is a low bridge ahead
- ❑ c there is a change in the road surface
- ❑ d the road ahead narrows

5.56

You are driving at 60 mph. As you approach this hazard you should

Mark one answer
- ❑ a maintain your speed
- ❑ b reduce your speed
- ❑ c take the next right turn
- ❑ d take the next left turn

5.57

What might you expect to happen in this situation?

Mark one answer
- ❑ a Traffic will move into the right-hand lane
- ❑ b Traffic speed will increase
- ❑ c Traffic will move into the left-hand lane
- ❑ d Traffic will not need to change position

Answers

5.50	b
5.51	b
5.52	b
5.53	a
5.54	d
5.55	a
5.56	b
5.57	c

5.58
You are driving on a road with several lanes. You see these signs above the lanes. What do they mean?

Mark one answer
- a The two right lanes are open
- b The two left lanes are open
- c Traffic in the left lanes should stop
- d Traffic in the right lanes should stop

5.59
You are invited to a pub lunch. You know that you will have to drive in the evening. What is your best course of action?
Mark one answer
- a Avoid mixing your alcoholic drinks
- b Not drink any alcohol at all
- c Have some milk before drinking alcohol
- d Eat a hot meal with your alcoholic drinks

5.60
You have been convicted of driving while unfit through drink or drugs. You will find this is likely to cause the cost of one of the following to rise considerably. Which one?

Mark one answer
- a Road fund licence
- b Insurance premiums
- c Vehicle test certificate
- d Driving licence

5.61
What advice should you give to a driver who has had a few alcoholic drinks at a party?
Mark one answer
- a Have a strong cup of coffee and then drive home
- b Drive home carefully and slowly
- c Go home by public transport
- d Wait a short while and then drive home

5.62
You have been taking medicine for a few days which made you feel drowsy. Today you feel better but still need to take the medicine. You should only drive
Mark one answer
- a if your journey is necessary
- b at night on quiet roads
- c if someone goes with you
- d after checking with your doctor

5.63
You are about to return home from holiday when you become ill. A doctor prescribes drugs which are likely to affect your driving. You should
Mark one answer
- a drive only if someone is with you
- b avoid driving on motorways
- c not drive yourself
- d never drive at more than 30 mph

5.64
During periods of illness your ability to drive may be impaired. You MUST
Mark two answers
- a see your doctor each time before you drive
- b only take smaller doses of any medicines
- c be medically fit to drive
- d not drive after taking certain medicines
- e take all your medicines with you when you drive

5.65

You feel drowsy when driving. You should
Mark two answers

- ❑ a stop and rest as soon as possible
- ❑ b turn the heater up to keep you warm and comfortable
- ❑ c make sure you have a good supply of fresh air
- ❑ d continue with your journey but drive more slowly
- ❑ e close the car windows to help you concentrate

5.66

You are driving along a motorway and become tired. You should
Mark two answers

- ❑ a stop at the next service area and rest
- ❑ b leave the motorway at the next exit and rest
- ❑ c increase your speed and turn up the radio volume
- ❑ d close all your windows and set heating to warm
- ❑ e pull up on the hard shoulder and change drivers

5.67

You are taking drugs that are likely to affect your driving. What should you do?
Mark one answer

- ❑ a Seek medical advice before driving
- ❑ b Limit your driving to essential journeys
- ❑ c Only drive if accompanied by a full licence-holder
- ❑ d Drive only for short distances

5.68

You are about to drive home. You feel very tired and have a severe headache. You should
Mark one answer

- ❑ a wait until you are fit and well before driving
- ❑ b drive home, but take a tablet for headaches
- ❑ c drive home if you can stay awake for the journey
- ❑ d wait for a short time, then drive home slowly

5.69

If you are feeling tired it is best to stop as soon as you can. Until then you should
Mark one answer

- ❑ a increase your speed to find a stopping place quickly
- ❑ b ensure a supply of fresh air
- ❑ c gently tap the steering wheel
- ❑ d keep changing speed to improve concentration

Answers

5.58	b
5.59	b
5.60	b
5.61	c The only sensible answer is don't drink and drive.
5.62	d
5.63	c
5.64	c, d
5.65	a, c
5.66	a, b
5.67	a A significant number of drugs, even those you can buy in the chemist, can affect your ability to drive. Sometimes a warning is given on the packet, but if in any doubt seek medical advice.
5.68	a
5.69	b

5.70

Driving long distances can be tiring. You can prevent this by

Mark three answers

- ❑ a stopping every so often for a walk
- ❑ b opening a window for some fresh air
- ❑ c ensuring plenty of refreshment breaks
- ❑ d completing the journey without stopping
- ❑ e eating a large meal before driving

5.71

You go to a social event and need to drive a short time after. What precaution should you take?

Mark one answer

- ❑ a Avoid drinking alcohol on an empty stomach
- ❑ b Drink plenty of coffee after drinking alcohol
- ❑ c Avoid drinking alcohol completely
- ❑ d Drink plenty of milk before drinking alcohol

5.72

You take some cough medicine given to you by a friend. What should you do before driving?

Mark one answer

- ❑ a Ask your friend if taking the medicine affected their driving
- ❑ b Drink some strong coffee one hour before driving
- ❑ c Check the label to see if the medicine will affect your driving
- ❑ d Drive a short distance to see if the medicine is affecting your driving

5.73

You take the wrong route and find you are on a one-way street. You should

Mark one answer

- ❑ a reverse out of the road
- ❑ b turn round in a side road
- ❑ c continue to the end of the road
- ❑ d reverse into a driveway

5.74

Which THREE are likely to make you lose concentration while driving?

Mark three answers

- ❑ a Looking at road maps
- ❑ b Listening to loud music
- ❑ c Using your windscreen washers
- ❑ d Looking in your wing mirror
- ❑ e Using a mobile phone

5.75

You are driving along this road. The driver on the left is reversing from a driveway. You should

Mark one answer

- ❑ a move to the opposite side of the road
- ❑ b drive through as you have priority
- ❑ c sound your horn and be prepared to stop
- ❑ d speed up and drive through quickly

5.76

You have been involved in an argument before starting your journey. This has made you feel angry. You should
Mark one answer

❏ a start to drive, but open a window
❏ b drive slower than normal and turn your radio on
❏ c have an alcoholic drink to help you relax before driving
❏ d calm down before you start to drive

5.77

You start to feel tired while driving. What should you do?
Mark one answer

❏ a Increase your speed slightly
❏ b Decrease your speed slightly
❏ c Find a less busy route
❏ d Pull over at a safe place to rest

5.78

You have just been overtaken by this motorcyclist who is cutting in sharply. You should

Mark one answer

❏ a sound the horn
❏ b brake firmly
❏ c keep a safe gap
❏ d flash your lights

5.79

You are about to drive home. You cannot find the glasses you need to wear. You should
Mark one answer

❏ a drive home slowly, keeping to quiet roads
❏ b borrow a friend's glasses and use those
❏ c drive home at night, so that the lights will help you
❏ d find a way of getting home without driving

5.80

Which THREE result from drinking alcohol?
Mark three answers

❏ a Less control
❏ b A false sense of confidence
❏ c Faster reactions
❏ d Poor judgement of speed
❏ e Greater awareness of danger

Answers

5.70	a, b, c
5.71	c
5.72	c
5.73	c
5.74	a, b, e Answers 'c' and 'd' are normal parts of the driving task.
5.75	c
5.76	d
5.77	d
5.78	c
5.79	d
5.80	a, b, d

5.81

Which THREE of these are likely effects of drinking alcohol?

Mark three answers

- ❑ a Reduced co-ordination
- ❑ b Increased confidence
- ❑ c Poor judgement
- ❑ d Increased concentration
- ❑ e Faster reactions
- ❑ f Colour blindness

5.82

You are driving along this motorway. It is raining. When following this lorry you should

Mark two answers

- ❑ a allow at least a two-second gap
- ❑ b move left and drive on the hard shoulder
- ❑ c allow at least a four-second gap
- ❑ d be aware of spray reducing your vision
- ❑ e move right and stay in the right-hand lane

5.83

You are driving towards this left-hand bend. What dangers should you be aware of?

Mark one answer

- ❑ a A vehicle overtaking you
- ❑ b No white lines in the centre of the road
- ❑ c No sign to warn you of the bend
- ❑ d Pedestrians walking towards you

5.84

The traffic ahead of you in the left-hand lane is slowing. You should

Mark two answers

- ❑ a be wary of cars on your right cutting in
- ❑ b accelerate past the vehicles in the left-hand lane
- ❑ c pull up on the left-hand verge
- ❑ d move across and continue in the right-hand lane
- ❑ e slow down, keeping a safe separation distance

5.85

How does alcohol affect you?

Mark one answer

- ❑ a It speeds up your reactions
- ❑ b It increases your awareness
- ❑ c It improves your co-ordination
- ❑ d It reduces your concentration

5.86

Your doctor has given you a course of medicine. Why should you ask how it will affect you?

Mark one answer

- ❑ a Drugs make you a better driver by quickening your reactions
- ❑ b You will have to let your insurance company know about the medicine
- ❑ c Some types of medicine can cause your reactions to slow down
- ❑ d The medicine you take may affect your hearing

5.87
You are on a motorway. You feel tired.
You should
Mark one answer
- [ ] a carry on but go slowly
- [ ] b leave the motorway at the next exit
- [ ] c complete your journey as quickly as possible
- [ ] d stop on the hard shoulder

5.88
You find that you need glasses to read vehicle number plates at the required distance. When MUST you wear them?
Mark one answer
- [ ] a Only in bad weather conditions
- [ ] b At all times when driving
- [ ] c Only when you think it necessary
- [ ] d Only in bad light or at night time

5.89
Which TWO things would help to keep you alert during a long journey?
Mark two answers
- [ ] a Finishing your journey as fast as you can
- [ ] b Keeping off the motorways and using country roads
- [ ] c Making sure that you get plenty of fresh air
- [ ] d Making regular stops for refreshments

5.90
Drinking any amount of alcohol is likely to
Mark three answers
- [ ] a slow down your reactions to hazards
- [ ] b increase the speed of your reactions
- [ ] c worsen your judgement of speed
- [ ] d improve your awareness of danger
- [ ] e give a false sense of confidence

5.91
What else can seriously affect your concentration, other than alcoholic drinks?
Mark three answers
- [ ] a Drugs
- [ ] b Tiredness
- [ ] c Tinted windows
- [ ] d Contact lenses
- [ ] e Loud music

Answers

5.81 a, b, c
5.82 c, d
5.83 d
5.84 a, e
5.85 d You may well feel, after drinking, that 'a', 'b' and 'c' are true. However, this is never correct and makes you dangerous.
5.86 c
5.87 b If you feel tired you greatly increase your chances of having an accident. You must stop, but as you are on a motorway you cannot do this unless you leave at the next exit or find a service station before it.
5.88 b If you need glasses to drive you must wear them whenever you are driving.
5.89 c, d
5.90 a, c, e
5.91 a, b, e

5.92

As a driver you find that your eyesight has become very poor. Your optician says they cannot help you. The law says that you should tell

Mark one answer

- ❑ a the licensing authority
- ❑ b your own doctor
- ❑ c the local police station
- ❑ d another optician

5.93

As a provisional licence holder, you must not drive a motor car

Mark two answers

- ❑ a at more than 40 mph
- ❑ b on your own
- ❑ c on the motorway
- ❑ d under the age of 18 years at night
- ❑ e with passengers in the rear seats

5.94

If your motorway journey seems boring and you feel drowsy while driving, you should

Mark one answer

- ❑ a open a window and drive to the next service area
- ❑ b stop on the hard shoulder for a sleep
- ❑ c speed up to arrive at your destination sooner
- ❑ d slow down and let other drivers overtake

5.95

You are not sure if your cough medicine will affect you. What TWO things should you do?

Mark two answers

- ❑ a Ask your doctor
- ❑ b Check the medicine label
- ❑ c Drive if you feel alright
- ❑ d Ask a friend or relative for advice

5.96

After passing your driving test, you suffer from ill health. This affects your driving. You MUST

Mark one answer

- ❑ a inform your local police station
- ❑ b avoid using motorways
- ❑ c always drive accompanied
- ❑ d inform the licensing authority

5.97

Why should the junction on the left be kept clear?

Mark one answer

- ❑ a To allow vehicles to enter and emerge
- ❑ b To allow the bus to reverse
- ❑ c To allow vehicles to make a U-turn
- ❑ d To allow vehicles to park

5.98

You are riding up to a zebra crossing. You intend to stop for waiting pedestrians. How could you let them know you are stopping?

Mark one answer

- ❑ a By signalling with your left arm
- ❑ b By waving them across
- ❑ c By flashing your headlight
- ❑ d By signalling with your right arm

5.99

Which of the following types of glasses should NOT be worn when riding at night?

Mark one answer

- ❑ a Half-moon
- ❑ b Round
- ❑ c Bi-focal
- ❑ d Tinted

5.100

For which of these may you use hazard warning lights?

Mark one answer

- ❑ a When riding on a motorway to warn traffic behind of a hazard ahead
- ❑ b When you are double-parked on a two-way road
- ❑ c When your direction indicators are not working
- ❑ d When warning oncoming traffic that you intend to stop

5.101

When should you use hazard warning lights?

Mark one answer

- ❑ a When you are double-parked on a two-way road
- ❑ b When your direction indicators are not working
- ❑ c When warning oncoming traffic that you intend to stop
- ❑ d When your motorcycle has broken down and is causing an obstruction

5.102

It is a very hot day. What would you expect to find?

Mark one answer

- ❑ a Mud on the road
- ❑ b A soft road surface
- ❑ c Roadworks ahead
- ❑ d Banks of fog

5.103

You see this road marking in between queuing traffic. What should you look out for?

Mark one answer

- ❑ a Overhanging trees
- ❑ b Roadworks
- ❑ c Traffic wardens
- ❑ d Traffic emerging

Answers

5.92	a You must not drive if your eyesight becomes so poor that you can no longer meet the minimum legal requirements, wearing glasses or contact lenses if necessary.
5.93	b, c
5.94	a
5.95	a, b
5.96	d In the event of a short-term illness, like flu, that affects your ability to drive, you would simply not drive until you are recovered.
5.97	a
5.98	d
5.99	d
5.100	a
5.101	d
5.102	b
5.103	d

5.104

You get cold and wet when riding. Which TWO are likely to happen?

Mark two answers

- ☐ a You may lose concentration
- ☐ b You may slide off the seat
- ☐ c Your visor may freeze up
- ☐ d Your reaction times may be slower
- ☐ e Your helmet may loosen

5.105

You are about to ride home. You cannot find the glasses you need to wear. You should

Mark one answer

- ☐ a ride home slowly, keeping to quiet roads
- ☐ b borrow a friend's glasses and use those
- ☐ c ride home at night, so that the lights will help you
- ☐ d find a way of getting home without riding

5.106

Which THREE of these are likely effects of drinking alcohol?

Mark three answers

- ☐ a Reduced co-ordination
- ☐ b Increased confidence
- ☐ c Poor judgement
- ☐ d Increased concentration
- ☐ e Faster reactions
- ☐ f Colour blindness

5.107

You find that you need glasses to read vehicle number plates at the required distance. When MUST you wear them?

Mark one answer

- ☐ a Only in bad weather conditions
- ☐ b At all times when riding
- ☐ c Only when you think it necessary
- ☐ d Only in bad light or at night time

5.108

Drinking any amount of alcohol is likely to

Mark three answers

- ☐ a slow down your reactions to hazards
- ☐ b increase the speed of your reactions
- ☐ c worsen your judgement of speed
- ☐ d improve your awareness of danger
- ☐ e give a false sense of confidence

5.109

When riding how can you help to reduce the risk of hearing damage?

Mark one answer

- ☐ a Wearing goggles
- ☐ b Using ear plugs
- ☐ c Wearing a scarf
- ☐ d Keeping the visor up

5.110

When riding long distances at speed, noise can cause fatigue. What can you do to help reduce this?

Mark one answer

- ☐ a Vary your speed
- ☐ b Wear ear plugs
- ☐ c Use an open-face helmet
- ☐ d Ride in an upright position

5.111

Why should you wear ear plugs when riding a motorcycle?

Mark one answer

- ☐ a To help to prevent ear damage
- ☐ b To make you less aware of traffic
- ☐ c To help to keep you warm
- ☐ d To make your helmet fit better

5.112

You are going out to a social event and alcohol will be available. You will be riding your motorcycle shortly afterwards. What is the safest thing to do?

Mark one answer

- ❑ a Stay just below the legal limit
- ❑ b Have soft drinks and alcohol in turn
- ❑ c Don't go beyond the legal limit
- ❑ d Stick to non-alcoholic drinks

5.113

You are convicted of riding after drinking too much alcohol. How could this affect your insurance?

Mark one answer

- ❑ a Your insurance may become invalid
- ❑ b The amount of excess you pay will be reduced
- ❑ c You will only be able to get third party cover
- ❑ d Cover will only be given for riding smaller motorcycles

5.114

Why should you check over your shoulder before turning right into a side road?

Mark one answer

- ❑ a To make sure the side road is clear
- ❑ b To check for emerging traffic
- ❑ c To check for overtaking vehicles
- ❑ d To confirm your intention to turn

5.115

You are not sure if your cough medicine will affect you. What TWO things should you do?

Mark two answers

- ❑ a Ask your doctor
- ❑ b Check the medicine label
- ❑ c Ride if you feel alright
- ❑ d Ask a friend or relative for advice

Answers

5.104	a, d
5.105	d
5.106	a, b, c
5.107	b
5.108	a, c, e
5.109	b
5.110	b
5.111	a
5.112	d Any alcohol will affect your balance and judgement on a motorcycle.
5.113	a
5.114	c
5.115	a, b

99

Theory Test Questions
for Car Drivers and Motorcyclists

Section 6   Vulnerable road users

6.1

Which sign means that there may be people walking along the road?

Mark one answer

❑ a ❑ b

❑ c ❑ d

6.2

You are turning left at a junction. Pedestrians have started to cross the road. You should

Mark one answer
- ❑ a go on, giving them plenty of room
- ❑ b stop and wave at them to cross
- ❑ c blow your horn and proceed
- ❑ d give way to them

6.3

You are turning left from a main road into a side road. People are already crossing the road into which you are turning. You should

Mark one answer
- ❑ a continue, as it is your right of way
- ❑ b signal to them to continue crossing
- ❑ c wait and allow them to cross
- ❑ d sound your horn to warn them of your presence

6.4

You are at a road junction, turning into a minor road. There are pedestrians crossing the minor road. You should

Mark one answer
- ❑ a stop and wave the pedestrians across
- ❑ b sound your horn to let the pedestrians know that you are there
- ❑ c give way to the pedestrians who are already crossing
- ❑ d carry on; the pedestrians should give way to you

6.5

You are turning left into a side road. What hazards should you be especially aware of?
Mark one answer

- ❑ a One-way street
- ❑ b Pedestrians
- ❑ c Traffic congestion
- ❑ d Parked vehicles

6.6

You intend to turn right into a side road. Just before turning you should check for motorcyclists who might be
Mark one answer

- ❑ a overtaking on your left
- ❑ b following you closely
- ❑ c emerging from the side road
- ❑ d overtaking on your right

6.7

A toucan crossing is different from other crossings because
Mark one answer

- ❑ a moped riders can use it
- ❑ b it is controlled by a traffic warden
- ❑ c it is controlled by two flashing lights
- ❑ d cyclists can use it

6.8

At toucan crossings
Mark two answers

- ❑ a there is no flashing amber light
- ❑ b cyclists are not permitted
- ❑ c there is a continuously flashing amber beacon
- ❑ d pedestrians and cyclists may cross
- ❑ e you only stop if someone is waiting to cross

6.9

How will a school-crossing patrol signal you to stop?
Mark one answer

- ❑ a By pointing to children on the opposite pavement
- ❑ b By displaying a red light
- ❑ c By displaying a stop sign
- ❑ d By giving you an arm signal

6.10

Where would you see this sign?

Mark one answer

- ❑ a In the window of a car taking children to school
- ❑ b At the side of the road
- ❑ c At playground areas
- ❑ d On the rear of a school bus or coach

Answers

6.1   d Red triangles give warnings, in this case of people walking along the road. Sign 'c' is a warning of a pedestrian crossing

6.2   d
6.3   c
6.4   c
6.5   b
6.6   d
6.7   d
6.8   a, d
6.9   c
6.10   d

6.11

Which sign tells you that pedestrians may be walking in the road as there is no pavement?
Mark one answer

❏ a

❏ b

❏ c

❏ d

6.12

What does this sign mean?

Mark one answer
❏ a No route for pedestrians and cyclists
❏ b A route for pedestrians only
❏ c A route for cyclists only
❏ d A route for pedestrians and cyclists

6.13

You see a pedestrian with a white stick and red band. This means that the person is
Mark one answer
❏ a physically disabled
❏ b deaf only
❏ c blind only
❏ d deaf and blind

6.14

What action would you take when elderly people are crossing the road?

Mark one answer
❏ a Wave them across so they know that you have seen them
❏ b Be patient and allow them to cross in their own time
❏ c Rev the engine to let them know that you are waiting
❏ d Tap the horn in case they are hard of hearing

6.15

You see two elderly pedestrians about to cross the road ahead. You should
Mark one answer
❏ a expect them to wait for you to pass
❏ b speed up to get past them quickly
❏ c stop and wave them across the road
❏ d be careful, they may misjudge your speed

6.16

You are coming up to a roundabout. A cyclist is signalling to turn right. What should you do?
Mark one answer
❏ a Overtake on the right
❏ b Give a horn warning
❏ c Signal the cyclist to move across
❏ d Give the cyclist plenty of room

6.17
When you are overtaking a cyclist you should leave as much room as you would give to a car. What is the main reason for this?
Mark one answer
❑ a The cyclist might change lanes
❑ b The cyclist might get off the bike
❑ c The cyclist might swerve
❑ d The cyclist might have to make a right turn

6.18
Which TWO should you allow extra room when overtaking?
Mark two answers
❑ a Motorcycles
❑ b Tractors
❑ c Bicycles
❑ d Road-sweeping vehicles

6.19
Why should you look particularly for motorcyclists and cyclists at junctions?
Mark one answer
❑ a They may want to turn into the side road
❑ b They may slow down to let you turn
❑ c They are harder to see
❑ d They might not see you turn

6.20
You are waiting to come out of a side road. Why should you watch carefully for motorcycles?
Mark one answer
❑ a Motorcycles are usually faster than cars
❑ b Police patrols often use motorcycles
❑ c Motorcycles are small and hard to see
❑ d Motorcycles have right of way

6.21
In daylight, an approaching motorcyclist is using a dipped headlight. Why?
Mark one answer
❑ a So that the rider can be seen more easily
❑ b To stop the battery overcharging
❑ c To improve the rider's vision
❑ d The rider is inviting you to proceed

6.22
Motorcyclists should wear bright clothing mainly because
Mark one answer
❑ a they must do so by law
❑ b it helps keep them cool in summer
❑ c the colours are popular
❑ d drivers often do not see them

Answers

6.11 a
6.12 d
6.13 d
6.14 b
6.15 d The ability to judge speed tends to deteriorate as you get older.
6.16 d
6.17 c The answer is 'c', but you should also be aware that cyclists can be unpredictable.
6.18 a, c Motorcycles and bicycles can easily swerve and you need to allow them extra room.
6.19 c
6.20 c
6.21 a
6.22 d

6.23

There is a slow-moving motorcyclist ahead of you. You are unsure what the rider is going to do. You should
Mark one answer

- ❑ a pass on the left
- ❑ b pass on the right
- ❑ c stay behind
- ❑ d move closer

6.24

Motorcyclists will often look round over their right shoulder just before turning right. This is because
Mark one answer

- ❑ a they need to listen for following traffic
- ❑ b motorcycles do not have mirrors
- ❑ c looking around helps them balance as they turn
- ❑ d they need to check for traffic in their blind area

6.25

At road junctions which of the following are most vulnerable?
Mark three answers

- ❑ a Cyclists
- ❑ b Motorcyclists
- ❑ c Pedestrians
- ❑ d Car drivers
- ❑ e Lorry drivers

6.26

Motorcyclists are particularly vulnerable
Mark one answer

- ❑ a when moving off
- ❑ b on dual carriageways
- ❑ c when approaching junctions
- ❑ d on motorways

6.27

An injured motorcyclist is lying unconscious in the road. You should
Mark one answer

- ❑ a remove the safety helmet
- ❑ b seek medical assistance
- ❑ c move the person off the road
- ❑ d remove the leather jacket

6.28

You are approaching a roundabout. There are horses just ahead of you. You should
Mark two answers

- ❑ a be prepared to stop
- ❑ b treat them like any other vehicle
- ❑ c give them plenty of room
- ❑ d accelerate past as quickly as possible
- ❑ e sound your horn as a warning

6.29

Which THREE should you do when passing sheep on a road?
Mark three answers

- ❑ a Allow plenty of room
- ❑ b Go very slowly
- ❑ c Pass quickly but quietly
- ❑ d Be ready to stop
- ❑ e Briefly sound your horn

6.30

As you approach a pelican crossing the lights change to green. Elderly people are halfway across. You should
Mark one answer

- ❑ a wave them to cross as quickly as they can
- ❑ b rev your engine to make them hurry
- ❑ c flash your lights in case they have not heard you
- ❑ d wait because they will take longer to cross

6.31

There are flashing amber lights under a school warning sign. What action should you take?

Mark one answer

- ❑ a Reduce speed until you are clear of the area
- ❑ b Keep up your speed and sound the horn
- ❑ c Increase your speed to clear the area quickly
- ❑ d Wait at the lights until they change to green

6.32

These road markings must be kept clear to allow

⋀-SCHOOL KEEP CLEAR-⋀

Mark one answer

- ❑ a school children to be dropped off
- ❑ b for teachers to park
- ❑ c school children to be picked up
- ❑ d a clear view of the crossing area

6.33

Where would you see this sign?

Mark one answer

- ❑ a Near a school crossing
- ❑ b At a playground entrance
- ❑ c On a school bus
- ❑ d At a 'pedestrians only' area

6.34

You are following two cyclists. They approach a roundabout in the left-hand lane. In which direction should you expect the cyclists to go?

Mark one answer

- ❑ a Left
- ❑ b Right
- ❑ c Any direction
- ❑ d Straight ahead

6.35

You are travelling behind a moped. You want to turn left just ahead. You should

Mark one answer

- ❑ a overtake the moped before the junction
- ❑ b pull alongside the moped and stay level until just before the junction
- ❑ c sound your horn as a warning and pull in front of the moped
- ❑ d stay behind until the moped has passed the junction

Answers

6.23 c
6.24 d
6.25 a, b, c
6.26 c
6.27 b
6.28 a, c
6.29 a, b, d
6.30 d
6.31 a
6.32 d You must not park on these yellow zig zag lines, not even to drop off or pick up children.
6.33 c
6.34 c
6.35 d

6.36

Which THREE of the following are hazards motorcyclists present in queues of traffic?

Mark three answers

- ❏ a Cutting in just in front of you
- ❏ b Riding in single file
- ❏ c Passing very close to you
- ❏ d Riding with their headlight on dipped beam
- ❏ e Filtering between the lanes

6.37

You see a horse rider as you approach a roundabout. They are signalling right but keeping well to the left. You should

Mark one answer

- ❏ a proceed as normal
- ❏ b keep close to them
- ❏ c cut in front of them
- ❏ d stay well back

6.38

How would you react to drivers who appear to be inexperienced?

Mark one answer

- ❏ a Sound your horn to warn them of your presence
- ❏ b Be patient and prepare for them to react more slowly
- ❏ c Flash your headlights to indicate that it is safe for them to proceed
- ❏ d Overtake them as soon as possible

6.39

You are following a learner driver who stalls at a junction. You should

Mark one answer

- ❏ a be patient as you expect them to make mistakes
- ❏ b stay very close behind and flash your headlights
- ❏ c start to rev your engine if they take too long to restart
- ❏ d immediately steer around them and drive on

6.40

You are on a country road. What should you expect to see coming towards you on YOUR side of the road?

Mark one answer

- ❏ a Motorcycles
- ❏ b Bicycles
- ❏ c Pedestrians
- ❏ d Horse riders

6.41

You are turning left into a side road. Pedestrians are crossing the road near the junction. You must

Mark one answer

- ❏ a wave them on
- ❏ b sound your horn
- ❏ c switch on your hazard lights
- ❏ d wait for them to cross

6.42

You are following a car driven by an elderly driver. You should

Mark one answer

- ❑ a expect the driver to drive badly
- ❑ b flash your lights and overtake
- ❑ c be aware that the driver's reactions may not be as fast as yours
- ❑ d stay very close behind but be careful

6.43

You are following a cyclist. You wish to turn left just ahead. You should

Mark one answer

- ❑ a overtake the cyclist before the junction
- ❑ b pull alongside the cyclist and stay level until after the junction
- ❑ c hold back until the cyclist has passed the junction
- ❑ d go around the cyclist on the junction

6.44

A horse rider is in the left-hand lane approaching a roundabout. You should expect the rider to

Mark one answer

- ❑ a go in any direction
- ❑ b turn right
- ❑ c turn left
- ❑ d go ahead

6.45

Powered vehicles used by disabled people are small and hard to see. How do they give early warning when on a dual carriageway?

Mark one answer

- ❑ a They will have a flashing red light
- ❑ b They will have a flashing green light
- ❑ c They will have a flashing blue light
- ❑ d They will have a flashing amber light

Answers

6.36 a, c, e Check all your mirrors, especially before moving forwards or changing lanes.

6.37 d

6.38 b

6.39 a

6.40 c Pedestrians are the most likely as country roads often have no pavements and pedestrians are advised to walk on the right. This is so that they can see oncoming traffic on their side of the road. However, you should always expect the unexpected when driving.

6.41 d When you turn into a side road pedestrians who are already crossing have priority so you must give way.

6.42 c

6.43 c As the question states you are turning left JUST ahead, you have no time to overtake the cyclist safely which is why 'c' is correct.

6.44 a

6.45 d

6.46

You should never attempt to overtake a cyclist·

Mark one answer

- ❑ a just before you turn left
- ❑ b on a left hand bend
- ❑ c on a one-way street
- ❑ d on a dual carriageway

6.47

Ahead of you there is a moving vehicle with a flashing amber beacon. This means it is

Mark one answer

- ❑ a slow moving
- ❑ b broken down
- ❑ c a doctor's car
- ❑ d a school crossing patrol

6.48

What does this sign mean?

Mark one answer

- ❑ a Contraflow pedal cycle lane
- ❑ b With-flow pedal cycle lane
- ❑ c Pedal cycles and buses only
- ❑ d No pedal cycles or buses

6.49

You notice horse riders in front. What should you do FIRST?

Mark one answer

- ❑ a Pull out to the middle of the road
- ❑ b Slow down and be ready to stop
- ❑ c Accelerate around them
- ❑ d Signal right

6.50

At night you see a pedestrian wearing reflective clothing and carrying a bright red light. What does this mean?

Mark one answer

- ❑ a You are approaching roadworks
- ❑ b You are approaching an organised walk
- ❑ c You are approaching a slow-moving vehicle
- ❑ d You are approaching an accident blackspot

6.51

You must not stop on these road markings because you may obstruct

⋀-SCHOOL KEEP CLEAR-⋀

Mark one answer

- ❑ a children's view of the crossing area
- ❑ b teachers' access to the school
- ❑ c delivery vehicles' access to the school
- ❑ d emergency vehicles' access to the school

6.52

The left-hand pavement is closed due to street repairs. What should you do?

Mark one answer

- ❑ a Watch out for pedestrians walking in the road
- ❑ b Use your right-hand mirror more often
- ❑ c Speed up to get past the roadworks quicker
- ❑ d Position close to the left-hand kerb

6.53

You are following a motorcyclist on an uneven road. You should

Mark one answer

- ❑ a allow less room so you can be seen in their mirrors
- ❑ b overtake immediately
- ❑ c allow extra room in case they swerve to avoid potholes
- ❑ d allow the same room as normal because road surfaces do not affect motorcyclists

6.54

You have just passed your test. How can you decrease your risk of accidents on the motorway?

Mark one answer

- ❑ a By keeping up with the car in front
- ❑ b By never going over 40 mph
- ❑ c By staying only in the left-hand lane
- ❑ d By taking further training

6.55

What does this sign tell you?

Mark one answer

- ❑ a No cycling
- ❑ b Cycle route ahead
- ❑ c Cycle parking only
- ❑ d End of cycle route

6.56

You are approaching this roundabout and see the cyclist signal right. Why is the cyclist keeping to the left?

Mark one answer

- ❑ a It is a quicker route for the cyclist
- ❑ b The cyclist is going to turn left instead
- ❑ c The cyclist thinks The Highway Code does not apply to bicycles
- ❑ d The cyclist is slower and more vulnerable

Answers

6.46   a Hang back until the cyclist has passed the junction.

6.47   a For example, a tractor or a breakdown recovery vehicle.

6.48   b

6.49   b Horses and their riders can be unpredictable so 'b' is the safest first action.

6.50   b

6.51   a

6.52   a Remember that pedestrians walking in the road may have their backs to you, so give them plenty of space.

6.53   c

6.54   d In many countries motorway tuition is compulsory. Motorway driving contains many new challenges and tuition is strongly recommended. Speak to your instructor for advice.

6.55   b

6.56   d

6.57

You are approaching this crossing. You should

Mark one answer

- ❑ a prepare to slow down and stop
- ❑ b stop and wave the pedestrians across
- ❑ c speed up and pass by quickly
- ❑ d continue unless the pedestrians step out

6.58

You see a pedestrian with a dog. The dog has a yellow or burgundy coat. This especially warns you that the pedestrian is

Mark one answer

- ❑ a elderly
- ❑ b dog training
- ❑ c colour blind
- ❑ d deaf

6.59

You are driving past parked cars. You notice a bicycle wheel sticking out between them. What should you do?

Mark one answer

- ❑ a Accelerate past quickly and sound your horn
- ❑ b Slow down and wave the cyclist across
- ❑ c Brake sharply and flash your headlights
- ❑ d Slow down and be prepared to stop for a cyclist

6.60

A friend wants to help you learn to drive. They must be

Mark one answer

- ❑ a over 21 and have held a full licence for at least two years
- ❑ b over 18 and hold an advanced driver's certificate
- ❑ c over 18 and have fully comprehensive insurance
- ❑ d over 21 and have held a full licence for at least three years

6.61

You are dazzled at night by a vehicle behind you. You should

Mark one answer

- ❑ a set your mirror to anti-dazzle
- ❑ b set your mirror to dazzle the other driver
- ❑ c brake sharply to a stop
- ❑ d switch your rear lights on and off

6.62

Yellow zigzag lines on the road outside schools mean

∿-SCHOOL KEEP CLEAR-∿

Mark one answer

- ❑ a sound your horn to alert other road users
- ❑ b stop to allow children to cross
- ❑ c you must not wait or park on these lines
- ❑ d you must not drive over these lines

6.63
What do these road markings outside a school mean?

W-SCHOOL KEEP CLEAR-W

Mark one answer
- [ ] a You may park here if you are a teacher
- [ ] b Sound your horn before parking
- [ ] c When parking, use your hazard warning lights
- [ ] d You must not wait or park your vehicle here

6.64
Which age group of drivers is most likely to be involved in a road accident?

Mark one answer
- [ ] a 17 - 25 year olds
- [ ] b 36 - 45 year olds
- [ ] c 46 - 55 year olds
- [ ] d Over 55 year olds

6.65
You are driving towards a zebra crossing. A person in a wheelchair is waiting to cross. What should you do?

Mark one answer
- [ ] a Continue on your way
- [ ] b Wave to the person to cross
- [ ] c Wave to the person to wait
- [ ] d Be prepared to stop

6.66
You want to reverse into a side road. You are not sure that the area behind your car is clear. What should you do?

Mark one answer
- [ ] a Look through the rear window only
- [ ] b Get out and check
- [ ] c Check the mirrors only
- [ ] d Carry on, assuming it is clear

6.67
You are about to reverse into a side road. A pedestrian wishes to cross behind you. You should

Mark one answer
- [ ] a wave to the pedestrian to stop
- [ ] b give way to the pedestrian
- [ ] c wave to the pedestrian to cross
- [ ] d reverse before the pedestrian starts to cross

6.68
Who is especially in danger of not being seen as you reverse your car?

Mark one answer
- [ ] a Motorcyclists
- [ ] b Car drivers
- [ ] c Cyclists
- [ ] d Children

Answers

6.57 a
6.58 d
6.59 d
6.60 d
6.61 a
6.62 c
6.63 d
6.64 a
6.65 d
6.66 b
6.67 b
6.68 d Children are small and you may not be able to see them through your rear windscreen.

6.69

You are reversing around a corner when you notice a pedestrian walking behind you. What should you do?

Mark one answer

- ❏ a Slow down and wave the pedestrian across
- ❏ b Continue reversing and steer round the pedestrian
- ❏ c Stop and give way
- ❏ d Continue reversing and sound your horn

6.70

You want to turn right from a junction but your view is restricted by parked vehicles. What should you do?

Mark one answer

- ❏ a Move out quickly, but be prepared to stop
- ❏ b Sound your horn and pull out if there is no reply
- ❏ c Stop, then move slowly forward until you have a clear view
- ❏ d Stop, get out and look along the main road to check

6.71

You are at the front of a queue of traffic waiting to turn right into a side road. Why is it important to check your right mirror just before turning?

Mark one answer

- ❏ a To look for pedestrians about to cross
- ❏ b To check for overtaking vehicles
- ❏ c To make sure the side road is clear
- ❏ d To check for emerging traffic

6.72

What must a driver do at a pelican crossing when the amber light is flashing?

Mark one answer

- ❏ a Signal the pedestrian to cross
- ❏ b Always wait for the green light before proceeding
- ❏ c Give way to any pedestrians on the crossing
- ❏ d Wait for the red-and-amber light before proceeding

6.73

You have stopped at a pelican crossing. A disabled person is crossing slowly in front of you. The lights have now changed to green. You should

Mark two answers

- ❏ a allow the person to cross
- ❏ b drive in front of the person
- ❏ c drive behind the person
- ❏ d sound your horn
- ❏ e be patient
- ❏ f edge forward slowly

6.74

You want to turn right from a main road into a side road. Just before turning you should

Mark one answer

- ❏ a cancel your right-turn signal
- ❏ b select first gear
- ❏ c check for traffic overtaking on your right
- ❏ d stop and set the handbrake

6.75

You are driving past a line of parked cars. You notice a ball bouncing out into the road ahead. What should you do?

Mark one answer

- ❑ a Continue driving at the same speed and sound your horn
- ❑ b Continue driving at the same speed and flash your headlights
- ❑ c Slow down and be prepared to stop for children
- ❑ d Stop and wave the children across to fetch their ball

6.76

You are driving in slow-moving queues of traffic. Just before changing lane you should

Mark one answer

- ❑ a sound the horn
- ❑ b look for motorcyclists filtering through the traffic
- ❑ c give a 'slowing down' arm signal
- ❑ d change down to first gear

6.77

You are driving in town. There is a bus at the bus stop on the other side of the road. Why should you be careful?

Mark one answer

- ❑ a The bus may have broken down
- ❑ b Pedestrians may come from behind the bus
- ❑ c The bus may move off suddenly
- ❑ d The bus may remain stationary

6.78

How should you overtake horse riders?

Mark one answer

- ❑ a Drive up close and overtake as soon as possible
- ❑ b Speed is not important but allow plenty of room
- ❑ c Use your horn just once to warn them
- ❑ d Drive slowly and leave plenty of room

6.79

You have a collision whilst your car is moving. What is the first thing you must do?

Mark one answer

- ❑ a Stop only if there are injured people
- ❑ b Call the emergency services
- ❑ c Stop at the scene of the accident
- ❑ d Call your insurance company

Answers

6.69 c
6.70 c You should not turn right until you can see it is safe to do so. You should stop and then edge slowly forwards until you can see clearly to the left and right.
6.71 b
6.72 c
6.73 a, e
6.74 c Use your right-door mirror and look particularly for motorcyclists.
6.75 c
6.76 b
6.77 b
6.78 d
6.79 c

6.80

You are driving on a main road. You intend to turn right into a side road. Just before turning you should

Mark one answer

- ❑ a adjust your interior mirror
- ❑ b flash your headlamps
- ❑ c steer over to the left
- ❑ d check for traffic overtaking on your right

6.81

Why should you allow extra room when overtaking a motorcyclist on a windy day?

Mark one answer

- ❑ a The rider may turn off suddenly to get out of the wind
- ❑ b The rider may be blown across in front of you
- ❑ c The rider may stop suddenly
- ❑ d The rider may be travelling faster than normal

6.82

Where in particular should you look out for motorcyclists?

Mark one answer

- ❑ a In a filling station
- ❑ b At a road junction
- ❑ c Near a service area
- ❑ d When entering a car park

6.83

Where should you take particular care to look out for motorcyclists and cyclists?

Mark one answer

- ❑ a On dual carriageways
- ❑ b At junctions
- ❑ c At zebra crossings
- ❑ d On one-way streets

6.84

The road outside this school is marked with yellow zigzag lines. What do these lines mean?

Mark one answer

- ❑ a You may park on the lines when dropping off schoolchildren
- ❑ b You may park on the lines when picking schoolchildren up
- ❑ c You must not wait or park your vehicle here at all
- ❑ d You must stay with your vehicle if you park here

6.85

You should not ride too closely behind a lorry because

Mark one answer

- ❏ a you will breathe in the lorry's exhaust fumes
- ❏ b wind from the lorry will slow you down
- ❏ c drivers behind you may not be able to see you
- ❏ d it will reduce your view ahead

6.86

You are riding along a main road with many side roads. Why should you be particularly careful?

Mark one answer

- ❏ a Gusts of wind from the side roads may push you off course
- ❏ b Drivers coming out from side roads may not see you
- ❏ c The road will be more slippery where cars have been turning
- ❏ d Drivers will be travelling slowly when they approach a junction

6.87

You are riding on a country lane. You see cattle on the road. You should

Mark three answers

- ❏ a slow down
- ❏ b stop if necessary
- ❏ c give plenty of room
- ❏ d rev your engine
- ❏ e sound your horn
- ❏ f ride up close behind them

6.88

A learner driver has begun to emerge into your path from a side road on the left. You should

Mark one answer

- ❏ a be ready to slow down and stop
- ❏ b let them emerge then ride close behind
- ❏ c turn into the side road
- ❏ d brake hard, then wave them out

6.89

The vehicle ahead is being driven by a learner. You should

Mark one answer

- ❏ a keep calm and be patient
- ❏ b ride up close behind
- ❏ c put your headlight on full beam
- ❏ d sound your horn and overtake

6.90

You are riding in fast-flowing traffic. The vehicle behind is following too closely. You should

Mark one answer

- ❏ a slow down gradually to increase the gap in front of you
- ❏ b slow down as quickly as possible by braking
- ❏ c accelerate to get away from the vehicle behind you
- ❏ d apply the brakes sharply to warn the driver behind

Answers

6.80	d
6.81	b
6.82	b
6.83	b
6.84	c
6.85	d
6.86	b
6.87	a, b, c
6.88	a
6.89	a
6.90	a

6.91

You are riding towards a zebra crossing.
Waiting to cross is a person in a wheelchair.
You should

Mark one answer

- ❑ a continue on your way
- ❑ b wave to the person to cross
- ❑ c wave to the person to wait
- ❑ d be prepared to stop

6.92

Why should you allow extra room when
overtaking another motorcyclist on a windy
day?

Mark one answer

- ❑ a The rider may turn off suddenly to get out of the wind
- ❑ b The rider may be blown across in front of you
- ❑ c The rider may stop suddenly
- ❑ d The rider may be travelling faster than normal

6.93

You have stopped at a pelican crossing.
A disabled person is crossing slowly in front of
you. The lights have now changed to green.
You should

Mark two answers

- ❑ a allow the person to cross
- ❑ b ride in front of the person
- ❑ c ride behind the person
- ❑ d sound your horn
- ❑ e be patient
- ❑ f edge forward slowly

6.94

Where should you take particular care to look
out for other motorcyclists and cyclists?

Mark one answer

- ❑ a On dual carriageways
- ❑ b At junctions
- ❑ c At zebra crossings
- ❑ d On one-way streets

6.95

What is a main cause of accidents among
young and new motorcyclists?

Mark one answer

- ❑ a Using borrowed equipment
- ❑ b Lack of experience and judgement
- ❑ c Riding in bad weather conditions
- ❑ d Riding on country roads

6.96

Young motorcyclists can often be the cause
of accidents due to

Mark one answer

- ❑ a being too cautious at junctions
- ❑ b riding in the middle of their lane
- ❑ c showing off and being competitive
- ❑ d riding when the weather is poor

6.97

Which of the following is applicable to young
motorcyclists?

Mark one answer

- ❑ a They are normally better than experienced riders
- ❑ b They are usually less likely to have accidents
- ❑ c They are often over-confident of their own ability
- ❑ d They are more likely to get cheaper insurance

6.98

Why is it vital for a rider to make a 'lifesaver'
check before turning right?

Mark one answer

- ❑ a To check for any overtaking traffic
- ❑ b To confirm that they are about to turn
- ❑ c To make sure the side road is clear
- ❑ d To check that the rear indicator is flashing

6.99

You are about to overtake horse riders. Which TWO of the following could scare the horses?

Mark two answers

- ☐ a Sounding your horn
- ☐ b Giving arm signals
- ☐ c Riding slowly
- ☐ d Revving your engine

6.100

The road outside this school is marked with yellow zigzag lines. What do these lines mean?

Mark one answer

- ☐ a You may park on the lines when dropping off schoolchildren
- ☐ b You may park on the lines when picking up schoolchildren
- ☐ c You must not wait or park your motorcycle here
- ☐ d You must stay with your motorcycle if you park here

Answers

6.91 d
6.92 b
6.93 a, e
6.94 b
6.95 b
6.96 c
6.97 c
6.98 a
6.99 a, d
6.100 c

119

Theory Test Questions
for Car Drivers and Motorcyclists

Section 7 | Other road users

7.1

You are about to overtake a slow-moving motorcyclist. Which one of these signs would make you take special care?

Mark one answer

❏ a ❏ b

❏ c ❏ d

7.2

You are waiting to emerge left from a minor road. A large vehicle is approaching from the right. You have time to turn, but you should wait. Why?

Mark one answer

❏ a The large vehicle can easily hide an overtaking vehicle
❏ b The large vehicle can turn suddenly
❏ c The large vehicle is difficult to steer in a straight line
❏ d The large vehicle can easily hide vehicles from the left

7.3

You are following a long vehicle. It approaches a crossroads and signals left, but moves out to the right. You should

Mark one answer

❏ a get closer in order to pass it quickly
❏ b stay well back and give it room
❏ c assume the signal is wrong and it is really turning right
❏ d overtake as it starts to slow down

7.4

You are following a long vehicle approaching a crossroads. The driver signals right but moves close to the left-hand kerb. What should you do?

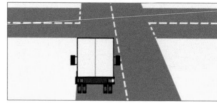

Mark one answer

❏ a Warn the driver of the wrong signal
❏ b Wait behind the long vehicle
❏ c Report the driver to the police
❏ d Overtake on the right-hand side

7.5

You are approaching a mini-roundabout. The long vehicle in front is signalling left but positioned over to the right. You should

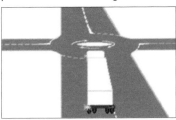

Mark one answer

- ❏ a sound your horn
- ❏ b overtake on the left
- ❏ c follow the same course as the lorry
- ❏ d keep well back

7.6

Before overtaking a large vehicle you should keep well back. Why is this?

Mark one answer

- ❏ a To give acceleration space to overtake quickly on blind bends
- ❏ b To get the best view of the road ahead
- ❏ c To leave a gap in case the vehicle stops and rolls back
- ❏ d To offer other drivers a safe gap if they want to overtake you

7.7

Why is passing a lorry more risky than passing a car?

Mark one answer

- ❏ a Lorries are longer than cars
- ❏ b Lorries may suddenly pull up
- ❏ c The brakes of lorries are not as good
- ❏ d Lorries climb hills more slowly

7.8

You are travelling behind a bus that pulls up at a bus stop. What should you do?

Mark two answers

- ❏ a Accelerate past the bus sounding your horn
- ❏ b Watch carefully for pedestrians
- ❏ c Be ready to give way to the bus
- ❏ d Pull in closely behind the bus

7.9

You are following a large lorry on a wet road. Spray makes it difficult to see. You should

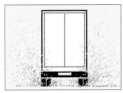

Mark one answer

- ❏ a drop back until you can see better
- ❏ b put your headlights on full beam
- ❏ c keep close to the lorry, away from the spray
- ❏ d speed up and overtake quickly

Answers

7.1   a The motorcyclist may wobble as you pass by in a windy situation.

7.2   a

7.3   b Long vehicles require more space to turn and often need to position for this.

7.4   b

7.5   d

7.6   b

7.7   a Overtaking takes time, so the longer the vehicle you overtake the greater the danger, as you will take longer to pass it.

7.8   b, c

7.9   a

7.10

You are following a large articulated vehicle. It is going to turn left into a narrow road. What action should you take?

Mark one answer

- ☐ a Move out and overtake on the right
- ☐ b Pass on the left as the vehicle moves out
- ☐ c Be prepared to stop behind
- ☐ d Overtake quickly before the lorry moves out

7.11

You keep well back while waiting to overtake a large vehicle. A car fills the gap. You should

Mark one answer

- ☐ a sound your horn
- ☐ b drop back further
- ☐ c flash your headlights
- ☐ d start to overtake

7.12

You are following a long lorry. The driver signals to turn left into a narrow road. What should you do?

Mark one answer

- ☐ a Overtake on the left before the lorry reaches the junction
- ☐ b Overtake on the right as soon as the lorry slows down
- ☐ c Do not overtake unless you can see there is no oncoming traffic
- ☐ d Do not overtake, stay well back and be prepared to stop

7.13

When you approach a bus signalling to move off from a bus stop you should

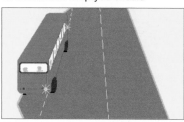

Mark one answer

- ☐ a get past before it moves
- ☐ b allow it to pull away, if it is safe to do so
- ☐ c flash your headlights as you approach
- ☐ d signal left and wave the bus on

7.14

You wish to overtake a long, slow-moving vehicle on a busy road. You should

Mark one answer

- ☐ a follow it closely and keep moving out to see the road ahead
- ☐ b flash your headlights for the oncoming traffic to give way
- ☐ c stay behind until the driver waves you past
- ☐ d keep well back until you can see that it is clear

7.15

Which of these is LEAST likely to be affected by crosswinds?

Mark one answer

- ☐ a Cyclists
- ☐ b Motorcyclists
- ☐ c High-sided vehicles
- ☐ d Cars

7.16

What should you do as you approach this lorry?

- ❏ a Slow down and be prepared to wait
- ❏ b Make the lorry wait for you
- ❏ c Flash your lights at the lorry
- ❏ d Move to the right-hand side of the road

7.17

You are following a large vehicle approaching crossroads. The driver signals to turn left. What should you do?
Mark one answer
- ❏ a Overtake if you can leave plenty of room
- ❏ b Overtake only if there are no oncoming vehicles
- ❏ c Do not overtake until the vehicle begins to turn
- ❏ d Do not overtake when at or approaching a junction

7.18

Powered vehicles, such as wheelchairs or scooters, used by disabled people have a maximum speed of
Mark one answer
- ❏ a 8 mph
- ❏ b 12 mph
- ❏ c 16 mph
- ❏ d 20 mph

7.19

In front of you is a powered vehicle (powered wheelchair) driven by a disabled person. These vehicles have a maximum speed of
Mark one answer
- ❏ a 8 mph
- ❏ b 18 mph
- ❏ c 28 mph
- ❏ d 38 mph

Answers

7.10 c The large articulated vehicle may need to position to the right in order to turn left into the narrow road.

7.11 b

7.12 d

7.13 b This helps traffic flow without giving confusing signals.

7.14 d

7.15 d Of the four mentioned, cars are by far the most stable and least affected by crosswinds.

7.16 a

7.17 d

7.18 a These small vehicles can be used on the pavement as well as on the road. On dual carriageways they will have an amber flashing light but on other roads they can be difficult to see.

7.19 a

7.20

It is very windy. You are behind a motorcyclist who is overtaking a high-sided vehicle. What should you do?

Mark one answer

❑ a Overtake the motorcyclist immediately
❑ b Keep well back
❑ c Stay level with the motorcyclist
❑ d Keep close to the motorcyclist

7.21

It is very windy. You are about to overtake a motorcyclist. You should

Mark one answer

❑ a overtake slowly
❑ b allow extra room
❑ c sound your horn
❑ d keep close as you pass

7.22

You are driving in town. Ahead of you a bus is at a bus stop. Which TWO of the following should you do?

Mark two answers

❑ a Be prepared to give way if the bus suddenly moves off
❑ b Continue at the same speed but sound your horn as a warning
❑ c Watch carefully for the sudden appearance of pedestrians
❑ d Pass the bus as quickly as you possibly can

7.23

You are driving along this road. What should you be prepared to do?

Mark one answer

❑ a Sound your horn and continue
❑ b Slow down and give way
❑ c Report the driver to the police
❑ d Squeeze through the gap

7.24

As a driver why should you be more careful where trams operate?

Mark one answer

❑ a Because they do not have a horn
❑ b Because they do not stop for cars
❑ c Because they do not have lights
❑ d Because they cannot steer to avoid you

7.25

You are towing a caravan. Which is the safest type of rear-view mirror to use?

Mark one answer

❑ a Interior wide-angle mirror
❑ b Extended-arm side mirrors
❑ c Ordinary door mirrors
❑ d Ordinary interior mirror

7.26

You are driving in heavy traffic on a wet road. Spray makes it difficult to be seen. You should use your
Mark two answers
- ❑ a full beam headlights
- ❑ b rear fog lights if visibility is less than 100 metres (328 feet)
- ❑ c rear fog lights if visibility is more than 100 metres (328 feet)
- ❑ d dipped headlights
- ❑ e sidelights only

7.27

It is a very windy day and you are about to overtake a cyclist. What should you do?
Mark one answer
- ❑ a Overtake very closely
- ❑ b Keep close as you pass
- ❑ c Sound your horn repeatedly
- ❑ d Allow extra room

7.28

You are riding behind a long vehicle. There is a mini-roundabout ahead. The vehicle is signalling left, but positioned to the right. You should
Mark one answer
- ❑ a sound your horn
- ❑ b overtake on the left
- ❑ c keep well back
- ❑ d flash your headlights

7.29

Why should you be careful when riding on roads where electric trams operate?
Mark two answers
- ❑ a They cannot steer to avoid you
- ❑ b They move quickly and quietly
- ❑ c They are noisy and slow
- ❑ d They can steer to avoid you
- ❑ e They give off harmful exhaust fumes

Answers

7.20 b Let the motorcyclist complete the overtake before even thinking about following.

7.21 b Motorcycles may have problems with strong crosswinds.

7.22 a, c

7.23 b

7.24 d

7.25 b

7.26 b, d

7.27 d Cyclists are vulnerable to the weather conditions. A strong gust of wind could blow a cyclist right off course so it is important to allow extra room when overtaking.

7.28 c

7.29 a, b

Theory Test Questions
for Car Drivers and Motorcyclists

Section 8 Vehicle and motorcycle handling

8.1

In which THREE of these situations may you overtake another vehicle on the left?

Mark three answers

- ❑ a When you are in a one-way street
- ❑ b When approaching a motorway slip road where you will be turning off
- ❑ c When the vehicle in front is signalling to turn right
- ❑ d When a slower vehicle is travelling in the right-hand lane of a dual carriageway
- ❑ e In slow-moving traffic queues when traffic in the right-hand lane is moving more slowly

8.2

You are travelling in very heavy rain. Your overall stopping distance is likely to be

Mark one answer

- ❑ a doubled
- ❑ b halved
- ❑ c up to ten times greater
- ❑ d no different

8.3

Which TWO of the following are correct? When overtaking at night you should

Mark two answers

- ❑ a wait until a bend so that you can see the oncoming headlights
- ❑ b sound your horn twice before moving out
- ❑ c be careful because you can see less
- ❑ d beware of bends in the road ahead
- ❑ e put headlights on full beam

8.4

When may you wait in a box junction?

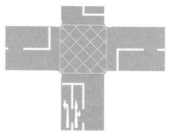

Mark one answer

- ❑ a When you are stationary in a queue of traffic
- ❑ b When approaching a pelican crossing
- ❑ c When approaching a zebra crossing
- ❑ d When oncoming traffic prevents you turning right

8.5

Which of these plates normally appear with this road sign?

Mark one answer

Humps for ½ mile	HumpBridge
❑ a	❑ b

Low Bridge	Soft Verge
❑ c	❑ d

8.6

Traffic calming measures are used to

Mark one answer

- ☐ a stop road rage
- ☐ b help overtaking
- ☐ c slow traffic down
- ☐ d help parking

8.7

You are on a motorway in fog. The left-hand edge of the motorway can be identified by reflective studs. What colour are they?

Mark one answer

- ☐ a Green
- ☐ b Amber
- ☐ c Red
- ☐ d White

8.8

A rumble device is designed to

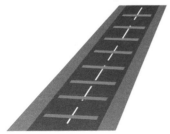

Mark two answers

- ☐ a give directions
- ☐ b prevent cattle escaping
- ☐ c alert you to low tyre pressure
- ☐ d alert you to a hazard
- ☐ e encourage you to reduce speed

8.9

You are on a narrow road at night. A slower-moving vehicle ahead has been signalling right for some time. What should you do?

Mark one answer

- ☐ a Overtake on the left
- ☐ b Flash your headlights before overtaking
- ☐ c Signal right and sound your horn
- ☐ d Wait for the signal to be cancelled before overtaking

8.10

You have to make a journey in foggy conditions. You should

Mark one answer

- ☐ a follow other vehicles' tail lights closely
- ☐ b avoid using dipped headlights
- ☐ c leave plenty of time for your journey
- ☐ d keep two seconds behind other vehicles

Answers

8.1   a, c, e

8.2   a

8.3   c, d

8.4   d You may wait in a box junction if your exit is clear but oncoming traffic prevents you from turning right.

8.5   a

8.6   c

8.7   c Red reflective studs separate the left-hand lane and the hard shoulder

8.8   d, e A rumble device is normally raised strips or markings on the surface of the road.

8.9   d

8.10   c The Highway Code advises you to allow more time for your journey in foggy conditions. However, always ask yourself if the journey really is necessary.

131

8.11

You are overtaking a car at night. You must be sure that

Mark one answer

- ❏ a you flash your headlights before overtaking
- ❏ b you select a higher gear
- ❏ c you have switched your lights to full beam before overtaking
- ❏ d you do not dazzle other road users

8.12

You are on a road which has speed humps. A driver in front is travelling slower than you. You should

Mark one answer

- ❏ a sound your horn
- ❏ b overtake as soon as you can
- ❏ c flash your headlights
- ❏ d slow down and stay behind

8.13

You are following other vehicles in fog with your lights on. How else can you reduce the chances of being involved in an accident?

Mark one answer

- ❏ a Keep close to the vehicle in front
- ❏ b Use your main beam instead of dipped headlights
- ❏ c Keep together with the faster vehicles
- ❏ d Reduce your speed and increase the gap

8.14

You see these markings on the road. Why are they there?

Mark one answer

- ❏ a To show a safe distance between vehicles
- ❏ b To keep the area clear of traffic
- ❏ c To make you aware of your speed
- ❏ d To warn you to change direction

8.15

Areas reserved for trams may have

Mark three answers

- ❏ a metal studs around them
- ❏ b white line markings
- ❏ c zigzag markings
- ❏ d a different coloured surface
- ❏ e yellow hatch markings
- ❏ f a different surface texture

8.16

You see a vehicle coming towards you on a single-track road. You should

Mark one answer

- ❏ a go back to the main road
- ❏ b do an emergency stop
- ❏ c stop at a passing place
- ❏ d put on your hazard warning lights

8.17

The road is wet. Why might a motorcyclist steer round drain covers on a bend?

Mark one answer

- ❑ a To avoid puncturing the tyres on the edge of the drain covers
- ❑ b To prevent the motorcycle sliding on the metal drain covers
- ❑ c To help judge the bend using the drain covers as marker points
- ❑ d To avoid splashing pedestrians on the pavement

8.18

After this hazard you should test your brakes. Why is this?

Mark one answer

- ❑ a You will be on a slippery road
- ❑ b Your brakes will be soaking wet
- ❑ c You will be going down a long hill
- ❑ d You will have just crossed a long bridge

8.19

Why should you always reduce your speed when travelling in fog?

Mark one answer

- ❑ a The brakes do not work as well
- ❑ b You will be dazzled by other headlights
- ❑ c The engine will take longer to warm up
- ❑ d It is more difficult to see events ahead

8.20

Hills can affect the performance of your vehicle. Which TWO apply when driving up steep hills?

Mark two answers

- ❑ a Higher gears will pull better
- ❑ b You will slow down sooner
- ❑ c Overtaking will be easier
- ❑ d The engine will work harder
- ❑ e The steering will feel heavier

8.21

You are driving on the motorway in windy conditions. When passing high-sided vehicles you should

Mark one answer

- ❑ a increase your speed
- ❑ b be wary of a sudden gust
- ❑ c drive alongside very closely
- ❑ d expect normal conditions

Answers

8.11 d You may need to switch to full-beam headlights as you overtake, but not before.

8.12 d
8.13 d
8.14 c
8.15 b, d, f
8.16 c Bear in mind that single-track roads may have passing places at long intervals. You may meet an oncoming vehicle at a point where one of you will need to reverse to the previous nearest passing point.
8.17 b
8.18 b
8.19 d Everybody knows this but an alarming number of people don't put the knowledge into practice. Collisions happen as a result.
8.20 b, d
8.21 b

8.22

To correct a rear-wheel skid you should

Mark one answer

❑ a not steer at all
❑ b steer away from it
❑ c steer into it
❑ d apply your handbrake

8.23

You are driving in fog. Why should you keep well back from the vehicle in front?

Mark one answer

❑ a In case it changes direction suddenly
❑ b In case its fog lights dazzle you
❑ c In case it stops suddenly
❑ d In case its brake lights dazzle you

8.24

You should switch your rear fog lights on when visibility drops below

Mark one answer

❑ a your overall stopping distance
❑ b ten car lengths
❑ c 200 metres (656 feet)
❑ d 100 metres (328 feet)

8.25

While driving, the fog clears and you can see more clearly. You must remember to

Mark one answer

❑ a switch off the fog lights
❑ b reduce your speed
❑ c switch off the demister
❑ d close any open windows

8.26

You have to park on the road in fog.
You should

Mark one answer

❑ a leave sidelights on
❑ b leave dipped headlights and fog lights on
❑ c leave dipped headlights on
❑ d leave main beam headlights on

8.27

On a foggy day you unavoidably have to park your car on the road. You should

Mark one answer

❑ a leave your headlights on
❑ b leave your fog lights on
❑ c leave your sidelights on
❑ d leave your hazard lights on

8.28

You are travelling at night. You are dazzled by headlights coming towards you. You should

Mark one answer

❑ a pull down your sun visor
❑ b slow down or stop
❑ c switch on your main beam headlights
❑ d put your hand over your eyes

8.29

Front fog lights may be used ONLY if

Mark one answer

❑ a visibility is seriously reduced
❑ b they are fitted above the bumper
❑ c they are not as bright as the headlights
❑ d an audible warning device is used

8.30

Front fog lights may be used ONLY if

Mark one answer

❑ a your headlights are not working
❑ b they are operated with rear fog lights
❑ c they were fitted by the vehicle manufacturer
❑ d visibility is seriously reduced

8.31

You are driving with your front fog lights switched on. Earlier fog has now cleared. What should you do?

Mark one answer

- ❑ a Leave them on if other drivers have their lights on
- ❑ b Switch them off as long as visibility remains good
- ❑ c Flash them to warn oncoming traffic that it is foggy
- ❑ d Drive with them on instead of your headlights

8.32

Front fog lights should be used ONLY when

Mark one answer

- ❑ a travelling in very light rain
- ❑ b visibility is seriously reduced
- ❑ c daylight is fading
- ❑ d driving after midnight

8.33

You are driving on a clear dry night with your rear fog lights switched on. This may

Mark two answers

- ❑ a reduce glare from the road surface
- ❑ b make other drivers think you are braking
- ❑ c give a better view of the road ahead
- ❑ d dazzle following drivers
- ❑ e help your indicators to be seen more clearly

8.34

You forget to switch off your rear fog lights when the fog has cleared. This may

Mark three answers

- ❑ a dazzle other road users
- ❑ b reduce battery life
- ❑ c cause brake lights to be less clear
- ❑ d be breaking the law
- ❑ e seriously affect engine power

8.35

You have been driving in thick fog which has now cleared. You must switch OFF your rear fog lights because

Mark one answer

- ❑ a they use a lot of power from the battery
- ❑ b they make your brake lights less clear
- ❑ c they will cause dazzle in your rear view mirrors
- ❑ d they may not be properly adjusted

8.36

Front fog lights should be used

Mark one answer

- ❑ a when visibility is reduced to 100 metres (328 feet)
- ❑ b as a warning to oncoming traffic
- ❑ c when driving during the hours of darkness
- ❑ d in any conditions and at any time

Answers

8.22 c

8.23 c If the car in front stops suddenly you may run into it if you have been driving too close.

8.24 d Remember to switch them off when visibility improves.

8.25 a Fog lights should only be used where visibility is down to about 100 metres. Otherwise you risk dazzling other drivers.

8.26 a
8.27 c
8.28 b
8.29 a
8.30 d
8.31 b
8.32 b
8.33 b, d
8.34 a, c, d
8.35 b
8.36 a

8.37

Using rear fog lights in clear daylight will

Mark one answer

- ❏ a be useful when towing a trailer
- ❏ b give extra protection
- ❏ c dazzle other drivers
- ❏ d make following drivers keep back

8.38

Using front fog lights in clear daylight will

Mark one answer

- ❏ a flatten the battery
- ❏ b dazzle other drivers
- ❏ c improve your visibility
- ❏ d increase your awareness

8.39

You may use front fog lights with headlights ONLY when visibility is reduced to less than

Mark one answer

- ❏ a 100 metres (328 feet)
- ❏ b 200 metres (656 feet)
- ❏ c 300 metres (984 feet)
- ❏ d 400 metres (1312 feet)

8.40

Chains can be fitted to your wheels to help prevent

Mark one answer

- ❏ a damage to the road surface
- ❏ b wear to the tyres
- ❏ c skidding in deep snow
- ❏ d the brakes locking

8.41

How can you use the engine of your vehicle to control your speed?

Mark one answer

- ❏ a By changing to a lower gear
- ❏ b By selecting reverse gear
- ❏ c By changing to a higher gear
- ❏ d By selecting neutral

8.42

Why could keeping the clutch down or selecting neutral for long periods of time be dangerous?

Mark one answer

- ❏ a Fuel spillage will occur
- ❏ b Engine damage may be caused
- ❏ c You will have less steering and braking control
- ❏ d It will wear tyres out more quickly

8.43

You are driving on an icy road. What distance should you drive from the car in front?

Mark one answer

- ❏ a Four times the normal distance
- ❏ b Six times the normal distance
- ❏ c Eight times the normal distance
- ❏ d Ten times the normal distance

8.44

You are on a well-lit motorway at night. You must

Mark one answer

- ❏ a use only your sidelights
- ❏ b always use your headlights
- ❏ c always use rear fog lights
- ❏ d use headlights only in bad weather

8.45

You are on a motorway at night with other vehicles just ahead of you. Which lights should you have on?

Mark one answer

- ❏ a Front fog lights
- ❏ b Main beam headlights
- ❏ c Sidelights only
- ❏ d Dipped headlights

8.46

Which THREE of the following will affect your stopping distance?

Mark three answers

- ☐ a How fast you are going
- ☐ b The tyres on your vehicle
- ☐ c The time of day
- ☐ d The weather
- ☐ e The street lighting

8.47

You are on a motorway at night. You MUST have your headlights switched on unless

Mark one answer

- ☐ a there are vehicles close in front of you
- ☐ b you are travelling below 50 mph
- ☐ c the motorway is lit
- ☐ d your vehicle is broken down on the hard shoulder

8.48

You will feel the effects of engine braking when you

Mark one answer

- ☐ a only use the handbrake
- ☐ b only use neutral
- ☐ c change to a lower gear
- ☐ d change to a higher gear

8.49

Daytime visibility is poor but not seriously reduced. You should switch on

Mark one answer

- ☐ a headlights and fog lights
- ☐ b front fog lights
- ☐ c dipped headlights
- ☐ d rear fog lights

8.50

Why are vehicles fitted with rear fog lights?

Mark one answer

- ☐ a To be seen when driving at high speed
- ☐ b To use if broken down in a dangerous position
- ☐ c To make them more visible in thick fog
- ☐ d To warn drivers following closely to drop back

Answers

8.37 c
8.38 b
8.39 a
8.40 c
8.41 a On a long, downhill slope changing to a lower gear before the descent means that you may not need to use the footbrake the whole time and will not risk the brakes overheating.
8.42 c
8.43 d Stopping distances can be up to ten times longer in snow and ice. Give yourself plenty of time to stop.
8.44 b
8.45 d Full-beam headlights would dazzle the drivers in front by reflecting in their mirrors.
8.46 a, b, d
8.47 d You must use your headlights when driving on a motorway at night, even if the motorway is lit.
8.48 c
8.49 c
8.50 c

8.51

While you are driving in fog, it becomes necessary to use front fog lights. You should

Mark one answer

- ❏ a only turn them on in heavy traffic conditions
- ❏ b remember not to use them on motorways
- ❏ c only use them on dual carriageways
- ❏ d remember to switch them off as visibility improves

8.52

When snow is falling heavily you should

Mark one answer

- ❏ a only drive with your hazard lights on
- ❏ b not drive unless you have a mobile phone
- ❏ c only drive when your journey is short
- ❏ d not drive unless it is essential

8.53

You are driving down a long steep hill. You suddenly notice your brakes are not working as well as normal. What is the usual cause of this?

Mark one answer

- ❏ a The brakes overheating
- ❏ b Air in the brake fluid
- ❏ c Oil on the brakes
- ❏ d Badly adjusted brakes

8.54

You have to make a journey in fog. What are the TWO most important things you should do before you set out?

Mark two answers

- ❏ a Top up the radiator with anti-freeze
- ❏ b Make sure that you have a warning triangle in the vehicle
- ❏ c Check that your lights are working
- ❏ d Check the battery
- ❏ e Make sure that the windows are clean

8.55

You have just driven out of fog. Visibility is now good. You MUST

Mark one answer

- ❏ a switch off all your fog lights
- ❏ b keep your rear fog lights on
- ❏ c keep your front fog lights on
- ❏ d leave fog lights on in case fog returns

8.56

You may drive with front fog lights switched on

Mark one answer

- ❏ a when visibility is less than 100 metres (328 feet)
- ❏ b at any time to be noticed
- ❏ c instead of headlights on high speed roads
- ❏ d when dazzled by the lights of oncoming vehicles

8.57

Why is it dangerous to leave rear fog lights on when they are not needed?

Mark two answers

- ❏ a Brake lights are less clear
- ❏ b Following drivers can be dazzled
- ❏ c Electrical systems could be overloaded
- ❏ d Direction indicators may not work properly
- ❏ e The battery could fail

8.58

Holding the clutch pedal down or rolling in neutral for too long while driving will

Mark one answer

- ❏ a use more fuel
- ❏ b cause the engine to overheat
- ❏ c reduce your control
- ❏ d improve tyre wear

8.59

You are driving down a steep hill. Why could keeping the clutch down or rolling in neutral for too long be dangerous?

Mark one answer

- ❑ a Fuel consumption will be higher
- ❑ b Your vehicle will pick up speed
- ❑ c It will damage the engine
- ❑ d It will wear tyres out more quickly

8.60

What are TWO main reasons why coasting downhill is wrong?

Mark two answers

- ❑ a Fuel consumption will be higher
- ❑ b The vehicle will get faster
- ❑ c It puts more wear and tear on the tyres
- ❑ d You have less braking and steering control
- ❑ e It damages the engine

8.61

Which FOUR of the following may apply when dealing with this hazard?

Mark four answers

- ❑ a It could be more difficult in winter
- ❑ b Use a low gear and drive slowly
- ❑ c Use a high gear to prevent wheelspin
- ❑ d Test your brakes afterwards
- ❑ e Always switch on fog lamps
- ❑ f There may be a depth gauge

8.62

Why is travelling in neutral for long distances (known as coasting) wrong?

Mark one answer

- ❑ a It will cause the car to skid
- ❑ b It will make the engine stall
- ❑ c The engine will run faster
- ❑ d There is no engine braking

8.63

When MUST you use dipped headlights during the day?

Mark one answer

- ❑ a All the time
- ❑ b Along narrow streets
- ❑ c In poor visibility
- ❑ d When parking

Answers

8.51 d

8.52 d

8.53 a Selecting a lower gear before descending a long, steep hill allows the engine to control the speed of the car and helps prevent the brakes overheating. With a lower gear selected, the footbrake can be used when necessary, rather than the whole time.

8.54 c, e See and be seen are the two most crucial safety aspects of driving in fog.

8.55 a

8.56 a

8.57 a, b

8.58 c

8.59 b

8.60 b, d

8.61 a, b, d, f

8.62 d

8.63 c

8.64

When you are seated on a stationary motorcycle, your position should allow you to

Mark one answer

- ❑ a just touch the ground with your toes
- ❑ b place both feet on the ground
- ❑ c operate the centre stand
- ❑ d reach the switches by stretching

8.65

As a safety measure before starting your engine, you should

Mark two answers

- ❑ a push the motorcycle forward to check the rear wheel turns freely
- ❑ b engage first gear and apply the rear brake
- ❑ c engage first gear and apply the front brake
- ❑ d glance at the neutral light on your instrument panel

8.66

You are approaching this junction. As the motorcyclist you should

Mark two answers

- ❑ a prepare to slow down
- ❑ b sound your horn
- ❑ c keep near the left kerb
- ❑ d speed up to clear the junction
- ❑ e stop, as the car has right of way

8.67

What can you do to improve your safety on the road as a motorcyclist?

Mark one answer

- ❑ a Anticipate the actions of others
- ❑ b Stay just above the speed limits
- ❑ c Keep positioned close to the kerbs
- ❑ d Remain well below speed limits

8.68

Which THREE of these can cause skidding?

Mark three answers

- ❑ a Braking too gently
- ❑ b Leaning too far over when cornering
- ❑ c Staying upright when cornering
- ❑ d Braking too hard
- ❑ e Changing direction suddenly

8.69

It is very cold and the road looks wet. You cannot hear any road noise. You should

Mark two answers

- ❑ a continue riding at the same speed
- ❑ b ride slower in as high a gear as possible
- ❑ c ride in as low a gear as possible
- ❑ d keep revving your engine
- ❑ e slow down as there may be black ice

8.70

When riding a motorcycle you should wear full protective clothing

Mark one answer

- ❑ a at all times
- ❑ b only on faster, open roads
- ❑ c just on long journeys
- ❑ d only during bad weather

8.71

You have to make a journey in fog. What are the TWO most important things you should do before you set out?
Mark two answers
- ❑ a Fill up with fuel
- ❑ b Make sure that you have a warm drink with you
- ❑ c Check that your lights are working
- ❑ d Check the battery
- ❑ e Make sure that your visor is clean

8.72

The best place to park your motorcycle is
Mark one answer
- ❑ a on soft tarmac
- ❑ b on bumpy ground
- ❑ c on grass
- ❑ d on firm, level ground

8.73

When riding in windy conditions, you should
Mark one answer
- ❑ a stay close to large vehicles
- ❑ b keep your speed up
- ❑ c keep your speed down
- ❑ d stay close to the gutter

8.74

In normal riding your position on the road should be
Mark one answer
- ❑ a about a foot from the kerb
- ❑ b about central in your lane
- ❑ c on the right of your lane
- ❑ d near the centre of the road

8.75

Your motorcycle is parked on a two-way road. You should get on from the
Mark one answer
- ❑ a right and apply the rear brake
- ❑ b left and leave the brakes alone
- ❑ c left and apply the front brake
- ❑ d right and leave the brakes alone

8.76

To gain basic skills in how to ride a motorcycle you should
Mark one answer
- ❑ a practise off-road with an approved training body
- ❑ b ride on the road on the first dry day
- ❑ c practise off-road in a public park or in a quiet cul-de-sac
- ❑ d ride on the road as soon as possible

Answers

8.64 b
8.65 a, d
8.66 a, b
8.67 a
8.68 b, d, e
8.69 b, e
8.70 a
8.71 c, e See and be seen are the two most crucial safety aspects of riding in fog.
8.72 d
8.73 c
8.74 b Your exact position will depend on the width of the road, the road surface, your view ahead and any obstructions.
8.75 c Always mount on the side away from traffic and apply the front brake to stop the motorcycle moving.
8.76 a

8.77

You should not ride with your clutch lever pulled in for longer than necessary because it

Mark one answer

- ❏ a increases wear on the gearbox
- ❏ b increases petrol consumption
- ❏ c reduces your control of the motorcycle
- ❏ d reduces the grip of the tyres

8.78

You are approaching a road with a surface of loose chippings. What should you do?

Mark one answer

- ❏ a Ride normally
- ❏ b Speed up
- ❏ c Slow down
- ❏ d Stop suddenly

8.79

It rains after a long dry, hot spell. This may cause the road surface to

Mark one answer

- ❏ a be unusually slippery
- ❏ b give better grip
- ❏ c become covered in grit
- ❏ d melt and break up

8.80

The main causes of a motorcycle skidding are

Mark three answers

- ❏ a heavy and sharp braking
- ❏ b excessive acceleration
- ❏ c leaning too far when cornering
- ❏ d riding in wet weather
- ❏ e riding in the winter

8.81

To stop your motorcycle quickly in an emergency you should apply

Mark one answer

- ❏ a the rear brake only
- ❏ b the front brake only
- ❏ c the front brake just before the rear
- ❏ d the rear brake just before the front

8.82

Riding with the side stand down could cause an accident. This is most likely to happen when

Mark one answer

- ❏ a going uphill
- ❏ b accelerating
- ❏ c braking
- ❏ d cornering

8.83

You leave the choke on for too long. This causes the engine to run too fast. When is this likely to make your motorcycle most difficult to control?

Mark one answer

- ❏ a Accelerating
- ❏ b Going uphill
- ❏ c Slowing down
- ❏ d On motorways

8.84

You should NOT look down at the front wheel when riding because it can

Mark one answer

- ❏ a make your steering lighter
- ❏ b improve your balance
- ❏ c use less fuel
- ❏ d upset your balance

8.85

You are entering a bend. Your side stand is not fully raised. This could

Mark one answer

- ❏ a cause an accident
- ❏ b improve your balance
- ❏ c alter the motorcycle's centre of gravity
- ❏ d make the motorcycle more stable

8.86

In normal riding conditions you should brake

Mark one answer

- ❏ a by using the rear brake first and then the front
- ❏ b when the motorcycle is being turned or ridden through a bend
- ❏ c by pulling in the clutch before using the front brake
- ❏ d when the motorcycle is upright and moving in a straight line

8.87

Which THREE of the following will affect your stopping distance?

Mark three answers

- ❏ a How fast you are going
- ❏ b The tyres on your motorcycle
- ❏ c The time of day
- ❏ d The weather
- ❏ e The street lighting

8.88

You are on a motorway at night. You MUST have your headlights switched on unless

Mark one answer

- ❏ a there are vehicles close in front of you
- ❏ b you are travelling below 50 mph
- ❏ c the motorway is lit
- ❏ d your motorcycle is broken down on the hard shoulder

8.89

You have to park on the road in fog. You should

Mark one answer

- ❏ a leave parking lights on
- ❏ b leave no lights on
- ❏ c leave dipped headlights on
- ❏ d leave main beam headlights on

Answers

8.77	c
8.78	c
8.79	a
8.80	a, b, c
8.81	c
8.82	d
8.83	c
8.84	d
8.85	a
8.86	d
8.87	a, b, d
8.88	d
8.89	a

8.90

You leave the choke on for too long.
This could make the engine run faster than
normal. This will make your motorcycle

Mark one answer

- ❑ a handle much better
- ❑ b corner much safer
- ❑ c stop much more quickly
- ❑ d more difficult to control

8.91

You are riding on a wet road. When braking
you should
Mark one answer

- ❑ a apply the rear brake well before the front
- ❑ b apply the front brake just before the rear
- ❑ c avoid using the front brake at all
- ❑ d avoid using the rear brake at all

8.92

You ride over broken glass and get a sudden
puncture. What should you do?
Mark one answer

- ❑ a Close the throttle and roll to a stop
- ❑ b Brake to a stop as quickly as possible
- ❑ c Release your grip on the handlebars
- ❑ d Steer from side to side to keep your
  balance

8.93

You are riding in wet weather. You see diesel
fuel on the road. What should you do?
Mark one answer

- ❑ a Swerve to avoid the area
- ❑ b Accelerate through quickly
- ❑ c Brake sharply to a stop
- ❑ d Slow down in good time

8.94

Spilt fuel on the road can be very dangerous
for you as a motorcyclist. How can this hazard
be seen?
Mark one answer

- ❑ a By a rainbow pattern on the surface
- ❑ b By a series of skid marks
- ❑ c By a pitted road surface
- ❑ d By a highly polished surface

8.95

Which FOUR types of road surface increase
the risk of skidding for motorcyclists?
Mark four answers

- ❑ a White lines
- ❑ b Dry tarmac
- ❑ c Tar banding
- ❑ d Yellow grid lines
- ❑ e Loose chippings

8.96

The road is wet. You are passing a line of
queuing traffic and riding on the painted road
markings. You should take extra care,
particularly when
Mark one answer

- ❑ a signalling
- ❑ b braking
- ❑ c carrying a passenger
- ❑ d checking your mirrors

8.97

You are going ahead and will have to cross tram lines. Why should you be especially careful ?

Mark one answer

- ❏ a Tram lines are always 'live'
- ❏ b Trams will be stopping here
- ❏ c Pedestrians will be crossing here
- ❏ d The steel rails can be slippery

8.98

You have to brake sharply and your motorcycle starts to skid. You should

Mark one answer

- ❏ a continue braking and select a low gear
- ❏ b apply the brakes harder for better grip
- ❏ c select neutral and use the front brake only
- ❏ d release the brakes and reapply

8.99

You see a rainbow-coloured pattern across the road. What will this warn you of?

Mark one answer

- ❏ a A soft uneven road surface
- ❏ b A polished road surface
- ❏ c Fuel spilt on the road
- ❏ d Water on the road

8.100

Traction Control Systems (TCS) are fitted to some motorcycles. What does this help to prevent?

Mark one answer

- ❏ a Wheelspin when accelerating
- ❏ b Skidding when braking too hard
- ❏ c Uneven front tyre wear
- ❏ d Uneven rear tyre wear

8.101

Braking too hard has caused both wheels to skid. What should you do?

Mark one answer

- ❏ a Release both brakes together
- ❏ b Release the front then the rear brake
- ❏ c Release the front brake only
- ❏ d Release the rear brake only

8.102

Your motorcycle does NOT have linked brakes. What should you do when braking to a normal stop?

Mark one answer

- ❏ a Only apply the front brake
- ❏ b Rely just on the rear brake
- ❏ c Apply both brakes smoothly
- ❏ d Apply either of the brakes gently

Answers

8.90	d
8.91	b
8.92	a
8.93	d
8.94	a
8.95	a, c, d, e
8.96	b
8.97	d
8.98	d
8.99	c
8.100	a
8.101	a
8.102	c

Theory Test Questions
for Car Drivers and Motorcyclists

Section 9   Motorway rules

9.1

When joining a motorway you must always
Mark one answer
- ❑ a use the hard shoulder
- ❑ b stop at the end of the acceleration lane
- ❑ c come to a stop before joining the motorway
- ❑ d give way to traffic already on the motorway

9.2

What is the national speed limit for cars and motorcycles in the centre lane of a three-lane motorway?
Mark one answer
- ❑ a 40 mph
- ❑ b 50 mph
- ❑ c 60 mph
- ❑ d 70 mph

9.3

What is the national speed limit on motorways for cars and motorcycles?
Mark one answer
- ❑ a 30 mph
- ❑ b 50 mph
- ❑ c 60 mph
- ❑ d 70 mph

9.4

The left-hand lane on a three-lane motorway is for use by

Mark one answer
- ❑ a any vehicle
- ❑ b large vehicles only
- ❑ c emergency vehicles only
- ❑ d slow vehicles only

9.5

Which of these IS NOT allowed to travel in the right-hand lane of a three-lane motorway?
Mark one answer
- ❑ a A small delivery van
- ❑ b A motorcycle
- ❑ c A vehicle towing a trailer
- ❑ d A motorcycle and side-car

9.6

You are travelling on a motorway. You decide you need a rest. You should
Mark two answers
- ❑ a stop on the hard shoulder
- ❑ b go to a service area
- ❑ c park on the slip road
- ❑ d park on the central reservation
- ❑ e leave at the next exit

9.7

You break down on a motorway. You need to call for help. Why may it be better to use an emergency roadside telephone rather than a mobile phone?
Mark one answer
- ❑ a It connects you to a local garage
- ❑ b Using a mobile phone will distract other drivers
- ❑ c It allows easy location by the emergency services
- ❑ d Mobile phones do not work on motorways

9.8

After a breakdown you need to rejoin the main carriageway of a motorway from the hard shoulder. You should

Mark one answer

- ❏ a move out onto the carriageway then build up your speed
- ❏ b move out onto the carriageway using your hazard lights
- ❏ c gain speed on the hard shoulder before moving out onto the carriageway
- ❏ d wait on the hard shoulder until someone flashes their headlights at you

9.9

A crawler lane on a motorway is found

Mark one answer

- ❏ a on a steep gradient
- ❏ b before a service area
- ❏ c before a junction
- ❏ d along the hard shoulder

9.10

What do these motorway signs show?

Mark one answer

- ❏ a They are countdown markers to a bridge
- ❏ b They are distance markers to the next telephone
- ❏ c They are countdown markers to the next exit
- ❏ d They warn of a police control ahead

9.11

On a motorway the amber reflective studs can be found between

Mark one answer

- ❏ a the hard shoulder and the carriageway
- ❏ b the acceleration lane and the carriageway
- ❏ c the central reservation and the carriageway
- ❏ d each pair of the lanes

9.12

What colour are the reflective studs between the lanes on a motorway?

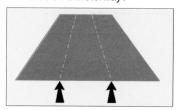

Mark one answer

- ❏ a Green
- ❏ b Amber
- ❏ c White
- ❏ d Red

Answers

9.1 d

9.2 d

9.3 d Speed limits may be altered due to weather conditions. Look out for signs on the central reservation or above your lane.

9.4 a Strictly speaking, any vehicle which is allowed on a motorway.

9.5 c

9.6 b, e

9.7 c

9.8 c

9.9 a

9.10 c

9.11 c

9.12 c

9.13

What colour are the reflective studs between a motorway and its slip road?
Mark one answer
- ❑ a Amber
- ❑ b White
- ❑ c Green
- ❑ d Red

9.14

You have broken down on a motorway. To find the nearest emergency telephone you should always walk
Mark one answer
- ❑ a with the traffic flow
- ❑ b facing oncoming traffic
- ❑ c in the direction shown on the marker posts
- ❑ d in the direction of the nearest exit

9.15

You are joining a motorway. Why is it important to make full use of the slip road?
Mark one answer
- ❑ a Because there is space available to turn round if you need to
- ❑ b To allow you direct access to the overtaking lanes
- ❑ c To build up a speed similar to traffic on the motorway
- ❑ d Because you can continue on the hard shoulder

9.16

How should you use the emergency telephone on a motorway?
Mark one answer
- ❑ a Stay close to the carriageway
- ❑ b Face the oncoming traffic
- ❑ c Keep your back to the traffic
- ❑ d Stand on the hard shoulder

9.17

You are on a motorway. What colour are the reflective studs on the left of the carriageway?
Mark one answer
- ❑ a Green
- ❑ b Red
- ❑ c White
- ❑ d Amber

9.18

On a three-lane motorway which lane should you normally use?
Mark one answer
- ❑ a Left
- ❑ b Right
- ❑ c Centre
- ❑ d Either the right or centre

9.19

When going through a contraflow system on a motorway you should

Mark one answer
- ❑ a ensure that you do not exceed 30 mph
- ❑ b keep a good distance from the vehicle ahead
- ❑ c switch lanes to keep the traffic flowing
- ❑ d stay close to the vehicle ahead to reduce queues

9.20

You are on a three-lane motorway. There are red reflective studs on your left and white ones to your right. Where are you?

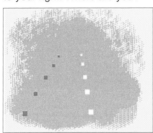

Mark one answer
- ❏ a In the right-hand lane
- ❏ b In the middle lane
- ❏ c On the hard shoulder
- ❏ d In the left-hand lane

9.21

You are approaching roadworks on a motorway. What should you do?

Mark one answer
- ❏ a Speed up to clear the area quickly
- ❏ b Always use the hard shoulder
- ❏ c Obey all speed limits
- ❏ d Stay very close to the vehicle in front

9.22

Which FOUR of these must NOT use motorways?

Mark four answers
- ❏ a Learner car drivers
- ❏ b Motorcycles over 50cc
- ❏ c Double-deck buses
- ❏ d Farm tractors
- ❏ e Horse riders
- ❏ f Cyclists

9.23

Which FOUR of these must NOT use motorways?

Mark four answers
- ❏ a Learner car drivers
- ❏ b Motorcycles over 50cc
- ❏ c Double-deck buses
- ❏ d Farm tractors
- ❏ e Learner motorcyclists
- ❏ f Cyclists

Answers

9.13 c
9.14 c
9.15 c You need to build up your speed to that of the traffic already on the motorway so you can ease into a gap in the flow of traffic.
9.16 b
9.17 b
9.18 a The other lanes should be used for overtaking.
9.19 b In these circumstances there may also be a speed limit – keep to it.
9.20 d
9.21 c In motorway roadworks you are sometimes, but not always, directed to use the hard shoulder, especially where the right-hand lane is closed. Therefore, 'b' is not correct. There often are lower speed limits to protect the traffic in contraflows or narrow lanes and you must obey these.
9.22 a, d, e, f
9.23 a, d, e, f

9.24

Immediately after joining a motorway you should normally

Mark one answer

- ❑ a try to overtake
- ❑ b readjust your mirrors
- ❑ c position your vehicle in the centre lane
- ❑ d keep in the left-hand lane

9.25

What is the right-hand lane used for on a three-lane motorway?

Mark one answer

- ❑ a Emergency vehicles only
- ❑ b Overtaking
- ❑ c Vehicles towing trailers
- ❑ d Coaches only

9.26

What should you use the hard shoulder of a motorway for?

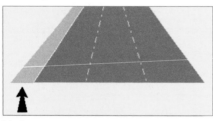

Mark one answer

- ❑ a Stopping in an emergency
- ❑ b Leaving the motorway
- ❑ c Stopping when you are tired
- ❑ d Joining the motorway

9.27

You are in the right-hand lane on a motorway. You see these overhead signs. This means

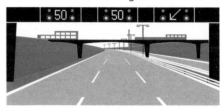

Mark one answer

- ❑ a move to the left and reduce your speed to 50 mph
- ❑ b there are roadworks 50 metres (55 yards) ahead
- ❑ c use the hard shoulder until you have passed the hazard
- ❑ d leave the motorway at the next exit

9.28

You are allowed to stop on a motorway when you

Mark one answer

- ❑ a need to walk and get fresh air
- ❑ b wish to pick up hitchhikers
- ❑ c are told to do so by flashing red lights
- ❑ d need to use a mobile telephone

9.29

You are travelling along the left-hand lane of a three-lane motorway. Traffic is joining from a slip road. You should

Mark one answer

- ❑ a race the other vehicles
- ❑ b move to another lane
- ❑ c maintain a steady speed
- ❑ d switch on your hazard flashers

9.30

A basic rule when on motorways is
Mark one answer
- ❏ a use the lane that has least traffic
- ❏ b keep to the left-hand lane unless overtaking
- ❏ c overtake on the side that is clearest
- ❏ d try to keep above 50 mph to prevent congestion

9.31

On motorways you should never overtake on the left unless
Mark one answer
- ❏ a you can see well ahead that the hard shoulder is clear
- ❏ b the traffic in the right-hand lane is signalling right
- ❏ c you warn drivers behind by signalling left
- ❏ d there is a queue of slow-moving traffic to your right that is moving more slowly than you are

9.32

Motorway emergency telephones are usually linked to the police. In some areas they are now linked to
Mark one answer
- ❏ a the Highways Agency Control Centre
- ❏ b the Driver Vehicle Licensing Agency
- ❏ c the Driving Standards Agency
- ❏ d the local Vehicle Registration Office

9.33

An Emergency Refuge Area is an area
Mark one answer
- ❏ a on a motorway for use in cases of emergency or breakdown
- ❏ b for use if you think you will be involved in a road rage incident
- ❏ c on a motorway for a police patrol to park and watch traffic
- ❏ d for construction and road workers to store emergency equipment

9.34

What is an Emergency Refuge Area on a motorway for?
Mark one answer
- ❏ a An area to park in when you want to use a mobile phone
- ❏ b To use in cases of emergency or breakdown
- ❏ c For an emergency recovery vehicle to park in a contra-flow system
- ❏ d To drive in when there is queuing traffic ahead

Answers

9.24 d
9.25 b
9.26 a You may only stop on the hard shoulder in an emergency.
9.27 a
9.28 c
9.29 b
9.30 b
9.31 d
9.32 a In some areas The Highways Agency Control Centre operates the phone network, taking the calls and passing the information on where appropriate to the relevant emergency service.
9.33 a Emergency refuge areas will be available in areas where the hard shoulder is being used as a running lane. They are 100 metres long, wider than the hard shoulder and are located every 500 metres. They are designed to be used in cases of emergency or breakdown.
9.34 b

9.35

Highways Agency Traffic Officers

❑ a will not be able to assist at a breakdown or emergency

❑ b are not able to stop and direct anyone on a motorway

❑ c will tow a broken down vehicle and its passengers home

❑ d are able to stop and direct anyone on a motorway

9.36

You are on a motorway. A red cross is displayed above the hard shoulder. What does this mean?

❑ a Pull up in this lane to answer your mobile phone

❑ b Use this lane as a running lane

❑ c This lane can be used if you need a rest

❑ d You should not travel in this lane

9.37

You are on a motorway in an Active Traffic Management (ATM) area. A mandatory speed limit is displayed above the hard shoulder. What does this mean?

❑ a You should not travel in this lane

❑ b The hard shoulder can be used as a running lane

❑ c You can park on the hard shoulder if you feel tired

❑ d You can pull up in this lane to answer a mobile phone

9.38

The aim of an Active Traffic Management scheme on a motorway is to

❑ a prevent overtaking

❑ b reduce rest stops

❑ c prevent tailgating

❑ d reduce congestion

9.39

You are in an Active Traffic Management area on a motorway. When the Actively Managed mode is operating

❑ a speed limits are only advisory

❑ b the national speed limit will apply

❑ c the speed limit is always 30 mph

❑ d all speed limit signals are set

9.40

You are travelling on a motorway. A red cross is shown above the hard shoulder and mandatory speed limits above all other lanes. This means

Mark one answer

❑ a the hard shoulder can be used as a rest area if you feel tired
❑ b the hard shoulder is for emergency or breakdown use only
❑ c the hard shoulder can be used as a normal running lane
❑ d the hard shoulder has a speed limit of 50 mph

9.41

You are travelling on a motorway. A red cross is shown above the hard shoulder. What does this mean?

Mark one answer

❑ a Use this lane as a rest area
❑ b Use this as a normal running lane
❑ c Do not use this lane to travel in
❑ d National speed limit applies in this lane

Answers

9.35 d Highways Agency Traffic Officers are there to help and guide you, usually at the scene of an accident or at road works. Follow their directions.

9.36 d The red cross means the same displayed above any lane – do not travel any further in this lane. When it is displayed above the hard shoulder it indicates you are travelling in an Active Traffic Management area.

9.37 b Active Traffic Management (ATM) aims to reduce congestion and make journey times more reliable. A pilot scheme is being carried out on a 17km stretch of the M42. In an ATM the hard shoulder can be used as an additional running lane under controlled conditions.

9.38 d See the explanation to 9.37 above.

9.39 d This allows the managed area to be controlled so that congestion is reduced.

9.40 b The red cross indicates you are driving in an actively managed area under normal motorway conditions, so the hard shoulder may only be used for emergency or breakdown. In addition to the hard shoulder you should make use of the emergency refuge areas, as these give additional distance from the carriageway.

9.41 c

9.42

You see this sign on a motorway. It means you can use

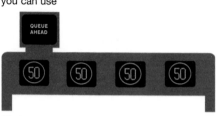

Mark one answer

❑ a any lane except the hard shoulder
❑ b the hard shoulder only
❑ c the three right-hand lanes only
❑ d all the lanes including the hard shoulder

9.43

Why can it be an advantage for traffic speed to stay constant over a longer distance?
Mark one answer
❑ a You will do more stop-start driving
❑ b You will use far more fuel
❑ c You will be able to use more direct routes
❑ d Your overall journey time will normally improve

9.44

You should not normally travel on the hard shoulder of a motorway. When can you use it?
Mark one answer
❑ a When taking the next exit
❑ b When traffic is stopped
❑ c When signs direct you to
❑ d When traffic is slow moving

9.45

For what reason may you use the right-hand lane of a motorway?
Mark one answer
❑ a For keeping out of the way of lorries
❑ b For travelling at more than 70 mph
❑ c For turning right
❑ d For overtaking other vehicles

9.46

On a motorway what is used to reduce traffic bunching?
Mark one answer
❑ a Variable speed limits
❑ b Contraflow systems
❑ c National speed limits
❑ d Lane closures

9.47

When should you stop on a motorway?
Mark three answers
❑ a If you have to read a map
❑ b When you are tired and need a rest
❑ c If red lights show above every lane
❑ d When told to by the police
❑ e If your mobile phone rings
❑ f When signalled by a Highways Agency Traffic Officer

9.48

When may you stop on a motorway?
Mark one answer
❑ a If you have to read a map
❑ b When you are tired and need a rest
❑ c If your mobile phone rings
❑ d In an emergency or breakdown

9.49

You are travelling on a motorway. Unless signs show a lower speed limit you must NOT exceed
Mark one answer
❑ a 50 mph
❑ b 60 mph
❑ c 70 mph
❑ d 80 mph

9.50

Motorway emergency telephones are usually linked to the police. In some areas they are now linked to

Mark one answer
- ❏ a the local ambulance service
- ❏ b an Highways Agency control centre
- ❏ c the local fire brigade
- ❏ d a breakdown service control centre

9.51

You are on a motorway. There are red flashing lights above every lane. You must

Mark one answer
- ❏ a pull onto the hard shoulder
- ❏ b slow down and watch for further signals
- ❏ c leave at the next exit
- ❏ d stop and wait

9.52

Your vehicle breaks down on the hard shoulder of a motorway. You decide to use your mobile phone to call for help. You should

Mark one answer
- ❏ a stand at the rear of the vehicle while making the call
- ❏ b try to repair the vehicle yourself
- ❏ c get out of the vehicle by the right-hand door
- ❏ d check your location from the marker posts on the left

9.53

You are on a three-lane motorway towing a trailer. You may use the right-hand lane when

Mark one answer
- ❏ a there are lane closures
- ❏ b there is slow-moving traffic
- ❏ c you can maintain a high speed
- ❏ d large vehicles are in the left and centre lanes

9.54

You are on a motorway. There is a contraflow system ahead. What would you expect to find?

Mark one answer
- ❏ a Temporary traffic lights
- ❏ b Lower speed limits
- ❏ c Wider lanes than normal
- ❏ d Speed humps

Answers

9.42 d

9.43 d It has been proven on roads such as the M25, that managing traffic speed to be more constant reduces journey time, pollution and the risk of accidents.

9.44 c

9.45 d

9.46 a When traffic is heavy on certain stretches of motorway variable speed limits are used. The traffic might be limited to a maximum of 50 mph over a certain distance which helps spread the traffic out and avoid congestion.

9.47 c, d, f Motorways are statistically the safest roads to drive on because the traffic travels at a constant speed and there are few distractions, such as stationary vehicles. You may only stop on a motorway in an emergency.

9.48 d

9.49 c

9.50 b

9.51 d

9.52 d

9.53 a

9.54 b

9.55

You are towing a trailer on a motorway. What is your maximum speed limit?

Mark one answer

- ❑ a 40 mph
- ❑ b 50 mph
- ❑ c 60 mph
- ❑ d 70 mph

9.56

The left-hand lane of a motorway should be used for

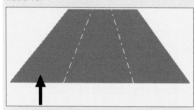

Mark one answer

- ❑ a breakdowns and emergencies only
- ❑ b overtaking slower traffic in the other lanes
- ❑ c slow vehicles only
- ❑ d normal driving

9.57

You are driving on a motorway. You have to slow down quickly due to a hazard. You should

Mark one answer

- ❑ a switch on your hazard lights
- ❑ b switch on your headlights
- ❑ c sound your horn
- ❑ d flash your headlights

9.58

You get a puncture on the motorway. You manage to get your vehicle onto the hard shoulder. You should

Mark one answer

- ❑ a change the wheel yourself immediately
- ❑ b use the emergency telephone and call for assistance
- ❑ c try to wave down another vehicle for help
- ❑ d only change the wheel if you have a passenger to help you

9.59

You are driving on a motorway. By mistake, you go past the exit that you wanted to take. You should

Mark one answer

- ❑ a carefully reverse on the hard shoulder
- ❑ b carry on to the next exit
- ❑ c carefully reverse in the left-hand lane
- ❑ d make a U-turn at the next gap in the central reservation

9.60

You are driving at 70 mph on a three-lane motorway. There is no traffic ahead. Which lane should you use?

Mark one answer

- ❑ a Any lane
- ❑ b Middle lane
- ❑ c Right lane
- ❑ d Left lane

9.61

Your vehicle has broken down on a motorway. You are not able to stop on the hard shoulder. What should you do?

Mark one answer

- ❑ a Switch on your hazard warning lights
- ❑ b Stop following traffic and ask for help
- ❑ c Attempt to repair your vehicle quickly
- ❑ d Stand behind your vehicle to warn others

9.62
Why is it particularly important to carry out a check on your vehicle before making a long motorway journey?
Mark one answer
- ❏ a You will have to do more harsh braking on motorways
- ❏ b Motorway service stations do not deal with breakdowns
- ❏ c The road surface will wear down the tyres faster
- ❏ d Continuous high speeds may increase the risk of your vehicle breaking down

9.63
On a motorway you may ONLY stop on the hard shoulder

Mark one answer
- ❏ a in an emergency
- ❏ b if you feel tired and need to rest
- ❏ c if you accidentally go past the exit that you wanted to take
- ❏ d to pick up a hitchhiker

9.64
You are driving on a motorway. The car ahead shows its hazard lights for a short time. This tells you that
Mark one answer
- ❏ a the driver wants you to overtake
- ❏ b the other car is going to change lanes
- ❏ c traffic ahead is slowing or stopping suddenly
- ❏ d there is a police speed check ahead

9.65
You are intending to leave the motorway at the next exit. Before you reach the exit you should normally position your vehicle
Mark one answer
- ❏ a in the middle lane
- ❏ b in the left-hand lane
- ❏ c on the hard shoulder
- ❏ d in any lane

9.66
As a provisional licence holder you should not drive a car
Mark one answer
- ❏ a over 30 mph
- ❏ b at night
- ❏ c on the motorway
- ❏ d with passengers in rear seats

Answers

9.55 c
9.56 d
9.57 a
9.58 b It is dangerous to attempt to change the wheel yourself. Try to keep as far from the carriageway as possible while waiting for assistance.
9.59 b
9.60 d You should always use the left-hand lane for normal driving.
9.61 a
9.62 d Check oil and windscreen washer levels and also check the tyres. Plan your rest stops.
9.63 a
9.64 c
9.65 b
9.66 c

9.67

On a motorway you may ONLY stop on the hard shoulder

Mark one answer

- ❏ a in an emergency
- ❏ b if you feel tired and need to rest
- ❏ c if you go past the exit that you wanted to take
- ❏ d to pick up a hitchhiker

9.68

You are intending to leave the motorway at the next exit. Before you reach the exit you should normally position your motorcycle

Mark one answer

- ❏ a in the middle lane
- ❏ b in the left-hand lane
- ❏ c on the hard shoulder
- ❏ d in any lane

9.69

You are joining a motorway from a slip road. You should

Mark one answer

- ❏ a adjust your speed to the speed of the traffic on the motorway
- ❏ b accelerate as quickly as you can and ride straight out
- ❏ c ride onto the hard shoulder until a gap appears
- ❏ d expect drivers on the motorway to give way to you

9.70

A motorcycle is not allowed on a motorway if it has an engine size smaller than

Mark one answer

- ❏ a 50 cc
- ❏ b 125 cc
- ❏ c 150 cc
- ❏ d 250 cc

9.71

To ride on a motorway your motorcycle must be

Mark one answer

- ❏ a 50 cc or more
- ❏ b 100 cc or more
- ❏ c 125 cc or more
- ❏ d 250 cc or more

9.72

On a three-lane motorway why should you normally ride in the left-hand lane?

Mark one answer

- ❏ a The left-hand lane is only for lorries and motorcycles
- ❏ b The left-hand lane should only be used by smaller vehicles
- ❏ c The lanes on the right are for overtaking
- ❏ d Motorcycles are not allowed in the far right-hand lane

9.73

You are riding at 70 mph on a three-lane motorway. There is no traffic ahead. Which lane should you use?

Mark one answer

- ❏ a Any lane
- ❏ b Middle lane
- ❏ c Right-hand lane
- ❏ d Left-hand lane

9.74

You are riding on a motorway. Unless signs show otherwise you must NOT exceed

Mark one answer

- ❏ a 50 mph
- ❏ b 60 mph
- ❏ c 70 mph
- ❏ d 80 mph

9.75

Why is it particularly important to carry out a check of your motorcycle before making a long motorway journey?

Mark one answer

❏ a You will have to do more harsh braking on motorways

❏ b Motorway service stations do not deal with breakdowns

❏ c The road surface will wear down the tyres faster

❏ d Continuous high speeds may increase the risk of your motorcycle breaking down

Answers

9.67 a
9.68 b
9.69 a The slip road gives you time and space to adjust your speed to that of the traffic on the motorway.
9.70 a
9.71 a
9.72 c
9.73 d
9.74 c
9.75 d

Theory Test Questions
for Car Drivers and Motorcyclists

Section 10   Rules of the road

10.1
What is the meaning of this sign?

Mark one answer
- ❑ a Local speed limit applies
- ❑ b No waiting on the carriageway
- ❑ c National speed limit applies
- ❑ d No entry to vehicular traffic

10.2
What is the national speed limit for cars and motorcycles on a dual carriageway?
Mark one answer
- ❑ a 30 mph
- ❑ b 50 mph
- ❑ c 60 mph
- ❑ d 70 mph

10.3
There are no speed limit signs on the road. How is a 30 mph limit indicated?
Mark one answer
- ❑ a By hazard warning lines
- ❑ b By street lighting
- ❑ c By pedestrian islands
- ❑ d By double or single yellow lines

10.4
Where you see street lights but no speed limit signs the limit is usually
Mark one answer
- ❑ a 30 mph
- ❑ b 40 mph
- ❑ c 50 mph
- ❑ d 60 mph

10.5
What does this sign mean?

Mark one answer
- ❑ a Minimum speed 30 mph
- ❑ b End of maximum speed
- ❑ c End of minimum speed
- ❑ d Maximum speed 30 mph

10.6
There is a tractor ahead of you. You wish to overtake but you are NOT sure if it is safe to do so. You should
Mark one answer
- ❑ a follow another overtaking vehicle through
- ❑ b sound your horn to the slow vehicle to pull over
- ❑ c speed through but flash your lights to oncoming traffic
- ❑ d not overtake if you are in doubt

10.7
Which three of the following are most likely to take an unusual course at roundabouts?
Mark three answers
- ❑ a Horse riders
- ❑ b Milk floats
- ❑ c Delivery vans
- ❑ d Long vehicles
- ❑ e Estate cars
- ❑ f Cyclists

10.8
On a clearway you must not stop
Mark one answer
- ❑ a at any time
- ❑ b when it is busy
- ❑ c in the rush hour
- ❑ d during daylight hours

10.9
What is the meaning of this sign?

Mark one answer
- ❑ a No entry
- ❑ b Waiting restrictions
- ❑ c National speed limit
- ❑ d School crossing patrol

10.10
You can park on the right-hand side of a road at night

Mark one answer
- ❑ a in a one-way street
- ❑ b with your sidelights on
- ❑ c more than 10 metres (32 feet) from a junction
- ❑ d under a lamp-post

10.11
On a three-lane dual carriageway the right-hand lane can be used for

Mark one answer
- ❑ a overtaking only, never turning right
- ❑ b overtaking or turning right
- ❑ c fast-moving traffic only
- ❑ d turning right only, never overtaking

10.12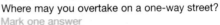
You are approaching a busy junction. There are several lanes with road markings. At the last moment you realise that you are in the wrong lane. You should

Mark one answer
- ❑ a continue in that lane
- ❑ b force your way across
- ❑ c stop until the area has cleared
- ❑ d use clear arm signals to cut across

10.13
Where may you overtake on a one-way street?

Mark one answer
- ❑ a Only on the left-hand side
- ❑ b Overtaking is not allowed
- ❑ c Only on the right-hand side
- ❑ d Either on the right or the left

Answers

10.1 c
10.2 d The national speed limit is 70 mph on a motorway or dual carriageway and 60 mph on two-way roads unless traffic signs denote anything different.
10.3 b
10.4 a
10.5 c
10.6 d
10.7 a, d, f
10.8 a
10.9 b
10.10 a
10.11 b
10.12 a All the other actions suggested could be dangerous.
10.13 d

10.14

When going straight ahead at a roundabout you should

Mark one answer

- ❑ a indicate left before leaving the roundabout
- ❑ b not indicate at any time
- ❑ c indicate right when approaching the roundabout
- ❑ d indicate left when approaching the roundabout

10.15

Which vehicle might have to use a different course to normal at roundabouts?

Mark one answer

- ❑ a Sports car
- ❑ b Van
- ❑ c Estate car
- ❑ d Long vehicle

10.16

You are going straight ahead at a roundabout. How should you signal?

Mark one answer

- ❑ a Signal right on the approach and then left to leave the roundabout
- ❑ b Signal left as you leave the roundabout
- ❑ c Signal left on the approach to the roundabout and keep the signal on until you leave
- ❑ d Signal left just after you pass the exit before the one you will take

10.17

You may only enter a box junction when

Mark one answer

- ❑ a there are less than two vehicles in front of you
- ❑ b the traffic lights show green
- ❑ c your exit road is clear
- ❑ d you need to turn left

10.18

You may wait in a yellow box junction when

Mark one answer

- ❑ a oncoming traffic is preventing you from turning right
- ❑ b you are in a queue of traffic turning left
- ❑ c you are in a queue of traffic to go ahead
- ❑ d you are on a roundabout

10.19

You MUST stop when signalled to do so by which THREE of these?

Mark three answers

- ❑ a A police officer
- ❑ b A pedestrian
- ❑ c A school crossing patrol
- ❑ d A bus driver
- ❑ e A red traffic light

10.20

Someone is waiting to cross at a zebra crossing. They are standing on the pavement. You should normally

Mark one answer

- ❑ a go on quickly before they step onto the crossing
- ❑ b stop before you reach the zigzag lines and let them cross
- ❑ c stop, let them cross, wait patiently
- ❑ d ignore them as they are still on the pavement

10.21

At toucan crossings, apart from pedestrians you should be aware of

Mark one answer

- ❑ a emergency vehicles emerging
- ❑ b buses pulling out
- ❑ c trams crossing in front
- ❑ d cyclists riding across

10.22

Who can use a toucan crossing?

Mark two answers

- ❑ a Trains
- ❑ b Cyclists
- ❑ c Buses
- ❑ d Pedestrians
- ❑ e Trams

10.23

At a pelican crossing, what does a flashing amber light mean?

Mark one answer

- ❑ a You must not move off until the lights stop flashing
- ❑ b You must give way to pedestrians still on the crossing
- ❑ c You can move off, even if pedestrians are still on the crossing
- ❑ d You must stop because the lights are about to change to red

10.24

You are waiting at a pelican crossing. The red light changes to flashing amber. This means you must

Mark one answer

- ❑ a wait for pedestrians on the crossing to clear
- ❑ b move off immediately without any hesitation
- ❑ c wait for the green light before moving off
- ❑ d get ready and go when the continuous amber light shows

Answers

10.14 a You should signal left just as you pass the exit before the one you want to take.

10.15 d

10.16 d This is correct for most roundabouts. Bear in mind that some roundabouts do not have an exit to the left, so the first exit is straight ahead.

10.17 c

10.18 a

10.19 a, c, e Note the word 'MUST' in the question, which is asking what the law says.

10.20 c

10.21 d Cyclists are allowed to ride across toucan crossings, unlike other crossings where they must dismount.

10.22 b, d Toucan crossings are shared by pedestrians and cyclists together.

10.23 b You may drive on as soon as the crossing is clear and before the flashing amber light changes to green.

10.24 a

10.25

When can you park on the left opposite these road markings?

Mark one answer
- ❑ a If the line nearest to you is broken
- ❑ b When there are no yellow lines
- ❑ c To pick up or set down passengers
- ❑ d During daylight hours only

10.26

You are intending to turn right at a crossroads. An oncoming driver is also turning right. It will normally be safer to

Mark one answer
- ❑ a keep the other vehicle to your RIGHT and turn behind it (offside to offside)
- ❑ b keep the other vehicle to your LEFT and turn in front of it (nearside to nearside)
- ❑ c carry on and turn at the next junction instead
- ❑ d hold back and wait for the other driver to turn first

10.27

You are on a road that has no traffic signs. There are street lights. What is the speed limit?

Mark one answer
- ❑ a 20 mph
- ❑ b 30 mph
- ❑ c 40 mph
- ❑ d 60 mph

10.28

You are going along a street with parked vehicles on the left-hand side. For which THREE reasons should you keep your speed down?

Mark three answers
- ❑ a So that oncoming traffic can see you more clearly
- ❑ b You may set off car alarms
- ❑ c Vehicles may be pulling out
- ❑ d Drivers' doors may open
- ❑ e Children may run out from between the vehicles

10.29

You meet an obstruction on your side of the road. You should

Mark one answer
- ❑ a carry on, you have priority
- ❑ b give way to oncoming traffic
- ❑ c wave oncoming vehicles through
- ❑ d accelerate to get past first

10.30

You are on a two-lane dual carriageway. For which TWO of the following would you use the right-hand lane?

Mark two answers
- ❑ a Turning right
- ❑ b Normal progress
- ❑ c Staying at the minimum allowed speed
- ❑ d Constant high speed
- ❑ e Overtaking slower traffic
- ❑ f Mending punctures

10.31

Who has priority at an unmarked crossroads?

Mark one answer
- ❑ a The larger vehicle
- ❑ b No one has priority
- ❑ c The faster vehicle
- ❑ d The smaller vehicle

10.32

What is the nearest you may park to a junction?

Mark one answer
- ❑ a 10 metres (32 feet)
- ❑ b 12 metres (39 feet)
- ❑ c 15 metres (49 feet)
- ❑ d 20 metres (66 feet)

10.33

In which THREE places must you NOT park?

Mark three answers
- ❑ a Near the brow of a hill
- ❑ b At or near a bus stop
- ❑ c Where there is no pavement
- ❑ d Within 10 metres (32 feet) of a junction
- ❑ e On a 40 mph road

10.34

You are waiting at a level crossing. A train has passed but the lights keep flashing. You must

Mark one answer
- ❑ a carry on waiting
- ❑ b phone the signal operator
- ❑ c edge over the stop line and look for trains
- ❑ d park and investigate

10.35

At a crossroads there are no signs or road markings. Two vehicles approach. Which has priority?

Mark one answer
- ❑ a Neither of the vehicles
- ❑ b The vehicle travelling the fastest
- ❑ c Oncoming vehicles turning right
- ❑ d Vehicles approaching from the right

10.36

What does this sign tell you?

Mark one answer
- ❑ a That it is a no-through road
- ❑ b End of traffic calming zone
- ❑ c Free parking zone ends
- ❑ d No waiting zone ends

Answers

10.25 c
10.26 a This is because when passing offside-to-offside your view will not be blocked by the oncoming car that also wishes to turn right.
10.27 b If there are street lights, the speed limit is 30 mph unless a road sign states otherwise.
10.28 c, d, e
10.29 b
10.30 a, e
10.31 b An unmarked crossroads has no road signs or road markings and no vehicle has priority even if one road is wider or busier than the other.
10.32 a
10.33 a, b, d
10.34 a
10.35 a You often find these on housing estates. Approach with caution and be prepared to give way.
10.36 d

10.37

You are entering an area of roadworks.
There is a temporary speed limit displayed.
You should
Mark one answer
- ❑ a not exceed the speed limit
- ❑ b obey the limit only during rush hour
- ❑ c ignore the displayed limit
- ❑ d obey the limit except at night

10.38

In which TWO places should you NOT park?
Mark two answers
- ❑ a Near a school entrance
- ❑ b Near a police station
- ❑ c In a side road
- ❑ d At a bus stop
- ❑ e In a one-way street

10.39

You are travelling on a well-lit road at night in
a built-up area. By using dipped headlights
you will be able to
Mark one answer
- ❑ a see further along the road
- ❑ b go at a much faster speed
- ❑ c switch to main beam quickly
- ❑ d be easily seen by others

10.40

The dual carriageway you are turning right
onto has a very narrow central reservation.
What should you do?
Mark one answer
- ❑ a Proceed to the central reservation and
  wait
- ❑ b Wait until the road is clear in both
  directions
- ❑ c Stop in the first lane so that other
  vehicles give way
- ❑ d Emerge slightly to show your intentions

10.41

What is the national speed limit on a single
carriageway road for cars and motorcycles?
Mark one answer
- ❑ a 30 mph
- ❑ b 50 mph
- ❑ c 60 mph
- ❑ d 70 mph

10.42

You park at night on a road with a 40 mph
speed limit. You should park
Mark one answer
- ❑ a facing the traffic
- ❑ b with parking lights on
- ❑ c with dipped headlights on
- ❑ d near a street light

10.43

You will see these red and white markers
when approaching

Mark one answer
- ❑ a the end of a motorway
- ❑ b a concealed level crossing
- ❑ c a concealed speed limit sign
- ❑ d the end of a dual carriageway

10.44

You are travelling on a motorway. You MUST
stop when signalled to do so by which of
these?
Mark one answer
- ❑ a Flashing amber lights above your lane
- ❑ b A Highways Agency Traffic Officer
- ❑ c Pedestrians on the hard shoulder
- ❑ d A driver who has broken down

10.45

At a busy unmarked crossroads, which of the following has priority?

Mark one answer

- ❑ a Vehicles going straight ahead
- ❑ b Vehicles turning right
- ❑ c None of the vehicles
- ❑ d The vehicles that arrived first

10.46

You may drive over a footpath

Mark one answer

- ❑ a to overtake slow-moving traffic
- ❑ b when the pavement is very wide
- ❑ c if no pedestrians are near
- ❑ d to get into a property

10.47

A single carriageway road has this sign. What is the maximum permitted speed for a car towing a trailer?

Mark one answer

- ❑ a 30 mph
- ❑ b 40 mph
- ❑ c 50 mph
- ❑ d 60 mph

10.48

You are towing a small caravan on a dual carriageway. You must not exceed

Mark one answer

- ❑ a 50 mph
- ❑ b 40 mph
- ❑ c 70 mph
- ❑ d 60 mph

10.49

You want to park and you see this sign. On the days and times shown you should

Meter ZONE
Mon - Fri 8.30 am - 6.30 pm Saturday 8.30 am - 1.30 pm

Mark one answer

- ❑ a park in a bay and not pay
- ❑ b park on yellow lines and pay
- ❑ c park on yellow lines and not pay
- ❑ d park in a bay and pay

Answers

10.37 a
10.38 a, d
10.39 d
10.40 b Because the central reservation is narrow, you would partly block the road if you drove to the middle and had to wait.
10.41 c
10.42 b
10.43 b These countdown markers indicate the distance to the stop line at the concealed level crossing.
10.44 b
10.45 c
10.46 d
10.47 c
10.48 d
10.49 d

10.50

You are driving along a road that has a cycle lane. The lane is marked by a solid white line. This means that during its period of operation
Mark one answer
- ❏ a the lane may be used for parking your car
- ❏ b you may drive in that lane at any time
- ❏ c the lane may be used when necessary
- ❏ d you must not drive in that lane

10.51

A cycle lane is marked by a solid white line. You must not drive or park in it
Mark one answer
- ❏ a at any time
- ❏ b during the rush hour
- ❏ c if a cyclist is using it
- ❏ d during its period of operation

10.52

While driving, you intend to turn left into a minor road. On the approach you should
Mark one answer
- ❏ a keep just left of the middle of the road
- ❏ b keep in the middle of the road
- ❏ c swing out wide just before turning
- ❏ d keep well to the left of the road

10.53

You are waiting at a level crossing. The red warning lights continue to flash after a train has passed by. What should you do?

Mark one answer
- ❏ a Get out and investigate
- ❏ b Telephone the signal operator
- ❏ c Continue to wait
- ❏ d Drive across carefully

10.54

You are driving over a level crossing. The warning lights come on and a bell rings. What should you do?

Mark one answer
- ❏ a Get everyone out of the vehicle immediately
- ❏ b Stop and reverse back to clear the crossing
- ❏ c Keep going and clear the crossing
- ❏ d Stop immediately and use your hazard warning lights

10.55

You are on a busy main road and find that you are travelling in the wrong direction. What should you do?
Mark one answer
- ❏ a Turn into a side road on the right and reverse into the main road
- ❏ b Make a U-turn in the main road
- ❏ c Make a 'three-point' turn in the main road
- ❏ d Turn round in a side road

10.56

You may remove your seat belt when carrying out a manoeuvre that involves
Mark one answer
- ❏ a reversing
- ❏ b a hill start
- ❏ c an emergency stop
- ❏ d driving slowly

10.57

You must not reverse
Mark one answer
- ❏ a for longer than necessary
- ❏ b for more than a car's length
- ❏ c into a side road
- ❏ d in a built-up area

10.58

When you are NOT sure that it is safe to reverse your vehicle you should
Mark one answer
- ❏ a use your horn
- ❏ b rev your engine
- ❏ c get out and check
- ❏ d reverse slowly

10.59

When may you reverse from a side road into a main road?
Mark one answer
- ❏ a Only if both roads are clear of traffic
- ❏ b Not at any time
- ❏ c At any time
- ❏ d Only if the main road is clear of traffic

10.60

You want to turn right at a box junction. There is oncoming traffic. You should
Mark one answer
- ❏ a wait in the box junction if your exit is clear
- ❏ b wait before the junction until it is clear of all traffic
- ❏ c drive on, you cannot turn right at a box junction
- ❏ d drive slowly into the box junction when signalled by oncoming traffic

10.61

You are reversing your vehicle into a side road. When would the greatest hazard to passing traffic occur?
Mark one answer
- ❏ a After you've completed the manoeuvre
- ❏ b Just before you actually begin to manoeuvre
- ❏ c After you've entered the side road
- ❏ d When the front of your vehicle swings out

Answers

10.50 d
10.51 d
10.52 d
10.53 c You should wait for three minutes. If no further train passes you should telephone the signal operator.
10.54 c You are already on the crossing when the warning lights come on, so 'c' is correct.
10.55 d It is illegal to reverse from a minor to a major road, so 'a' is wrong. Answers 'b' and 'c' would be dangerous because the road is busy.
10.56 a
10.57 a
10.58 c
10.59 b
10.60 a
10.61 d Always remember to check all round just before steering and give way to any road users.

10.62

Where is the safest place to park your vehicle at night?

Mark one answer

- ❑ a In a garage
- ❑ b On a busy road
- ❑ c In a quiet car park
- ❑ d Near a red route

10.63

You are driving on an urban clearway. You may stop only to

Mark one answer

- ❑ a set down and pick up passengers
- ❑ b use a mobile telephone
- ❑ c ask for directions
- ❑ d load or unload goods

10.64

You are looking for somewhere to park your vehicle. The area is full EXCEPT for spaces marked 'disabled use'. You can

Mark one answer

- ❑ a use these spaces when elsewhere is full
- ❑ b park if you stay with your vehicle
- ❑ c use these spaces, disabled or not
- ❑ d not park there unless permitted

10.65

Your vehicle is parked on the road at night. When must you use sidelights?

Mark one answer

- ❑ a Where there are continuous white lines in the middle of the road
- ❑ b Where the speed limit exceeds 30 mph
- ❑ c Where you are facing oncoming traffic
- ❑ d Where you are near a bus stop

10.66

You are on a road that is only wide enough for one vehicle. There is a car coming towards you. What should you do?

Mark one answer

- ❑ a Pull into a passing place on your right
- ❑ b Force the other driver to reverse
- ❑ c Pull into a passing place if your vehicle is wider
- ❑ d Pull into a passing place on your left

10.67

What MUST you have to park in a disabled space?

Mark one answer

- ❑ a An orange or blue badge
- ❑ b A wheelchair
- ❑ c An advanced driver certificate
- ❑ d A modified vehicle

10.68

You are driving at night with full beam headlights on. A vehicle is overtaking you. You should dip your lights

Mark one answer

- ❑ a some time after the vehicle has passed you
- ❑ b before the vehicle starts to pass you
- ❑ c only if the other driver dips their headlights
- ❑ d as soon as the vehicle passes you

10.69

When may you drive a motor car in this bus lane?

- ❑ a Outside its hours of operation
- ❑ b To get to the front of a traffic queue
- ❑ c You may not use it at any time
- ❑ d To overtake slow-moving traffic

10.70

Signals are normally given by direction indicators and
- ❑ a brake lights
- ❑ b side lights
- ❑ c fog lights
- ❑ d interior lights

10.71

As a car driver, which THREE lanes are you NOT normally allowed to use?
- ❑ a Crawler lane
- ❑ b Bus lane
- ❑ c Overtaking lane
- ❑ d Acceleration lane
- ❑ e Cycle lane
- ❑ f Tram lane

10.72

You are parked in a busy high street. What is the safest way to turn your vehicle around so you can go the opposite way?
- ❑ a Find a quiet side road to turn round in
- ❑ b Drive into a side road and reverse into the main road
- ❑ c Get someone to stop the traffic
- ❑ d Do a U-turn

10.73

To help keep your vehicle secure at night, where should you park?
- ❑ a Near a police station
- ❑ b In a quiet road
- ❑ c On a red route
- ❑ d In a well-lit area

Answers

10.62 a
10.63 a
10.64 d
10.65 b
10.66 d
10.67 a Since April 1, 2000 the Orange Badge scheme has been known as the Blue Badge scheme.
10.68 d If you dip your lights too early you may reduce your vision; too late and you may dazzle the driver who has overtaken.
10.69 a
10.70 a
10.71 b, e, f
10.72 a
10.73 d

10.74

You are in the right-hand lane of a dual carriageway. You see signs showing that the right-hand lane is closed 800 yards ahead. You should

Mark one answer
- [ ] a keep in that lane until you reach the queue
- [ ] b move to the left immediately
- [ ] c wait and see which lane is moving faster
- [ ] d move to the left in good time

10.75

On which THREE occasions MUST you stop your vehicle?

Mark three answers
- [ ] a When in an accident where damage or injury is caused
- [ ] b At a red traffic light
- [ ] c When signalled to do so by a police officer
- [ ] d At a junction with double broken white lines
- [ ] e At a pelican crossing when the amber light is flashing and no pedestrians are crossing

10.76

You are driving on a road that has a cycle lane. The lane is marked by a broken white line. This means that

Mark two answers
- [ ] a you should not drive in the lane unless it is unavoidable
- [ ] b you should not park in the lane unless it is unavoidable
- [ ] c cyclists can travel in both directions in that lane
- [ ] d the lane must be used by motorcyclists in heavy traffic

10.77

You are riding slowly in a town centre. Before turning left you should glance over your left shoulder to

Mark one answer
- [ ] a check for cyclists
- [ ] b help keep your balance
- [ ] c look for traffic signs
- [ ] d check for potholes

10.78

As a motorcycle rider which TWO lanes must you NOT use?

Mark two answers
- [ ] a Crawler lane
- [ ] b Overtaking lane
- [ ] c Acceleration lane
- [ ] d Cycle lane
- [ ] e Tram lane

10.79

You want to tow a trailer with your motorcycle. Your engine must be more than

Mark one answer
- [ ] a 50 cc
- [ ] b 125 cc
- [ ] c 525 cc
- [ ] d 1000 cc

10.80

You are turning right at a large roundabout. Just before you leave the roundabout you should

Mark one answer

- ❑ a take a 'lifesaver' glance over your left shoulder
- ❑ b take a 'lifesaver' glance over your right shoulder
- ❑ c put on your right indicator
- ❑ d cancel the left indicator

10.81

What does this sign mean?

Mark one answer

- ❑ a No parking for solo motorcycles
- ❑ b Parking for solo motorcycles
- ❑ c Passing place for motorcycles
- ❑ d Police motorcycles only

10.82

You are riding on a busy dual carriageway. When changing lanes you should

Mark one answer

- ❑ a rely totally on mirrors
- ❑ b always increase your speed
- ❑ c signal so others will give way
- ❑ d use mirrors and shoulder checks

10.83

You are looking for somewhere to park your motorcycle. The area is full EXCEPT for spaces marked 'disabled use'. You can

Mark one answer

- ❑ a use these spaces when elsewhere is full
- ❑ b park if you stay with your motorcycle
- ❑ c use these spaces, disabled or not
- ❑ d not park there unless permitted

10.84

On which THREE occasions MUST you stop your motorcycle?

Mark three answers

- ❑ a When involved in an accident
- ❑ b At a red traffic light
- ❑ c When signalled to do so by a police officer
- ❑ d At a junction with double broken white lines
- ❑ e At a pelican crossing when the amber light is flashing and no pedestrians are crossing

Answers

10.74 d
10.75 a, b, c 'd' is wrong – although the double, broken white lines at a junction mean 'give way', you do not necessarily have to stop in order to do so. 'e' is wrong – you may drive on at a pelican crossing when the amber light is flashing if no pedestrians are crossing.
10.76 a, b
10.77 a
10.78 d, e
10.79 b
10.80 a
10.81 b
10.82 d
10.83 d
10.84 a, b ,c

10.85

You are on a road with passing places. It is only wide enough for one vehicle. There is a car coming towards you. What should you do?

Mark one answer

- ❏ a Pull into a passing place on your right
- ❏ b Force the other driver to reverse
- ❏ c Turn round and ride back to the main road
- ❏ d Pull into a passing place on your left

10.86

You are both turning right at this crossroads. It is safer to keep the car to your right so you can

Mark one answer

- ❏ a see approaching traffic
- ❏ b keep close to the kerb
- ❏ c keep clear of following traffic
- ❏ d make oncoming vehicles stop

10.87

When filtering through slow-moving or stationary traffic you should

Mark three answers

- ❏ a watch for hidden vehicles emerging from side roads
- ❏ b continually use your horn as a warning
- ❏ c look for vehicles changing course suddenly
- ❏ d always ride with your hazard lights on
- ❏ e stand up on the footrests for a good view ahead
- ❏ f look for pedestrians walking between vehicles

10.88

You are riding towards roadworks. The temporary traffic lights are at red. The road ahead is clear. What should you do?

Mark one answer

- ❏ a Ride on with extreme caution
- ❏ b Ride on at normal speed
- ❏ c Carry on if approaching cars have stopped
- ❏ d Wait for the green light

10.89

You intend to go abroad and will be riding on the right-hand side of the road. What should you fit to your motorcycle?

Mark one answer

- ❏ a Twin headlights
- ❏ b Headlight deflectors
- ❏ c Tinted yellow brake lights
- ❏ d Tinted red indicator lenses

10.90

What is the national speed limit on a single carriageway?

Mark one answer

- ❏ a 40 mph
- ❏ b 50 mph
- ❏ c 60 mph
- ❏ d 70 mph

Answers

10.85 d
10.86 a
10.87 a, c, f
10.88 d
10.89 b If you do not fit deflectors you will dazzle other road users when travelling abroad.
10.90 c

Theory Test Questions
for Car Drivers and Motorcyclists

Section 11   Road and traffic signs

11.1

You MUST obey signs giving orders. These signs are mostly in

Mark one answer

- ❏ a green rectangles
- ❏ b red triangles
- ❏ c blue rectangles
- ❏ d red circles

11.2

Traffic signs giving orders are generally which shape?

Mark one answer

❏ a ❏ b

❏ c ❏ d

11.3

Which type of sign tells you NOT to do something?

Mark one answer

❏ a ❏ b

❏ c ❏ d

11.4

What does this sign mean?

Mark one answer

- ❏ a Maximum speed limit with traffic calming
- ❏ b Minimum speed limit with traffic calming
- ❏ c 20 cars only parking zone
- ❏ d Only 20 cars allowed at any one time

11.5

Which sign means 'no motor vehicles are allowed'?

Mark one answer

❏ a ❏ b

❏ c ❏ d

11.6
Which of these signs means 'no motor vehicles'?

Mark one answer

☐ a   ☐ b

☐ c   ☐ d

11.7
What does this sign mean?

Mark one answer

☐ a New speed limit 20 mph
☐ b No vehicles over 30 tonnes
☐ c Minimum speed limit 30 mph
☐ d End of 20 mph zone

11.8
What does this sign mean?

Mark one answer

☐ a No overtaking
☐ b No motor vehicles
☐ c Clearway (no stopping)
☐ d Cars and motorcycles only

11.9
What does this sign mean?

Mark one answer

☐ a No parking
☐ b No road markings
☐ c No through road
☐ d No entry

11.10
What does this sign mean?

Mark one answer

☐ a Bend to the right
☐ b Road on the right closed
☐ c No traffic from the right
☐ d No right turn

Answers

11.1 d
11.2 d
11.3 a Red circles tell you what you must not do. Rectangles usually give you information.
11.4 a
11.5 b
11.6 a
11.7 d
11.8 b
11.9 d
11.10 d

11.11

Which sign means 'no entry'?

Mark one answer

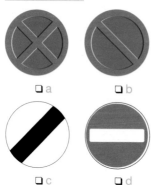

❏ a

❏ b

❏ c

❏ d

11.12

What does this sign mean?

Mark one answer

❏ a Route for trams only
❏ b Route for buses only
❏ c Parking for buses only
❏ d Parking for trams only

11.13

Which type of vehicle does this sign apply to?

Mark one answer

❏ a Wide vehicles
❏ b Long vehicles
❏ c High vehicles
❏ d Heavy vehicles

11.14

Which sign means 'NO motor vehicles allowed'?

Mark one answer

❏ a

❏ b

❏ c

❏ d

11.15

What does this sign mean?

Mark one answer

❏ a You have priority
❏ b No motor vehicles
❏ c Two-way traffic
❏ d No overtaking

11.16

What does this sign mean?

Mark one answer

❏ a Keep in one lane
❏ b Give way to oncoming traffic
❏ c Do not overtake
❏ d Form two lanes

11.17
Which sign means 'no overtaking'?
Mark one answer

❏ a

❏ b

❏ c

❏ d

11.18
What does this sign mean?

Mark one answer
❏ a Waiting restrictions apply
❏ b Waiting permitted
❏ c National speed limit applies
❏ d Clearway (no stopping)

11.19
What does this sign mean?

Mark one answer
❏ a End of restricted speed area
❏ b End of restricted parking area
❏ c End of clearway
❏ d End of cycle route

11.20
Which sign means 'no stopping'?
Mark one answer

❏ a

❏ b

❏ c

❏ d

11.21
What does this sign mean?

Mark one answer
❏ a Roundabout
❏ b Crossroads
❏ c No stopping
❏ d No entry

Answers

11.11 d
11.12 a
11.13 c
11.14 b
11.15 d
11.16 c
11.17 b
11.18 a There will also be a plate indicating when the restrictions apply.
11.19 b
11.20 b
11.21 c

11.22

You see this sign ahead. It means

Mark one answer

- ❑ a national speed limit applies
- ❑ b waiting restrictions apply
- ❑ c no stopping
- ❑ d no entry

11.23

What does this sign mean?

Mark one answer

- ❑ a Distance to parking place ahead
- ❑ b Distance to public telephone ahead
- ❑ c Distance to public house ahead
- ❑ d Distance to passing place ahead

11.24

What does this sign mean?

Mark one answer

- ❑ a Vehicles may not park on the verge or footway
- ❑ b Vehicles may park on the left-hand side of the road only
- ❑ c Vehicles may park fully on the verge or footway
- ❑ d Vehicles may park on the right-hand side of the road only

11.25

What does this traffic sign mean?

Mark one answer

- ❑ a No overtaking allowed
- ❑ b Give priority to oncoming traffic
- ❑ c Two-way traffic
- ❑ d One-way traffic only

11.26

What is the meaning of this traffic sign?

Mark one answer

- ❑ a End of two-way road
- ❑ b Give priority to vehicles coming towards you
- ❑ c You have priority over vehicles coming towards you
- ❑ d Bus lane ahead

11.27

What does this sign mean?

Mark one answer

- ❑ a No overtaking
- ❑ b You are entering a one-way street
- ❑ c Two-way traffic ahead
- ❑ d You have priority over vehicles from the opposite direction

184

11.28
What shape is a STOP sign at a junction?
Mark one answer

❏ a   ❏ b

❏ c   ❏ d

11.31
Which of these signs means turn left ahead?
Mark one answer

❏ a   ❏ b

❏ c   ❏ d

11.29
At a junction you see this sign partly covered by snow. What does it mean?

Mark one answer
❏ a Cross roads
❏ b Give way
❏ c Stop
❏ d Turn right

11.30
What does this sign mean?

Mark one answer
❏ a Service area 30 miles ahead
❏ b Maximum speed 30 mph
❏ c Minimum speed 30 mph
❏ d Lay-by 30 miles ahead

Answers

11.22 c This is a clearway sign and you must not stop at all.
11.23 a
11.24 c
11.25 b
11.26 c
11.27 d
11.28 d
11.29 c The Stop sign is the only octagonal sign, allowing easy identification.
11.30 c
11.31 b

11.32

What does this sign mean?

Mark one answer
- ❑ a Give way to oncoming vehicles
- ❑ b Approaching traffic passes you on both sides
- ❑ c Turn off at the next available junction
- ❑ d Pass either side to get to the same destination

11.33

What does this sign mean?

Mark one answer
- ❑ a Route for trams
- ❑ b Give way to trams
- ❑ c Route for buses
- ❑ d Give way to buses

11.34

What does a circular traffic sign with a blue background do?

Mark one answer
- ❑ a Give warning of a motorway ahead
- ❑ b Give directions to a car park
- ❑ c Give motorway information
- ❑ d Give an instruction

11.35

Which of these signs means that you are entering a one-way street?

Mark one answer

❑ a   ❑ b

❑ c   ❑ d

11.36

Where would you see a contraflow bus and cycle lane?

Mark one answer
- ❑ a On a dual carriageway
- ❑ b On a roundabout
- ❑ c On an urban motorway
- ❑ d On a one-way street

11.37

What does this sign mean?

Mark one answer
- ❑ a Bus station on the right
- ❑ b Contraflow bus lane
- ❑ c With-flow bus lane
- ❑ d Give way to buses

11.38
What does this sign mean?

Mark one answer
- ❏ a With-flow bus and cycle lane
- ❏ b Contraflow bus and cycle lane
- ❏ c No buses and cycles allowed
- ❏ d No waiting for buses and cycles

11.39
What does a sign with a brown background show?

Mark one answer
- ❏ a Tourist directions
- ❏ b Primary roads
- ❏ c Motorway routes
- ❏ d Minor routes

11.40
This sign means

Mark one answer
- ❏ a tourist attraction
- ❏ b beware of trains
- ❏ c level crossing
- ❏ d beware of trams

11.41
What are triangular signs for?

Mark one answer
- ❏ a To give warnings
- ❏ b To give information
- ❏ c To give orders
- ❏ d To give directions

11.42
What does this sign mean?

Mark one answer
- ❏ a Turn left ahead
- ❏ b T-junction
- ❏ c No through road
- ❏ d Give way

Answers

11.32 d
11.33 a
11.34 d Circular signs with blue backgrounds tell you what you must do.
11.35 b
11.36 d
11.37 b
11.38 a
11.39 a
11.40 a
11.41 a
11.42 b

11.43
What does this sign mean?

Mark one answer
- ❑ a Multi-exit roundabout
- ❑ b Risk of ice
- ❑ c Six roads converge
- ❑ d Place of historical interest

11.44
What does this sign mean?

Mark one answer
- ❑ a Crossroads
- ❑ b Level crossing with gate
- ❑ c Level crossing without gate
- ❑ d Ahead only

11.45
What does this sign mean?

Mark one answer
- ❑ a Ring road
- ❑ b Mini-roundabout
- ❑ c No vehicles
- ❑ d Roundabout

11.46
Which FOUR of these would be indicated by a triangular road sign?

Mark four answers
- ❑ a Road narrows
- ❑ b Ahead only
- ❑ c Low bridge
- ❑ d Minimum speed
- ❑ e Children crossing
- ❑ f T-junction

11.47
What does this sign mean?

Mark one answer
- ❑ a Cyclists must dismount
- ❑ b Cycles are not allowed
- ❑ c Cycle route ahead
- ❑ d Cycle in single file

11.48

Which sign means that pedestrians may be walking along the road?

Mark one answer

❑ a   ❑ b

❑ c   ❑ d

11.49

Which of these signs warn you of a pedestrian crossing?

Mark one answer

❑ a   ❑ b

❑ c   ❑ d

11.50

What does this sign mean?

Mark one answer

❑ a No footpath ahead
❑ b Pedestrians only ahead
❑ c Pedestrian crossing ahead
❑ d School crossing ahead

11.51

What does this sign mean?

Mark one answer

❑ a School crossing patrol
❑ b No pedestrians allowed
❑ c Pedestrian zone - no vehicles
❑ d Pedestrian crossing ahead

11.52

Which of these signs means there is a double bend ahead?

Mark one answer

❑ a   ❑ b

❑ c   ❑ d

Answers

11.43 b
11.44 a
11.45 d
11.46 a, c, e, f Red triangles usually give a warning.
11.47 c
11.48 a
11.49 a
11.50 c
11.51 d
11.52 b

11.53

What does this sign mean?

Mark one answer

- ☐ a Wait at the barriers
- ☐ b Wait at the crossroads
- ☐ c Give way to trams
- ☐ d Give way to farm vehicles

11.54

What does this sign mean?

Mark one answer

- ☐ a Humpback bridge
- ☐ b Humps in the road
- ☐ c Entrance to tunnel
- ☐ d Soft verges

11.55

What does this sign mean?

Mark one answer

- ☐ a Low bridge ahead
- ☐ b Tunnel ahead
- ☐ c Ancient monument ahead
- ☐ d Accident black spot ahead

11.56

Which sign means 'two-way traffic crosses a one-way road'?

Mark one answer

☐ a   ☐ b

☐ c   ☐ d

11.57

Which of these signs means the end of a dual carriageway?

Mark one answer

☐ a   ☐ b

☐ c   ☐ d

11.58
What does this sign mean?

Mark one answer
- ❏ a End of dual carriageway
- ❏ b Tall bridge
- ❏ c Road narrows
- ❏ d End of narrow bridge

11.59
What does this sign mean?

Mark one answer
- ❏ a Crosswinds
- ❏ b Road noise
- ❏ c Airport
- ❏ d Adverse camber

11.60
What does this traffic sign mean?

Mark one answer
- ❏ a Slippery road ahead
- ❏ b Tyres liable to punctures ahead
- ❏ c Danger ahead
- ❏ d Service area ahead

11.61
You are about to overtake when you see this sign. You should

Mark one answer
- ❏ a overtake the other driver as quickly as possible
- ❏ b move to the right to get a better view
- ❏ c switch your headlights on before overtaking
- ❏ d hold back until you can see clearly ahead

Answers

11.53 c
11.54 b
11.55 b
11.56 b
11.57 d
11.58 a
11.59 a
11.60 c
11.61 d It is dangerous to overtake when you see this sign because the dip in the road could be hiding oncoming traffic.

11.62
What does this sign mean?

Mark one answer
- ❑ a Level crossing with gate or barrier
- ❑ b Gated road ahead
- ❑ c Level crossing without gate or barrier
- ❑ d Cattle grid ahead

11.63
What does this sign mean?

Mark one answer
- ❑ a No trams ahead
- ❑ b Oncoming trams
- ❑ c Trams crossing ahead
- ❑ d Trams only

11.64
What does this sign mean?

Mark one answer
- ❑ a Adverse camber
- ❑ b Steep hill downwards
- ❑ c Uneven road
- ❑ d Steep hill upwards

11.65
What does this sign mean?

Mark one answer
- ❑ a Uneven road surface
- ❑ b Bridge over the road
- ❑ c Road ahead ends
- ❑ d Water across the road

11.66
What does this sign mean?

Mark one answer
- ❑ a Turn left for parking area
- ❑ b No through road on the left
- ❑ c No entry for traffic turning left
- ❑ d Turn left for ferry terminal

11.67
What does this sign mean?

Mark one answer
- ❑ a T-junction
- ❑ b No through road
- ❑ c Telephone box ahead
- ❑ d Toilet ahead

11.68

Which sign means 'no through road'?

Mark one answer

❑ a ❑ b

❑ c ❑ d

11.69

Which is the sign for a ring road?

Mark one answer

❑ a ❑ b

❑ c ❑ d

11.70

What does this sign mean?

Mark one answer

❑ a The right-hand lane ahead is narrow
❑ b Right-hand lane for buses only
❑ c Right-hand lane for turning right
❑ d The right-hand lane is closed

11.71

What does this sign mean?

Mark one answer

❑ a Change to the left lane
❑ b Leave at the next exit
❑ c Contraflow system
❑ d One-way street

Answers	
11.62	a
11.63	c
11.64	b
11.65	d
11.66	b
11.67	b
11.68	c
11.69	d
11.70	d
11.71	c

11.72
What does this sign mean?

Mark one answer
- ❏ a Leave motorway at next exit
- ❏ b Lane for heavy and slow vehicles
- ❏ c All lorries use the hard shoulder
- ❏ d Rest area for lorries

11.73
You are approaching a red traffic light. The signal will change from red to

Mark one answer
- ❏ a red and amber, then green
- ❏ b green, then amber
- ❏ c amber, then green
- ❏ d green and amber, then green

11.74
A red traffic light means

Mark one answer
- ❏ a you should stop unless turning left
- ❏ b stop, if you are able to brake safely
- ❏ c you must stop and wait behind the stop line
- ❏ d proceed with caution

11.75
At traffic lights, amber on its own means

Mark one answer
- ❏ a prepare to go
- ❏ b go if the way is clear
- ❏ c go if no pedestrians are crossing
- ❏ d stop at the stop line

11.76
You are at a junction controlled by traffic lights. When should you NOT proceed at green?

Mark one answer
- ❏ a When pedestrians are waiting to cross
- ❏ b When your exit from the junction is blocked
- ❏ c When you think the lights may be about to change
- ❏ d When you intend to turn right

11.77

You are in the left-hand lane at traffic lights. You are waiting to turn left. At which of these traffic lights must you NOT move on?

Mark one answer

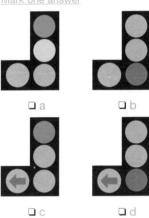

☐ a   ☐ b

☐ c   ☐ d

11.78

What does this sign mean?

Mark one answer
☐ a Traffic lights out of order
☐ b Amber signal out of order
☐ c Temporary traffic lights ahead
☐ d New traffic lights ahead

11.79

When traffic lights are out of order, who has priority?
Mark one answer
☐ a Traffic going straight on
☐ b Traffic turning right
☐ c Nobody
☐ d Traffic turning left

11.80

These flashing red lights mean STOP. In which THREE of the following places could you find them?

Mark three answers
☐ a Pelican crossings
☐ b Lifting bridges
☐ c Zebra crossings
☐ d Level crossings
☐ e Motorway exits
☐ f Fire stations

Answers

11.72 b
11.73 a The sequence of traffic lights is red, then red and amber, then green, then amber alone, then red.
11.74 c You must always stop at a red traffic light.
11.75 d An amber light means stop, and the lights will next change to red.
11.76 b
11.77 a
11.78 a
11.79 c
11.80 b, d, f

11.81

What do these zigzag lines at pedestrian crossings mean?

Mark one answer
- ❏ a No parking at any time
- ❏ b Parking allowed only for a short time
- ❏ c Slow down to 20 mph
- ❏ d Sounding horns is not allowed

11.82

When may you cross a double solid white line in the middle of the road?

Mark one answer
- ❏ a To pass traffic that is queuing back at a junction
- ❏ b To pass a car signalling to turn left ahead
- ❏ c To pass a road maintenance vehicle travelling at 10 mph or less
- ❏ d To pass a vehicle that is towing a trailer

11.83

What does this road marking mean?

Mark one answer
- ❏ a Do not cross the line
- ❏ b No stopping allowed
- ❏ c You are approaching a hazard
- ❏ d No overtaking allowed

11.84

Where would you see this road marking?

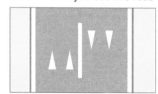

Mark one answer
- ❏ a At traffic lights
- ❏ b On road humps
- ❏ c Near a level crossing
- ❏ d At a box junction

11.85

Which is a hazard warning line?
Mark one answer

❏ a   ❏ b
❏ c   ❏ d

11.86

At this junction there is a stop sign with a solid white line on the road surface. Why is there a stop sign here?

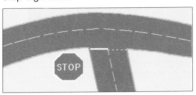

Mark one answer

- ❑ a Speed on the major road is de-restricted
- ❑ b It is a busy junction
- ❑ c Visibility along the major road is restricted
- ❑ d There are hazard warning lines in the centre of the road

11.87

You see this line across the road at the entrance to a roundabout. What does it mean?

Mark one answer

- ❑ a Give way to traffic from the right
- ❑ b Traffic from the left has right of way
- ❑ c You have right of way
- ❑ d Stop at the line

11.88

How will a police officer in a patrol vehicle normally get you to stop?

Mark one answer

- ❑ a Flash the headlights, indicate left and point to the left
- ❑ b Wait until you stop, then approach you
- ❑ c Use the siren, overtake, cut in front and stop
- ❑ d Pull alongside you, use the siren and wave you to stop

11.89

You approach a junction. The traffic lights are not working. A police officer gives this signal. You should

Mark one answer

- ❑ a turn left only
- ❑ b turn right only
- ❑ c stop level with the officer's arm
- ❑ d stop at the stop line

Answers

11.81 a
11.82 c
11.83 c
11.84 b
11.85 a Long lines with short gaps between them in the middle of the road are hazard warning lines. The more paint the more danger.
11.86 c Because the major road is on a bend, your vision is restricted to both left and right.
11.87 a
11.88 a
11.89 d

197

11.90

The driver of the car in front is giving this arm signal. What does it mean?

Mark one answer
- ❏ a The driver is slowing down
- ❏ b The driver intends to turn right
- ❏ c The driver wishes to overtake
- ❏ d The driver intends to turn left

11.91

Where would you see these road markings?

Mark one answer
- ❏ a At a level crossing
- ❏ b On a motorway slip road
- ❏ c At a pedestrian crossing
- ❏ d On a single-track road

11.92

When may you NOT overtake on the left?
Mark one answer
- ❏ a On a free-flowing motorway or dual carriageway
- ❏ b When the traffic is moving slowly in queues
- ❏ c On a one-way street
- ❏ d When the car in front is signalling to turn right

11.93

What does this motorway sign mean?

Mark one answer
- ❏ a Change to the lane on your left
- ❏ b Leave the motorway at the next exit
- ❏ c Change to the opposite carriageway
- ❏ d Pull up on the hard shoulder

11.94

What does this motorway sign mean?

Mark one answer
- ❏ a Temporary minimum speed 50 mph
- ❏ b No services for 50 miles
- ❏ c Obstruction 50 metres (164 feet) ahead
- ❏ d Temporary maximum speed 50 mph

11.95

What does this sign mean?

Mark one answer
- ❏ a Through traffic to use left lane
- ❏ b Right-hand lane T-junction only
- ❏ c Right-hand lane closed ahead
- ❏ d 11 tonne weight limit

11.96
On a motorway this sign means

Mark one answer
- a move over onto the hard shoulder
- b overtaking on the left only
- c leave the motorway at the next exit
- d move to the lane on your left

11.97
What does '25' mean on this motorway sign?

Mark one answer
- a The distance to the nearest town
- b The route number of the road
- c The number of the next junction
- d The speed limit on the slip road

11.98
The right-hand lane of a three-lane motorway is
Mark one answer
- a for lorries only
- b an overtaking lane
- c the right-turn lane
- d an acceleration lane

11.99
Where can you find reflective amber studs on a motorway?
Mark one answer
- a Separating the slip road from the motorway
- b On the left-hand edge of the road
- c On the right-hand edge of the road
- d Separating the lanes

11.100
Where on a motorway would you find green reflective studs?
Mark one answer
- a Separating driving lanes
- b Between the hard shoulder and the carriageway
- c At slip road entrances and exits
- d Between the carriageway and the central reservation

Answers

11.90 d
11.91 b
11.92 a You must not overtake on the left on a motorway or dual carriageway unless you are moving in queues of slow-moving traffic.
11.93 a Obviously you must make sure it is safe before doing so.
11.94 d
11.95 c Always look well ahead and you will have plenty of time to react.
11.96 d Obviously you must make sure it is safe before doing so.
11.97 c
11.98 b
11.99 c
11.100 c

11.101

You are travelling along a motorway. You see this sign. You should

Mark one answer
- ❏ a leave the motorway at the next exit
- ❏ b turn left immediately
- ❏ c change lane
- ❏ d move onto the hard shoulder

11.102

What does this sign mean?

Mark one answer
- ❏ a No motor vehicles
- ❏ b End of motorway
- ❏ c No through road
- ❏ d End of bus lane

11.103

What is the maximum speed on a single carriageway road?

Mark one answer
- ❏ a 50 mph
- ❏ b 60 mph
- ❏ c 40 mph
- ❏ d 70 mph

11.104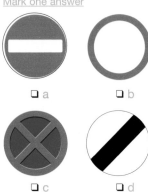

Which of these signs means that the national speed limit applies?

Mark one answer

❏ a   ❏ b

❏ c   ❏ d

11.105

What does this sign mean?

Mark one answer
- ❏ a End of motorway
- ❏ b End of restriction
- ❏ c Lane ends ahead
- ❏ d Free recovery ends

11.106

This sign is advising you to

Mark one answer
- ❏ a follow the route diversion
- ❏ b follow the signs to the picnic area
- ❏ c give way to pedestrians
- ❏ d give way to cyclists

11.107

Why would this temporary speed limit sign be shown?

Mark one answer
- ❑ a To warn of the end of the motorway
- ❑ b To warn you of a low bridge
- ❑ c To warn you of a junction ahead
- ❑ d To warn of road works ahead

11.108

This traffic sign means there is

Mark one answer
- ❑ a a compulsory maximum speed limit
- ❑ b an advisory maximum speed limit
- ❑ c a compulsory minimum speed limit
- ❑ d an advised separation distance

11.109

You are signalling to turn right in busy traffic. How would you confirm your intention safely?

Mark one answer
- ❑ a Sound the horn
- ❑ b Give an arm signal
- ❑ c Flash your headlights
- ❑ d Position over the centre line

11.110

You see this sign at a crossroads. You should

Mark one answer
- ❑ a maintain the same speed
- ❑ b carry on with great care
- ❑ c find another route
- ❑ d telephone the police

11.111

What does this sign mean?

Mark one answer
- ❑ a Motorcycles only
- ❑ b No cars
- ❑ c Cars only
- ❑ d No motorcycles

Answers

11.101	a
11.102	b
11.103	b
11.104	d
11.105	b
11.106	a
11.107	d
11.108	a
11.109	b
11.110	b
11.111	d

11.112

You are on a motorway. You see this sign on a lorry that has stopped in the right-hand lane. You should

Mark one answer
- ❏ a move into the right-hand lane
- ❏ b stop behind the flashing lights
- ❏ c pass the lorry on the left
- ❏ d leave the motorway at the next exit

11.113

You are on a motorway. Red flashing lights appear above your lane only. What should you do?

Mark one answer
- ❏ a Continue in that lane and look for further information
- ❏ b Move into another lane in good time
- ❏ c Pull onto the hard shoulder
- ❏ d Stop and wait for an instruction to proceed

11.114

A red traffic light means

Mark one answer
- ❏ a you must stop behind the white stop line
- ❏ b you may go straight on if there is no other traffic
- ❏ c you may turn left if it is safe to do so
- ❏ d you must slow down and prepare to stop if traffic has started to cross

11.115

The driver of this car is giving an arm signal. What are they about to do?

Mark one answer
- ❏ a Turn to the right
- ❏ b Turn to the left
- ❏ c Go straight ahead
- ❏ d Let pedestrians cross

11.116

Which arm signal tells you that the car you are following is going to turn left?

Mark one answer

❏ a   ❏ b

❏ c   ❏ d

11.117

When may you sound the horn?

Mark one answer
- ❏ a To give you right of way
- ❏ b To attract a friend's attention
- ❏ c To warn others of your presence
- ❏ d To make slower drivers move over

11.118

You must not use your horn when you are stationary

Mark one answer

- ❑ a unless a moving vehicle may cause you danger
- ❑ b at any time whatsoever
- ❑ c unless it is used only briefly
- ❑ d except for signalling that you have just arrived

11.119

What does this sign mean?

URBAN CLEARWAY
Monday to Friday
am 8.00 - 9.30
pm 4.30 - 6.30

Mark one answer

- ❑ a You can park on the days and times shown
- ❑ b No parking on the days and times shown
- ❑ c No parking at all from Monday to Friday
- ❑ d End of the urban clearway restrictions

11.120

What does this sign mean?

Mark one answer

- ❑ a Quayside or river bank
- ❑ b Steep hill downwards
- ❑ c Uneven road surface
- ❑ d Road liable to flooding

11.121

Which sign means you have priority over oncoming vehicles?

Mark one answer

❑ a

❑ b

❑ c

❑ d

Answers

11.112 c
11.113 b
11.114 a
11.115 b
11.116 a
11.117 c Sounding your horn has the same meaning as flashing your headlights – to warn of your presence.
11.118 a
11.119 b
11.120 a
11.121 c

11.122

A white line like this along the centre of the road is a

Mark one answer

- ❏ a bus lane marking
- ❏ b hazard warning
- ❏ c give way marking
- ❏ d lane marking

11.123

What is the reason for the yellow criss-cross lines painted on the road here?

Mark one answer

- ❏ a To mark out an area for trams only
- ❏ b To prevent queuing traffic from blocking the junction on the left
- ❏ c To mark the entrance lane to a car park
- ❏ d To warn you of the tram lines crossing the road

11.124

What is the reason for the area marked in red and white along the centre of this road?

Mark one answer

- ❏ a It is to separate traffic flowing in opposite directions
- ❏ b It marks an area to be used by overtaking motorcyclists
- ❏ c It is a temporary marking to warn of the roadworks
- ❏ d It is separating the two sides of the dual carriageway

11.125

Other drivers may sometimes flash their headlights at you. In which situation are they allowed to do this?

Mark one answer

- ❏ a To warn of a radar speed trap ahead
- ❏ b To show that they are giving way to you
- ❏ c To warn you of their presence
- ❏ d To let you know there is a fault with your vehicle

11.126

At roadworks which of the following can control traffic flow?

Mark three answers

- ❏ a A STOP-GO board
- ❏ b Flashing amber lights
- ❏ c A police officer
- ❏ d Flashing red lights
- ❏ e Temporary traffic lights

11.127

In some narrow residential streets you may find a speed limit of

Mark one answer

- ❑ a 20 mph
- ❑ b 25 mph
- ❑ c 35 mph
- ❑ d 40 mph

11.128

At a junction you see this signal. It means

Mark one answer

- ❑ a cars must stop
- ❑ b trams must stop
- ❑ c both trams and cars must stop
- ❑ d both trams and cars can continue

11.129

Where would you find these road markings?

Mark one answer

- ❑ a At a railway crossing
- ❑ b At a junction
- ❑ c On a motorway
- ❑ d On a pedestrian crossing

11.130

There is a police car following you. The police officer flashes the headlights and points to the left. What should you do?

Mark one answer

- ❑ a Turn left at the next junction
- ❑ b Pull up on the left
- ❑ c Stop immediately
- ❑ d Move over to the left

Answers

11.122 b
11.123 b
11.124 a
11.125 c Answer 'c' is correct because that is what flashing your headlights is supposed to mean. Not everyone knows or obeys the rules and they may flash their headlights for other reasons, so always try to make sure what they mean before you decide on any action.
11.126 a, c, e
11.127 a
11.128 b
11.129 b
11.130 b You must stop, but 'c' is wrong because it may not be safe to stop immediately.

11.131

You see this amber traffic light ahead.
Which light or lights, will come on next?

Mark one answer
- ❑ a Red alone
- ❑ b Red and amber together
- ❑ c Green and amber together
- ❑ d Green alone

11.132

This broken white line painted in the centre
of the road means

Mark one answer
- ❑ a oncoming vehicles have priority over you
- ❑ b you should give priority to oncoming
  vehicles
- ❑ c there is a hazard ahead of you
- ❑ d the area is a national speed limit zone

11.133

You see this signal overhead on the motorway.
What does it mean?

Mark one answer
- ❑ a Leave the motorway at the next exit
- ❑ b All vehicles use the hard shoulder
- ❑ c Sharp bend to the left ahead
- ❑ d Stop, all lanes ahead closed

11.134

What is the purpose of these yellow
criss-cross lines on the road?

Mark one answer
- ❑ a To make you more aware of the traffic
  lights
- ❑ b To guide you into position as you turn
- ❑ c To prevent the junction becoming blocked
- ❑ d To show you where to stop when the
  lights change

11.135

What MUST you do when you see this sign?

Mark one answer
- ❑ a Stop, only if traffic is approaching
- ❑ b Stop, even if the road is clear
- ❑ c Stop, only if children are waiting to cross
- ❑ d Stop, only if a red light is showing

11.136
Which shape is used for a 'give way' sign?

Mark one answer

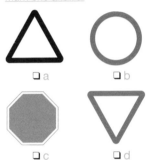

❏ a ❏ b

❏ c ❏ d

11.137
What does this sign mean?

Mark one answer
- ❏ a Buses turning
- ❏ b Ring road
- ❏ c Mini-roundabout
- ❏ d Keep right

11.138
What does this sign mean?

Mark one answer
- ❏ a Two-way traffic straight ahead
- ❏ b Two-way traffic crosses a one-way road
- ❏ c Two-way traffic over a bridge
- ❏ d Two-way traffic crosses a two-way road

11.139
What does this sign mean?

Mark one answer
- ❏ a Two-way traffic ahead across a one-way road
- ❏ b Traffic approaching you has priority
- ❏ c Two-way traffic straight ahead
- ❏ d Motorway contraflow system ahead

11.140
What does this sign mean?

Mark one answer
- ❏ a Hump-back bridge
- ❏ b Traffic calming hump
- ❏ c Low bridge
- ❏ d Uneven road

Answers

11.131 a
11.132 c
11.133 a
11.134 c
11.135 b You must always stop at a stop sign.
11.136 d The give way sign is the only triangular sign mounted this way up.
11.137 c
11.138 b
11.139 c
11.140 a

11.141

Which of the following signs informs you that you are coming to a 'no through road'?

Mark one answer

❏ a   ❏ b

❏ c   ❏ d

11.142

What does this sign mean?

Mark one answer
❏ a Direction to park-and-ride car park
❏ b No parking for buses or coaches
❏ c Directions to bus and coach park
❏ d Parking area for cars and coaches

11.143

You are approaching traffic lights.
Red and amber are showing. This means

Mark one answer
❏ a pass the lights if the road is clear
❏ b there is a fault with the lights - take care
❏ c wait for the green light before you cross the stop line
❏ d the lights are about to change to red

11.144

This marking appears on the road just before a

Mark one answer
❏ a 'no entry' sign
❏ b 'give way' sign
❏ c 'stop' sign
❏ d 'no through road' sign

11.145

At a railway level crossing the red light signal continues to flash after a train has gone by. What should you do?

Mark one answer
❏ a Phone the signal operator
❏ b Alert drivers behind you
❏ c Wait
❏ d Proceed with caution

11.146

You are in a tunnel and you see this sign. What does it mean?

Mark one answer
❏ a Direction to emergency pedestrian exit
❏ b Beware of pedestrians, no footpath ahead
❏ c No access for pedestrians
❏ d Beware of pedestrians crossing ahead

11.147

You are approaching a zebra crossing where pedestrians are waiting. Which arm signal might you give?

Mark one answer

❏ a   ❏ b

❏ c   ❏ d

11.148

The white line along the side of the road

Mark one answer

❏ a shows the edge of the carriageway
❏ b shows the approach to a hazard
❏ c means no parking
❏ d means no overtaking

11.149

You see this white arrow on the road ahead. It means

Mark one answer
❏ a entrance on the left
❏ b all vehicles turn left
❏ c keep left of the hatched markings
❏ d road bending to the left

Answers

11.141   c
11.142   a
11.143   c The next light will be green and you must wait for it to appear before driving on.
11.144   b
11.145   c
11.146   a
11.147   a
11.148   a
11.149   c

11.150

How should you give an arm signal to turn left?

Mark one answer

❑ a

❑ b

❑ c

❑ d

11.151

You are waiting at a T-junction. A vehicle is coming from the right with the left signal flashing. What should you do?

Mark one answer

❑ a Move out and accelerate hard
❑ b Wait until the vehicle starts to turn in
❑ c Pull out before the vehicle reaches the junction
❑ d Move out slowly

11.152

When may you use hazard warning lights when driving?

Mark one answer

❑ a Instead of sounding the horn in a built-up area between 11.30 pm and 7 am
❑ b On a motorway or unrestricted dual carriageway, to warn of a hazard ahead
❑ c On rural routes, after a warning sign of animals
❑ d On the approach to toucan crossings where cyclists are waiting to cross

11.153

You are driving on a motorway. There is a slow-moving vehicle ahead. On the back you see this sign. You should

Mark one answer

❑ a pass on the right
❑ b pass on the left
❑ c leave at the next exit
❑ d drive no further

11.154

You should NOT normally stop on these markings near schools

ᴧ-SCHOOL KEEP CLEAR-ᴧ

Mark one answer

❑ a except when picking up children
❑ b under any circumstances
❑ c unless there is nowhere else available
❑ d except to set down children

11.155

Why should you make sure that your indicators are cancelled after turning?
Mark one answer
- ❑ a To avoid flattening the battery
- ❑ b To avoid misleading other road users
- ❑ c To avoid dazzling other road users
- ❑ d To avoid damage to the indicator relay

11.156

You are driving in busy traffic. You want to pull up on the left just after a junction on the left. When should you signal?
Mark one answer
- ❑ a As you are passing or just after the junction
- ❑ b Just before you reach the junction
- ❑ c Well before you reach the junction
- ❑ d It would be better not to signal at all

11.157

How should you give an arm signal to turn left?
Mark one answer

- ❑ a
- ❑ b
- ❑ c
- ❑ d

11.158

You are giving an arm signal ready to turn left. Why should you NOT continue with the arm signal while you turn?

Mark one answer
- ❑ a Because you might hit a pedestrian on the corner
- ❑ b Because you will have less steering control
- ❑ c Because you will need to keep the clutch applied
- ❑ d Because other motorists will think that you are stopping on the corner

Answers

11.150 c
11.151 b The approaching vehicle might have left the signal on by mistake, or intends to stop after the junction. Always wait long enough to be sure the vehicle is really turning left.
11.152 b Note that the question states 'when driving'. The types of roads in 'b' are the only places where it is legal to use hazard warning lights while your car is moving.
11.153 b
11.154 b
11.155 b
11.156 a
11.157 c
11.158 b

11.159

This sign is of particular importance to motorcyclists. It means

Mark one answer
- ☐ a side winds
- ☐ b airport
- ☐ c slippery road
- ☐ d service area

11.160

Which one of these signs are you allowed to ride past on a solo motorcycle?

Mark one answer

☐ a ☐ b

☐ c ☐ d

11.161

Which of these signals should you give when slowing or stopping your motorcycle?

Mark one answer

☐ a ☐ b

☐ c ☐ d

11.162

When drivers flash their headlights at you it means

Mark one answer
- ☐ a that there is a radar speed trap ahead
- ☐ b that they are giving way to you
- ☐ c that they are warning you of their presence
- ☐ d that there is something wrong with your motorcycle

11.163

Why should you make sure that you cancel your indicators after turning?

Mark one answer
- ☐ a To avoid flattening the battery
- ☐ b To avoid misleading other road users
- ☐ c To avoid dazzling other road users
- ☐ d To avoid damage to the indicator relay

11.164

Your indicators are difficult to see due to bright sunshine. When using them you should

Mark one answer

- ❏ a also give an arm signal
- ❏ b sound your horn
- ❏ c flash your headlight
- ❏ d keep both hands on the handlebars

11.165

You are riding on a motorway. There is a slow-moving vehicle ahead. On the back you see this sign. What should you do?

Mark one answer

- ❏ a Pass on the right
- ❏ b Pass on the left
- ❏ c Leave at the next exit
- ❏ d Drive no further

Answers

11.159	a
11.160	d
11.161	a
11.162	c
11.163	b
11.164	a
11.165	b

Theory Test Questions
for Car Drivers and Motorcyclists

Section 12 Documents

12.1

An MOT certificate is normally valid for

Mark one answer

❑ a three years after the date it was issued
❑ b 10,000 miles
❑ c one year after the date it was issued
❑ d 30,000 miles

12.2

A cover note is a document issued before you receive your

Mark one answer

❑ a driving licence
❑ b insurance certificate
❑ c registration document
❑ d MOT certificate

12.3

You have just passed your practical test. You do not hold a full licence in another category. Within two years you get six penalty points on your licence. What will you have to do?

Mark two answers

❑ a Retake only your theory test
❑ b Retake your theory and practical tests
❑ c Retake only your practical test
❑ d Reapply for your full licence immediately
❑ e Reapply for your provisional licence

12.4

A police officer asks to see your documents. You do not have them with you. You may produce them at a police station within

Mark one answer

❑ a 5 days
❑ b 7 days
❑ c 14 days
❑ d 21 days

12.5

How long will a Statutory Off Road Notification (SORN) last for?

Mark one answer

❑ a 12 months
❑ b 24 months
❑ c 3 years
❑ d 10 years

12.6

What is a Statutory Off Road Notification (SORN) declaration?

Mark one answer

❑ a A notification to tell VOSA that a vehicle does not have a current MOT
❑ b Information kept by the police about the owner of the vehicle
❑ c A notification to tell DVLA that a vehicle is not being used on the road
❑ d Information held by insurance companies to check the vehicle is insured

12.7

A Statutory Off Road Notification (SORN) declaration is

Mark one answer

❑ a to tell DVLA that your vehicle is being used on the road but the MOT has expired
❑ b to tell DVLA that you no longer own the vehicle
❑ c to tell DVLA that your vehicle is not being used on the road
❑ d to tell DVLA that you are buying a personal number plate

12.8

A Statutory Off Road Notification (SORN) is valid

Mark one answer

❏ a for as long as the vehicle has an MOT
❏ b for 12 months only
❏ c only if the vehicle is more than 3 years old
❏ d provided the vehicle is insured

12.9

A Statutory Off Road Notification (SORN) will last

Mark one answer

❏ a for the life of the vehicle
❏ b for as long as you own the vehicle
❏ c for 12 months only
❏ d until the vehicle warranty expires

12.10

What is the maximum specified fine for driving without insurance?

Mark one answer

❏ a £50
❏ b £500
❏ c £1,000
❏ d £5,000

12.11

When should you update your Vehicle Registration Certificate (V5C)?

Mark one answer

❏ a When you pass your driving test
❏ b When you move house
❏ c When your vehicle needs an MOT
❏ d When you have an accident

12.12

Who is legally responsible for ensuring that a Vehicle Registration Certificate (V5C) is updated?

Mark one answer

❏ a The registered vehicle keeper
❏ b The vehicle manufacturer
❏ c Your insurance company
❏ d The licensing authority

Answers

12.1 c
12.2 b
12.3 b, e
12.4 b You may select the police station of your choice.
12.5 a A SORN is the document used by the vehicle owner to tell DVLA that a vehicle is not being used on the road. It lasts 12 months.
12.6 c
12.7 c
12.8 b
12.9 c
12.10 d All cars or motorcycles must be insured for the driver/rider's use on the road. The minimum cover required by law is third party only.
12.11 b
12.12 a Your Vehicle Registration Certificate registers your vehicle to you and your home address. You, as the registered vehicle keeper are responsible for keeping the Certificate up to date.

12.13

To drive on the road learners MUST

Mark one answer

- ❑ a have NO penalty points on their licence
- ❑ b have taken professional instruction
- ❑ c have a signed, valid provisional licence
- ❑ d apply for a driving test within 12 months

12.17

A newly qualified driver must

Mark one answer

- ❑ a display green L plates
- ❑ b not exceed 40 mph for 12 months
- ❑ c be accompanied on a motorway
- ❑ d have valid motor insurance

12.14

Before driving anyone else's motor vehicle you should make sure that

Mark one answer

- ❑ a the vehicle owner has third party insurance cover
- ❑ b your own vehicle has insurance cover
- ❑ c the vehicle is insured for your use
- ❑ d the owner has left the insurance documents in the vehicle

12.18

You have third party insurance. What does this cover?

Mark three answers

- ❑ a Damage to your own vehicle
- ❑ b Damage to your vehicle by fire
- ❑ c Injury to another person
- ❑ d Damage to someone's property
- ❑ e Damage to other vehicles
- ❑ f Injury to yourself

12.15

Your car needs an MOT certificate. If you drive without one this could invalidate your

Mark one answer

- ❑ a vehicle service record
- ❑ b insurance
- ❑ c road tax disc
- ❑ d vehicle registration document

12.19

For which TWO of these must you show your motor insurance certificate?

Mark two answers

- ❑ a When you are taking your driving test
- ❑ b When buying or selling a vehicle
- ❑ c When a police officer asks you for it
- ❑ d When you are taxing your vehicle
- ❑ e When having an MOT inspection

12.16

How old must you be to supervise a learner driver?

Mark one answer

- ❑ a 18 years old
- ❑ b 19 years old
- ❑ c 20 years old
- ❑ d 21 years old

12.20

Vehicle excise duty is often called 'Road Tax' or 'The Tax Disc'. You must

Mark one answer

- ❑ a keep it with your registration document
- ❑ b display it clearly on your vehicle
- ❑ c keep it concealed safely in your vehicle
- ❑ d carry it on you at all times

12.21

Your vehicle needs a current MOT certificate. You do not have one. Until you do have one you will not be able to renew your
Mark one answer

- ❑ a driving licence
- ❑ b vehicle insurance
- ❑ c road tax disc
- ❑ d vehicle registration document

12.22

Which THREE pieces of information are found on a vehicle registration document?
Mark three answers

- ❑ a Registered keeper
- ❑ b Make of the vehicle
- ❑ c Service history details
- ❑ d Date of the MOT
- ❑ e Type of insurance cover
- ❑ f Engine size

12.23

You have a duty to contact the licensing authority when
Mark three answers

- ❑ a you go abroad on holiday
- ❑ b you change your vehicle
- ❑ c you change your name
- ❑ d your job status is changed
- ❑ e your permanent address changes
- ❑ f your job involves travelling abroad

12.24

You must notify the licensing authority when
Mark three answers

- ❑ a your health affects your driving
- ❑ b your eyesight does not meet a set standard
- ❑ c you intend lending your vehicle
- ❑ d your vehicle requires an MOT certificate
- ❑ e you change your vehicle

12.25

Your motor insurance policy has an excess of £100. What does this mean?
Mark one answer

- ❑ a The insurance company will pay the first £100 of any claim
- ❑ b You will be paid £100 if you do not have an accident
- ❑ c Your vehicle is insured for a value of £100 if it is stolen
- ❑ d You will have to pay the first £100 of any claim

Answers

12.13 c You are not allowed to drive until you have applied for and received your provisional licence and have signed it in ink.

12.14 c Your own vehicle insurance may cover you as a passenger in another person's vehicle but very rarely covers you to drive it.

12.15 b

12.16 d

12.17 d

12.18 c, d, e

12.19 c, d

12.20 b

12.21 c When you renew your road tax disc you must produce a valid certificate of insurance and also a current MOT certificate if your car is over three years old.

12.22 a, b, f

12.23 b, c, e

12.24 a, b, e

12.25 d Agreeing to pay an excess may enable you to obtain a lower premium.

12.26

When you apply to renew your vehicle excise licence (tax disc) you must produce
Mark one answer
- ❏ a a valid insurance certificate
- ❏ b the old tax disc
- ❏ c the vehicle handbook
- ❏ d a valid driving licence

12.27

Which THREE of the following do you need before you can drive legally?
Mark three answers
- ❏ a A valid driving licence with signature
- ❏ b A valid tax disc displayed on your vehicle
- ❏ c A vehicle service record
- ❏ d Proper insurance cover
- ❏ e Breakdown cover
- ❏ f A vehicle handbook

12.28

The cost of your insurance may reduce if you
Mark one answer
- ❏ a are under 25 years old
- ❏ b do not wear glasses
- ❏ c pass the driving test first time
- ❏ d take the Pass Plus scheme

12.29

Which of the following may reduce the cost of your insurance?
Mark one answer
- ❏ a Having a valid MOT certificate
- ❏ b Taking a Pass Plus course
- ❏ c Driving a powerful car
- ❏ d Having penalty points on your licence

12.30

To supervise a learner driver you must
Mark two answers
- ❏ a have held a full licence for at least 3 years
- ❏ b be at least 21 years old
- ❏ c be an approved driving instructor
- ❏ d hold an advanced driving certificate

12.31

When is it legal to drive a car over three years old without an MOT certificate?
Mark one answer
- ❏ a Up to seven days after the old certificate has run out
- ❏ b When driving to an MOT centre to arrange an appointment
- ❏ c Just after buying a second-hand car with no MOT
- ❏ d When driving to an appointment at an MOT centre

12.32

Motor cars must first have an MOT test certificate when they are
Mark one answer
- ❏ a one year old
- ❏ b three years old
- ❏ c five years old
- ❏ d seven years old

12.33

The Pass Plus scheme has been created for new drivers. What is its main purpose?
Mark one answer
- ❏ a To allow you to drive faster
- ❏ b To allow you to carry passengers
- ❏ c To improve your basic skills
- ❏ d To let you drive on motorways

12.34
Your vehicle is insured third party only.
This covers
Mark two answers
- ❑ a damage to your vehicle
- ❑ b damage to other vehicles
- ❑ c injury to yourself
- ❑ d injury to others
- ❑ e all damage and injury

12.35
What is the legal minimum insurance cover
you must have to drive on public roads?
Mark one answer
- ❑ a Third party, fire and theft
- ❑ b Comprehensive
- ❑ c Third party only
- ❑ d Personal injury cover

12.36
You claim on your insurance to have your car
repaired. Your policy has an excess of £100.
What does this mean?
Mark one answer
- ❑ a The insurance company will pay the first
     £100 of any claim
- ❑ b You will be paid £100 if you do not claim
     within one year
- ❑ c Your vehicle is insured for a value of
     £100 if it is stolen
- ❑ d You will have to pay the first £100 of
     the cost of repair to your car

12.37
The Pass Plus scheme is designed to
Mark one answer
- ❑ a give you a discount on your MOT
- ❑ b improve your basic driving skills
- ❑ c increase your mechanical knowledge
- ❑ d allow you to drive anyone else's vehicle

12.38
By taking part in the Pass Plus scheme
you will
Mark one answer
- ❑ a never get any points on your licence
- ❑ b be able to service your own car
- ❑ c allow you to drive anyone else's vehicle
- ❑ d improve your basic driving skills

Answers

12.26 a

12.27 a, b, d

12.28 d

12.29 b

12.30 a, b

12.31 d If your car is over three years old
and has no valid MOT certificate,
you must pre-book an
appointment at an MOT centre
before you drive it there.

12.32 b

12.33 c

12.34 b, d

12.35 c This only covers damage to other
people and their property.

12.36 d Most insurance companies offer
policies with an excess. As a
general rule, the higher the excess,
the lower the premium.

12.37 b The Pass Plus scheme is open to
anyone, who has passed their
driving test. It is designed to help
keep you safer on the roads.

12.38 d

12.39

Your motorcycle road tax is due to expire. As well as the renewal form and fee you will also need to produce an MOT (if required). What else will you need?

Mark one answer

❑ a Proof of purchase receipt
❑ b Compulsory Basic Training certificate
❑ c A valid certificate of insurance
❑ d The Vehicle Registration Document

12.40

A Vehicle Registration Document will show

Mark one answer

❑ a the service history
❑ b the year of first registration
❑ c the purchase price
❑ d the tyre sizes

12.41

What is the purpose of having a vehicle test certificate (MOT)?

Mark one answer

❑ a To make sure your motorcycle is roadworthy
❑ b To certify how many miles per gallon it does
❑ c To prove you own the motorcycle
❑ d To allow you to park in restricted areas

12.42

After passing your motorcycle test you must exchange the pass certificate for a full motorcycle licence within

Mark one answer

❑ a six months
❑ b one year
❑ c two years
❑ d five years

12.43

For which TWO of these must you show your motorcycle insurance certificate?

Mark two answers

❑ a When you are taking your motorcycle test
❑ b When buying or selling a machine
❑ c When a police officer asks you for it
❑ d When you are taxing your machine
❑ e When having an MOT inspection

12.44

Which of the following information is found on your motorcycle registration document?

Mark three answers

❑ a Make and model
❑ b Service history record
❑ c Ignition key security number
❑ d Engine size and number
❑ e Purchase price
❑ f Year of first registration

12.45

A theory test pass certificate is valid for

Mark one answer

❑ a two years
❑ b three years
❑ c four years
❑ d five years

12.46

Compulsory Basic Training (CBT) can only be carried out by

Mark one answer

❑ a any ADI (Approved Driving Instructor)
❑ b any road safety officer
❑ c any DSA (Driving Standards Agency) approved training body
❑ d any motorcycle main dealer

12.47

Before riding anyone else's motorcycle you should make sure that

Mark one answer

- ❑ a the owner has third party insurance cover
- ❑ b your own motorcycle has insurance cover
- ❑ c the motorcycle is insured for your use
- ❑ d the owner has the insurance documents with them

12.48

Vehicle excise duty is often called 'Road Tax' or 'The Tax Disc'. You must

Mark one answer

- ❑ a keep it with your registration document
- ❑ b display it clearly on your motorcycle
- ❑ c keep it concealed safely in your motorcycle
- ❑ d carry it on you at all times

12.49

Motorcycles must FIRST have an MOT test certificate when they are

Mark one answer

- ❑ a one year old
- ❑ b three years old
- ❑ c five years old
- ❑ d seven years old

12.50

Your motorcycle needs a current MOT certificate. You do not have one. Until you do have one you will not be able to renew your

Mark one answer

- ❑ a driving licence
- ❑ b motorcycle insurance
- ❑ c road tax disc
- ❑ d motorcycle registration document

12.51

Which THREE of the following do you need before you can ride legally?

Mark three answers

- ❑ a A valid driving licence with signature
- ❑ b A valid tax disc displayed on your motorcycle
- ❑ c Proof of your identity
- ❑ d Proper insurance cover
- ❑ e Breakdown cover
- ❑ f A vehicle handbook

12.52

Which THREE pieces of information are found on a registration document?

Mark three answers

- ❑ a Registered keeper
- ❑ b Make of the motorcycle
- ❑ c Service history details
- ❑ d Date of the MOT
- ❑ e Type of insurance cover
- ❑ f Engine size

Answers

12.39 c
12.40 b
12.41 a
12.42 c
12.43 c, d
12.44 a, d, f
12.45 a
12.46 c
12.47 c Your own motorbike insurance is very unlikely to cover you to ride another person's motorcycle.
12.48 b
12.49 b
12.50 c
12.51 a, b, d
12.52 a, b, f

12.53

You have a duty to contact the licensing authority when

Mark three answers

- ❑ a you go abroad on holiday
- ❑ b you change your motorcycle
- ❑ c you change your name
- ❑ d your job status is changed
- ❑ e your permanent address changes
- ❑ f your job involves travelling abroad

12.54

Your motorcycle is insured third party only. This covers

Mark two answers

- ❑ a damage to your motorcycle
- ❑ b damage to other vehicles
- ❑ c injury to yourself
- ❑ d injury to others
- ❑ e all damage and injury

12.55

Your motorcycle insurance policy has an excess of £100. What does this mean?

Mark one answer

- ❑ a The insurance company will pay the first £100 of any claim
- ❑ b You will be paid £100 if you do not have an accident
- ❑ c Your motorcycle is insured for a value of £100 if it is stolen
- ❑ d You will have to pay the first £100 of any claim

12.56

When you apply to renew your motorcycle excise licence (tax disc) you must produce

Mark one answer

- ❑ a a valid insurance certificate
- ❑ b the old tax disc
- ❑ c the motorcycle handbook
- ❑ d a valid driving licence

12.57

What is the legal minimum insurance cover you must have to ride on public roads?

Mark one answer

- ❑ a Third party, fire and theft
- ❑ b Fully comprehensive
- ❑ c Third party only
- ❑ d Personal injury cover

12.58

Before taking a practical motorcycle test you need

Mark one answer

- ❑ a a full moped licence
- ❑ b a full car licence
- ❑ c a CBT (Compulsory Basic Training) certificate
- ❑ d 12 months' riding experience

12.59

You must notify the licensing authority when

Mark three answers

- ❑ a your health affects your riding
- ❑ b your eyesight does not meet a set standard
- ❑ c you intend lending your motorcycle
- ❑ d your motorcycle requires an MOT certificate
- ❑ e you change your motorcycle

12.60

You have just passed your practical motorcycle test. This is your first full licence. Within two years you get six penalty points. You will have to

Mark two answers

- ❑ a retake only your theory test
- ❑ b retake your theory and practical tests
- ❑ c retake only your practical test
- ❑ d reapply for your full licence immediately
- ❑ e reapply for your provisional licence

12.61

You are a learner motorcyclist. The law states that you can carry a passenger when

Mark one answer

- ❏ a your motorcycle is no larger than 125 cc
- ❏ b your pillion passenger is a full licence-holder
- ❏ c you have passed your test for a full licence
- ❏ d you have had three years' experience of riding

12.62

You hold a provisional motorcycle licence. This means you must NOT

Mark three answers

- ❏ a exceed 30 mph
- ❏ b ride on a motorway
- ❏ c ride after dark
- ❏ d carry a pillion passenger
- ❏ e ride without L plates displayed

12.63

A full category A1 licence will allow you to ride a motorcycle up to

Mark one answer

- ❏ a 125 cc
- ❏ b 250 cc
- ❏ c 350 cc
- ❏ d 425 cc

12.64

Which one of these details would you expect to see on an MOT?

Mark one answer

- ❏ a Your name, address and telephone number
- ❏ b The vehicle registration and chassis number
- ❏ c The previous owners' details
- ❏ d The next due date for servicing

12.65

You want a licence to ride a large motorcycle via Direct Access. You will

Mark one answer

- ❏ a not require L plates if you have passed a car test
- ❏ b require L plates only when learning on your own machine
- ❏ c require L plates while learning with a qualified instructor
- ❏ d not require L plates if you have passed a moped test

12.66

A theory test pass certificate will not be valid after

Mark one answer

- ❏ a six months
- ❏ b one year
- ❏ c eighteen months
- ❏ d two years

Answers

12.53 b, c, e
12.54 b, d
12.55 d
12.56 a
12.57 c
12.58 c
12.59 a, b, e
12.60 b, e
12.61 c
12.62 b, d, e
12.63 a
12.64 b
12.65 c
12.66 d

12.67

A motorcyclist may only carry a pillion passenger when

Mark three answers

- ❏ a the rider has successfully completed CBT (Compulsory Basic Training)
- ❏ b the rider holds a full licence for the category of motorcycle
- ❏ c the motorcycle is fitted with rear footrest
- ❏ d the rider has a full car licence and is over 21
- ❏ e there is a proper passenger seat fitted
- ❏ f there is no sidecar fitted to the machine

12.68

You have a CBT (Compulsory Basic Training) certificate. How long is it valid?

Mark one answer

- ❏ a one year
- ❏ b two years
- ❏ c three years
- ❏ d four years

Answers

12.67 b, c, e
12.68 b

Theory Test Questions
for Car Drivers and Motorcyclists

Section 13　Accidents

13.1

At the scene of an accident you should

Mark one answer

- ❑ a not put yourself at risk
- ❑ b go to those casualties who are screaming
- ❑ c pull everybody out of their vehicles
- ❑ d leave vehicle engines switched on

13.2

You are the first to arrive at the scene of an accident. Which FOUR of these should you do?

Mark four answers

- ❑ a Leave as soon as another motorist arrives
- ❑ b Switch off the vehicle engine(s)
- ❑ c Move uninjured people away from the vehicle(s)
- ❑ d Call the emergency services
- ❑ e Warn other traffic

13.3

You are the first person to arrive at an accident where people are badly injured. Which THREE should you do?

Mark three answers

- ❑ a Switch on your own hazard warning lights
- ❑ b Make sure that someone telephones for an ambulance
- ❑ c Try and get people who are injured to drink something
- ❑ d Move the people who are injured clear of their vehicles
- ❑ e Get people who are not injured clear of the scene

13.4

You arrive at the scene of a motorcycle accident. The rider is injured. When should the helmet be removed?

Mark one answer

- ❑ a Only when it is essential
- ❑ b Always straight away
- ❑ c Only when the motorcyclist asks
- ❑ d Always, unless they are in shock

13.5

Which of the following should you NOT do at the scene of an accident?

Mark one answer

- ❑ a Warn other traffic by switching on your hazard warning lights
- ❑ b Call the emergency services immediately
- ❑ c Offer someone a cigarette to calm them down
- ❑ d Ask drivers to switch off their engines

13.6

You arrive at the scene of a motorcycle accident. No other vehicle is involved. The rider is unconscious, lying in the middle of the road. The first thing you should do is

Mark one answer

- ❑ a move the rider out of the road
- ❑ b warn other traffic
- ❑ c clear the road of debris
- ❑ d give the rider reassurance

13.7

At an accident a casualty is unconscious but still breathing. You should only move them if

Mark one answer

- ❑ a an ambulance is on its way
- ❑ b bystanders advise you to
- ❑ c there is further danger
- ❑ d bystanders will help you

13.8

At an accident you suspect a casualty has back injuries. The area is safe. You should

Mark one answer

- ❑ a offer them a drink
- ❑ b not move them
- ❑ c raise their legs
- ❑ d offer them a cigarette

13.9

At an accident it is important to look after the casualty. When the area is safe, you should
Mark one answer
- ❏ a get them out of the vehicle
- ❏ b give them a drink
- ❏ c give them something to eat
- ❏ d keep them in the vehicle

13.10

A tanker is involved in an accident. Which sign would show that the tanker is carrying dangerous goods?
Mark one answer

 a  LONG VEHICLE

 b 2YE 1089 Newtown-on-Moors 0181 645 2830

❏ c

❏ d

13.11

The police may ask you to produce which three of these documents following an accident?
Mark three answers
- ❏ a Vehicle registration document
- ❏ b Driving licence
- ❏ c Theory test certificate
- ❏ d Insurance certificate
- ❏ e MOT test certificate
- ❏ f Road tax disc

13.12

You see a car on the hard shoulder of a motorway with a HELP pennant displayed. This means the driver is most likely to be
Mark one answer
- ❏ a a disabled person
- ❏ b first aid trained
- ❏ c a foreign visitor
- ❏ d a rescue patrol person

13.13

For which TWO should you use hazard warning lights?
Mark two answers
- ❏ a When you slow down quickly on a motorway because of a hazard ahead
- ❏ b When you have broken down
- ❏ c When you wish to stop on double yellow lines
- ❏ d When you need to park on the pavement

Answers
13.1 a
13.2 b, c, d, e
13.3 a, b, e
13.4 a
13.5 c
13.6 b Note that this is the FIRST thing to do. By warning other traffic you help reduce the risk of more collisions.
13.7 c
13.8 b If you move the casualty you may worsen their injury.
13.9 d
13.10 b
13.11 b, d, e
13.12 a
13.13 a, b

13.14

When are you allowed to use hazard warning lights?

Mark one answer

❏ a When stopped and temporarily obstructing traffic

❏ b When travelling during darkness without headlights

❏ c When parked for shopping on double yellow lines

❏ d When travelling slowly because you are lost

13.15

You are on a motorway. A large box falls onto the road from a lorry. The lorry does not stop. You should

Mark one answer

❏ a go to the next emergency telephone and inform the police

❏ b catch up with the lorry and try to get the driver's attention

❏ c stop close to the box until the police arrive

❏ d pull over to the hard shoulder, then remove the box

13.16

On the motorway, the hard shoulder should be used

Mark one answer

❏ a to answer a mobile phone

❏ b when an emergency arises

❏ c for a short rest when tired

❏ d to check a road atlas

13.17

You are going through a congested tunnel and have to stop. What should you do?

Mark one answer

❏ a Pull up very close to the vehicle in front to save space

❏ b Ignore any message signs as they are never up to date

❏ c Keep a safe distance from the vehicle in front

❏ d Make a U-turn and find another route

13.18

You arrive at a serious motorcycle accident. The motorcyclist is unconscious and bleeding. Your main priorities should be to

Mark three answers

❏ a try to stop the bleeding

❏ b make a list of witnesses

❏ c check the casualty's breathing

❏ d take the numbers of the vehicles involved

❏ e sweep up any loose debris

❏ f check the casualty's airways

13.19

You arrive at an accident. A motorcyclist is unconscious. Your FIRST priority is the casualty's

Mark one answer

❏ a breathing

❏ b bleeding

❏ c broken bones

❏ d bruising

13.20

At an accident a casualty is unconscious. Which THREE of the following should you check urgently?

Mark three answers

❏ a Circulation

❏ b Airway

❏ c Shock

❏ d Breathing

❏ e Broken bones

13.21

You arrive at the scene of an accident. It has just happened and someone is unconscious. Which of the following should be given urgent priority to help them?

Mark three answers

- ❑ a Clear the airway and keep it open
- ❑ b Try to get them to drink water
- ❑ c Check that they are breathing
- ❑ d Look for any witnesses
- ❑ e Stop any heavy bleeding
- ❑ f Take the numbers of vehicles involved

13.22

At an accident someone is unconscious. Your main priorities should be to

Mark three answers

- ❑ a sweep up the broken glass
- ❑ b take the names of witnesses
- ❑ c count the number of vehicles involved
- ❑ d check the airway is clear
- ❑ e make sure they are breathing
- ❑ f stop any heavy bleeding

13.23

You have stopped at the scene of an accident to give help. Which THREE things should you do?

Mark three answers

- ❑ a Keep injured people warm and comfortable
- ❑ b Keep injured people calm by talking to them reassuringly
- ❑ c Keep injured people on the move by walking them around
- ❑ d Give injured people a warm drink
- ❑ e Make sure that injured people are not left alone

13.24

You arrive at the scene of an accident. It has just happened and someone is injured. Which THREE of the following should be given urgent priority?

Mark three answers

- ❑ a Stop any severe bleeding
- ❑ b Get them a warm drink
- ❑ c Check that their breathing is OK
- ❑ d Take numbers of vehicles involved
- ❑ e Look for witnesses
- ❑ f Clear their airway and keep it open

13.25

There has been an accident. The driver is suffering from shock. You should

Mark two answers

- ❑ a give them a drink
- ❑ b reassure them
- ❑ c not leave them alone
- ❑ d offer them a cigarette
- ❑ e ask who caused the accident

Answers

13.14 a
13.15 a
13.16 b
13.17 c
13.18 a, c, f Injuries should be dealt with in the order Airway, Breathing then Circulation and bleeding.
13.19 a
13.20 a, b, d
13.21 a, c, e Note that these are the things to which you should give urgent priority.
13.22 d, e, f
13.23 a, b, e You should not move injured people unless they are in danger; nor should you give them anything to drink.
13.24 a, c, f
13.25 b, c

13.26

You have to treat someone for shock at the scene of an accident. You should

Mark one answer

- ❑ a reassure them constantly
- ❑ b walk them around to calm them down
- ❑ c give them something cold to drink
- ❑ d cool them down as soon as possible

13.27

At an accident a small child is not breathing. When giving mouth-to-mouth you should breathe

Mark one answer

- ❑ a sharply
- ❑ b gently
- ❑ c heavily
- ❑ d rapidly

13.28

When you are giving mouth-to-mouth you should only stop when

Mark one answer

- ❑ a you think the casualty is dead
- ❑ b the casualty can breathe without help
- ❑ c the casualty has turned blue
- ❑ d you think the ambulance is coming

13.29

You arrive at the scene of an accident. There has been an engine fire and someone's hands and arms have been burnt. You should NOT

Mark one answer

- ❑ a douse the burn thoroughly with cool liquid
- ❑ b lay the casualty down
- ❑ c remove anything sticking to the burn
- ❑ d reassure them constantly

13.30

You arrive at an accident where someone is suffering from severe burns. You should

Mark one answer

- ❑ a apply lotions to the injury
- ❑ b burst any blisters
- ❑ c remove anything stuck to the burns
- ❑ d douse the burns with cool liquid

13.31

You arrive at the scene of an accident. A pedestrian has a severe bleeding wound on their leg, although it is not broken. What should you do?

Mark two answers

- ❑ a Dab the wound to stop bleeding
- ❑ b Keep both legs flat on the ground
- ❑ c Apply firm pressure to the wound
- ❑ d Raise the leg to lessen bleeding
- ❑ e Fetch them a warm drink

13.32

You arrive at the scene of an accident. A passenger is bleeding badly from an arm wound. What should you do?

Mark one answer

- ❑ a Apply pressure over the wound and keep the arm down
- ❑ b Dab the wound
- ❑ c Get them a drink
- ❑ d Apply pressure over the wound and raise the arm

13.33

You arrive at the scene of an accident. A pedestrian is bleeding heavily from a leg wound but the leg is not broken. What should you do?

Mark one answer

- ❑ a Dab the wound to stop the bleeding
- ❑ b Keep both legs flat on the ground
- ❑ c Apply firm pressure to the wound
- ❑ d Fetch them a warm drink

13.34

After an accident, someone is unconscious in their vehicle. When should you call the emergency services?

Mark one answer

❑ a Only as a last resort
❑ b As soon as possible
❑ c After you have woken them up
❑ d After checking for broken bones

13.35

An accident casualty has an injured arm. They can move it freely, but it is bleeding. Why should you get them to keep it in a raised position?

Mark one answer

❑ a Because it will ease the pain
❑ b It will help them to be seen more easily
❑ c To stop them touching other people
❑ d It will help to reduce the bleeding

13.36

You are going through a tunnel. What should you look out for that warns of accidents or congestion?

Mark one answer

❑ a Hazard warning lines
❑ b Other drivers flashing their lights
❑ c Variable message signs
❑ d Areas marked with hatch markings

13.37

You are going through a tunnel. What systems are provided to warn of any accidents or congestion?

Mark one answer

❑ a Double white centre lines
❑ b Variable message signs
❑ c Chevron distance markers
❑ d Rumble strips

13.38

An accident has just happened. An injured person is lying in a busy road. What is the FIRST thing you should do to help?

Mark one answer

❑ a Treat the person for shock
❑ b Warn other traffic
❑ c Place them in the recovery position
❑ d Make sure the injured person is kept warm

13.39

At an accident a casualty has stopped breathing. You should

Mark two answers

❑ a remove anything that is blocking the mouth
❑ b keep the head tilted forwards as far as possible
❑ c raise the legs to help with circulation
❑ d try to give the casualty something to drink
❑ e tilt the head back gently to clear the airway

Answers

13.26 a
13.27 b
13.28 b
13.29 c
13.30 d
13.31 c, d
13.32 d
13.33 c
13.34 b
13.35 d
13.36 c
13.37 b
13.38 b Warning other traffic first helps stop the accident getting even worse.
13.39 a, e

13.40

You are at the scene of an accident.
Someone is suffering from shock. You should
Mark four answers
- □ a reassure them constantly
- □ b offer them a cigarette
- □ c keep them warm
- □ d avoid moving them if possible
- □ e avoid leaving them alone
- □ f give them a warm drink

13.41

To start mouth to mouth on a casualty you
should
Mark three answers
- □ a tilt their head forward
- □ b clear the airway
- □ c turn them on their side
- □ d tilt their head back gently
- □ e pinch the nostrils together
- □ f put their arms across their chest

13.42

There has been an accident. A motorcyclist
is lying injured and unconscious. Unless it's
essential, why should you usually not attempt
to remove their helmet?
Mark one answer
- □ a Because they may not want you to
- □ b This could result in more serious injury
- □ c They will get too cold if you do this
- □ d Because you could scratch the helmet

13.43

You have broken down on a two-way road.
You have a warning triangle. You should place
the warning triangle at least how far from your
vehicle?

Mark one answer
- □ a 5 metres (16 feet)
- □ b 25 metres (82 feet)
- □ c 45 metres (147 feet)
- □ d 100 metres (328 feet)

13.44

You break down on a level crossing. The lights
have not yet begun to flash. Which THREE
things should you do?
Mark three answers
- □ a Telephone the signal operator
- □ b Leave your vehicle and get everyone clear
- □ c Walk down the track and signal the next
       train
- □ d Move the vehicle if a signal operator tells
       you to
- □ e Tell drivers behind what has happened

13.45

Your vehicle has broken down on an
automatic railway level crossing. What should
you do FIRST?
Mark one answer
- □ a Get everyone out of the vehicle and clear
       of the crossing
- □ b Phone the signal operator so that trains
       can be stopped
- □ c Walk along the track to give warning
       to any approaching trains
- □ d Try to push the vehicle clear of the
       crossing as soon as possible

13.46
Your tyre bursts while you are driving.
Which TWO things should you do?
Mark two answers
- a Pull on the handbrake
- b Brake as quickly as possible
- c Pull up slowly at the side of the road
- d Hold the steering wheel firmly to keep control
- e Continue on at a normal speed

13.47
Which TWO things should you do when a front tyre bursts?
Mark two answers
- a Apply the handbrake to stop the vehicle
- b Brake firmly and quickly
- c Let the vehicle roll to a stop
- d Hold the steering wheel lightly
- e Grip the steering wheel firmly

13.48
Your vehicle has a puncture on a motorway.
What should you do?
Mark one answer
- a Drive slowly to the next service area to get assistance
- b Pull up on the hard shoulder. Change the wheel as quickly as possible
- c Pull up on the hard shoulder. Use the emergency phone to get assistance
- d Switch on your hazard lights. Stop in your lane

13.49
Which of these items should you carry in your vehicle for use in the event of an accident?
Mark three answers
- a Road map
- b Can of petrol
- c Jump leads
- d Fire extinguisher
- e First Aid kit
- f Warning triangle

13.50
You have stalled in the middle of a level crossing and cannot restart the engine.
The warning bell starts to ring. You should
Mark one answer
- a get out and clear of the crossing
- b run down the track to warn the signal operator
- c carry on trying to restart the engine
- d push the vehicle clear of the crossing

Answers

13.40 a, c, d, e
13.41 b, d, e
13.42 b
13.43 c 45 metres is recommended on two-way roads and 150 metres on a dual carriageway. You should not use a warning triangle on a motorway; it is too dangerous.
13.44 a, b, d
13.45 a Your first action is to get everyone to safety.
13.46 c, d You will need both hands firmly on the wheel in order to control the car, and using the gears or brakes is likely to make your car swerve. When possible, it is safest just to let your car roll to a halt at the side of the road.
13.47 c, e
13.48 c The hard shoulder of a motorway is a dangerous place and 'c' is the safest course of action. It can be particularly dangerous to try to change an offside wheel as you may be very close to fast-moving traffic in the left-hand lane.
13.49 d, e, f
13.50 a A train may arrive within seconds so 'a' is the only safe possibility.

13.51

You are on a motorway. When can you use hazard warning lights?

Mark two answers

- ☐ a When a vehicle is following too closely
- ☐ b When you slow down quickly because of danger ahead
- ☐ c When you are towing another vehicle
- ☐ d When driving on the hard shoulder
- ☐ e When you have broken down on the hard shoulder

13.52

You are involved in an accident with another vehicle. Someone is injured. Your vehicle is damaged. Which FOUR of the following should you find out?

Mark four answers

- ☐ a Whether the driver owns the other vehicle involved
- ☐ b The other driver's name, address and telephone number
- ☐ c The make and registration number of the other vehicle
- ☐ d The occupation of the other driver
- ☐ e The details of the other driver's vehicle insurance
- ☐ f Whether the other driver is licensed to drive

13.53

You have broken down on a motorway. When you use the emergency telephone you will be asked

Mark three answers

- ☐ a for the number on the telephone that you are using
- ☐ b for your driving licence details
- ☐ c for the name of your vehicle insurance company
- ☐ d for details of yourself and your vehicle
- ☐ e whether you belong to a motoring organisation

13.54

You lose control of your car and damage a garden wall. No one is around. What must you do?

Mark one answer

- ☐ a Report the accident to the police within 24 hours
- ☐ b Go back to tell the house owner the next day
- ☐ c Report the accident to your insurance company when you get home
- ☐ d Find someone in the area to tell them about it immediately

13.55

Before driving through a tunnel what should you do?

Mark one answer

- ☐ a Switch your radio off
- ☐ b Remove any sunglasses
- ☐ c Close your sunroof
- ☐ d Switch on windscreen wipers

13.56

You are driving through a tunnel and the traffic is flowing normally. What should you do?

Mark one answer

- ☐ a Use parking lights
- ☐ b Use front spot lights
- ☐ c Use dipped headlights
- ☐ d Use rear fog lights

13.57

Before entering a tunnel it is good advice to

Mark one answer

- ☐ a put on your sunglasses
- ☐ b check tyre pressures
- ☐ c change to a lower gear
- ☐ d tune your radio to a local channel

13.58
You are driving through a tunnel. Your vehicle breaks down. What should you do?

Mark one answer
- ❑ a Switch on hazard warning lights
- ❑ b Remain in your vehicle
- ❑ c Wait for the police to find you
- ❑ d Rely on CCTV cameras seeing you

13.59
When driving through a tunnel you should

Mark one answer
- ❑ a Look out for variable message signs
- ❑ b Use your air conditioning system
- ❑ c Switch on your rear fog lights
- ❑ d Always use your windscreen wipers

13.60
What TWO safeguards could you take against fire risk to your vehicle?

Mark two answers
- ❑ a Keep water levels above maximum
- ❑ b Carry a fire extinguisher
- ❑ c Avoid driving with a full tank of petrol
- ❑ d Use unleaded petrol
- ❑ e Check out any strong smell of petrol
- ❑ f Use low octane fuel

13.61
You are on the motorway. Luggage falls from your vehicle. What should you do?

Mark one answer
- ❑ a Stop at the next emergency telephone and contact the police
- ❑ b Stop on the motorway and put on hazard lights while you pick it up
- ❑ c Walk back up the motorway to pick it up
- ❑ d Pull up on the hard shoulder and wave traffic down

13.62
While driving, a warning light on your vehicle's instrument panel comes on. You should

Mark one answer
- ❑ a continue if the engine sounds all right
- ❑ b hope that it is just a temporary electrical fault
- ❑ c deal with the problem when there is more time
- ❑ d check out the problem quickly and safely

13.63
You are in an accident on a two-way road. You have a warning triangle with you. At what distance before the obstruction should you place the warning triangle?

Mark one answer
- ❑ a 25 metres (82 feet)
- ❑ b 45 metres (147 feet)
- ❑ c 100 metres (328 feet)
- ❑ d 150 metres (492 feet)

Answers

13.51 b, e
13.52 a, b, c, e
13.53 a, d, e
13.54 a
13.55 b
13.56 c
13.57 d Local radio could inform you of any breakdowns and congestion in the tunnel.
13.58 a
13.59 a
13.60 b, e
13.61 a
13.62 d
13.63 b

13.64

You have broken down on a two-way road. You have a warning triangle. It should be displayed

Mark one answer
- ❏ a on the roof of your vehicle
- ❏ b at least 150 metres (492 feet) behind your vehicle
- ❏ c at least 45 metres (147 feet) behind your vehicle
- ❏ d just behind your vehicle

13.65

Your engine catches fire. What should you do first?

Mark one answer
- ❏ a Lift the bonnet and disconnect the battery
- ❏ b Lift the bonnet and warn other traffic
- ❏ c Call a breakdown service
- ❏ d Call the fire brigade

13.66

Your vehicle breaks down in a tunnel. What should you do?

Mark one answer
- ❏ a Stay in your vehicle and wait for the police
- ❏ b Stand in the lane behind your vehicle to warn others
- ❏ c Stand in front of your vehicle to warn oncoming drivers
- ❏ d Switch on hazard lights then go and call for help immediately

13.67

You have an accident while driving through a tunnel. You are not injured but your vehicle cannot be driven. What should you do first?

Mark one answer
- ❏ a Rely on other drivers phoning for the police
- ❏ b Switch off the engine and switch on hazard lights
- ❏ c Take the names of witnesses and other drivers
- ❏ d Sweep up any debris that is in the road

13.68

Your vehicle catches fire while driving through a tunnel. It is still driveable. What should you do?

Mark one answer
- ❏ a Leave it where it is with the engine running
- ❏ b Pull up, then walk to an emergency telephone point
- ❏ c Park it away from the carriageway
- ❏ d Drive it out of the tunnel if you can do so

13.69

You are driving through a tunnel. Your vehicle catches fire. What should you do?

Mark one answer
- ❏ a Continue through the tunnel if you can
- ❏ b Turn your vehicle around immediately
- ❏ c Reverse out of the tunnel
- ❏ d Carry out an emergency stop

13.70

You are in a tunnel. Your vehicle is on fire and you CANNOT drive it. What should you do?

Mark two answers
- ❏ a Stay in the vehicle and close the windows
- ❏ b Switch on hazard warning lights
- ❏ c Leave the engine running
- ❏ d Try and put out the fire
- ❏ e Switch off all of your lights
- ❏ f Wait for other people to phone for help

13.71

You are driving through a tunnel. There has been an accident and the car in front is on fire and blocking the road. What should you do?

Mark one answer

- ❑ a Overtake and continue as quickly as you can
- ❑ b Lock all the doors and windows
- ❑ c Switch on hazard warning lights
- ❑ d Stop, then reverse out of the tunnel

13.72

Your motorcycle has broken down on a motorway. How will you know the direction of the nearest emergency telephone?

Mark one answer

- ❑ a By walking with the flow of traffic
- ❑ b By following an arrow on a marker post
- ❑ c By walking against the flow of traffic
- ❑ d By remembering where the last phone was

13.73

You are travelling on a motorway. A bag falls from your motorcycle. There are valuables in the bag. What should you do?

Mark one answer

- ❑ a Go back carefully and collect the bag as quickly as possible
- ❑ b Stop wherever you are and pick up the bag, but only when there is a safe gap
- ❑ c Stop on the hard shoulder and use the emergency telephone to inform the police
- ❑ d Stop on the hard shoulder and then retrieve the bag yourself

13.74

You should use the engine cut-out switch to

Mark one answer

- ❑ a stop the engine in an emergency
- ❑ b stop the engine on short journeys
- ❑ c save wear on the ignition switch
- ❑ d start the engine if you lose the key

13.75

You are riding on a motorway. The car in front switches on its hazard warning lights while moving. This means

Mark one answer

- ❑ a they are going to take the next exit
- ❑ b there is a danger ahead
- ❑ c there is a police car in the left lane
- ❑ d they are trying to change lanes

13.76

You are on the motorway. Luggage falls from your motorcycle. What should you do?

Mark one answer

- ❑ a Stop at the next emergency telephone and contact the police
- ❑ b Stop on the motorway and put on hazard lights whilst you pick it up
- ❑ c Walk back up the motorway to pick it up
- ❑ d Pull up on the hard shoulder and wave traffic down

Answers

13.64 c
13.65 d
13.66 d
13.67 b
13.68 d
13.69 a
13.70 b, d
13.71 c You cannot drive out of the tunnel. The safest thing to do is to switch on your hazard warning lights which alerts following drivers to the hazard ahead and the need to slow down and stop.
13.72 b
13.73 c It would be extremely dangerous to try to retrieve the bag yourself.
13.74 a
13.75 b
13.76 a

13.77

You are involved in an accident with another vehicle. Someone is injured. Your motorcycle is damaged. Which FOUR of the following should you find out?

Mark four answers

☐ a Whether the driver owns the other vehicle involved
☐ b The other driver's name, address and telephone number
☐ c The make and registration number of the other vehicle
☐ d The occupation of the other driver
☐ e The details of the other driver's vehicle insurance
☐ f Whether the other driver is licensed to drive

13.78

You have broken down on a motorway. When you use the emergency telephone you will be asked

Mark three answers

☐ a for the number on the telephone that you are using
☐ b for your driving licence details
☐ c for the name of your vehicle insurance company
☐ d for details of yourself and your motorcycle
☐ e whether you belong to a motoring organisation

13.79

You are on a motorway. When can you use hazard warning lights?

Mark one answer

☐ a When a vehicle is following too closely
☐ b When you slow down quickly because of danger ahead
☐ c When you are being towed by another vehicle
☐ d When riding on the hard shoulder

13.80

Your motorcycle breaks down in a tunnel. What should you do?

Mark one answer

☐ a Stay with your motorcycle and wait for the Police
☐ b Stand in the lane behind your motorcycle to warn others
☐ c Stand in front of your motorcycle to warn oncoming drivers
☐ d Switch on hazard lights then go and call for help immediately

13.81

You are riding through a tunnel. Your motorcycle breaks down. What should you do?

Mark one answer

☐ a Switch on hazard warning lights
☐ b Remain on your motorcycle
☐ c Wait for the police to find you
☐ d Rely on CCTV cameras seeing you

13.82

You are involved in an accident. How can you reduce the risk of fire to your motorcycle?

Mark one answer

☐ a Keep the engine running
☐ b Open the choke
☐ c Turn the fuel tap to reserve
☐ d Use the engine cut-out switch

Answers

13.77 a, b, c, e
13.78 a, d, e
13.79 b
13.80 d
13.81 a
13.82 d

Theory Test Questions
for Car Drivers and Motorcyclists

Section 14 Vehicle and motorcycle loading

14.1

You are towing a small trailer on a busy three-lane motorway. All the lanes are open. You must

Mark two answers

- ❑ a not exceed 60 mph
- ❑ b not overtake
- ❑ c have a stabiliser fitted
- ❑ d use only the left and centre lanes

14.2

If a trailer swerves or snakes when you are towing it you should

Mark one answer

- ❑ a ease off the accelerator and reduce your speed
- ❑ b let go of the steering wheel and let it correct itself
- ❑ c brake hard and hold the pedal down
- ❑ d increase your speed as quickly as possible

14.3

How can you stop a caravan snaking from side to side?

Mark one answer

- ❑ a Turn the steering wheel slowly to each side
- ❑ b Accelerate to increase your speed
- ❑ c Stop as quickly as you can
- ❑ d Slow down very gradually

14.4

On which TWO occasions might you inflate your tyres to more than the recommended normal pressure?

Mark two answers

- ❑ a When the roads are slippery
- ❑ b When driving fast for a long distance
- ❑ c When the tyre tread is worn below 2mm
- ❑ d When carrying a heavy load
- ❑ e When the weather is cold
- ❑ f When the vehicle is fitted with anti-lock brakes

14.5

A heavy load on your roof rack will

Mark one answer

- ❑ a improve the road holding
- ❑ b reduce the stopping distance
- ❑ c make the steering lighter
- ❑ d reduce stability

14.6

You are towing a caravan along a motorway. The caravan begins to swerve from side to side. What should you do?

Mark one answer

- ❑ a Ease off the accelerator slowly
- ❑ b Steer sharply from side to side
- ❑ c Do an emergency stop
- ❑ d Speed up very quickly

14.7

Overloading your vehicle can seriously affect the

Mark two answers

- ❑ a gearbox
- ❑ b steering
- ❑ c handling
- ❑ d battery life
- ❑ e journey time

14.8

Who is responsible for making sure that a vehicle is not overloaded?

Mark one answer

- ❑ a The driver of the vehicle
- ❑ b The owner of the items being carried
- ❑ c The person who loaded the vehicle
- ❑ d The licensing authority

14.9

Which of these is a suitable restraint for a child under three years?

Mark one answer

- ❑ a A child seat
- ❑ b An adult holding a child
- ❑ c An adult seat belt
- ❑ d A lap belt

14.10

A child under three years is being carried in your vehicle. They should be secured in a restraint. Which of these is suitable?

Mark one answer

- ❑ a An adult holding a child
- ❑ b A lap belt
- ❑ c A baby carrier
- ❑ d An adult seat belt

14.11

You are planning to tow a caravan. Which of these will mostly help to aid the vehicle handling?

Mark one answer

- ❑ a A jockey wheel fitted to the towbar
- ❑ b Power steering fitted to the towing vehicle
- ❑ c Anti-lock brakes fitted to the towing vehicle
- ❑ d A stabiliser fitted to the towbar

14.12

Are passengers allowed to ride in a caravan that is being towed?

Mark one answer

- ❑ a Yes, if they are over fourteen
- ❑ b No, not at any time
- ❑ c Only if all the seats in the towing vehicle are full
- ❑ d Only if a stabiliser is fitted

14.13

A trailer must stay securely hitched up to the towing vehicle. What additional safety device can be fitted to the trailer braking system?

Mark one answer

- ❑ a Stabiliser
- ❑ b Jockey wheel
- ❑ c Corner steadies
- ❑ d Breakaway cable

Answers

14.1	a, d
14.2	a Options 'b', 'c' or 'd' would all be likely to make the problem worse.
14.3	d
14.4	b, d
14.5	d A heavy load on the roof will shift the centre of gravity of your vehicle and could make you more likely to skid or roll over.
14.6	a
14.7	b, c
14.8	a
14.9	a
14.10	c
14.11	d
14.12	b
14.13	d

14.14

Why would you fit a stabiliser before towing a caravan?

Mark one answer

- ❑ a It will help with stability when driving in crosswinds
- ❑ b It will allow heavy items to be loaded behind the axle
- ❑ c It will help you to raise and lower the jockey wheel
- ❑ d It will allow you to tow without the breakaway cable

14.15

You wish to tow a trailer. Where would you find the maximum noseweight of your vehicle's tow ball?

Mark one answer

- ❑ a In the vehicle handbook
- ❑ b In The Highway Code
- ❑ c In your vehicle registration certificate
- ❑ d In your licence documents

14.16

Any load that is carried on a roof rack should be

Mark one answer

- ❑ a securely fastened when driving
- ❑ b loaded towards the rear of the vehicle
- ❑ c visible in your exterior mirror
- ❑ d covered with plastic sheeting

14.17

If a trailer swerves or snakes when you are towing it you should

Mark one answer

- ❑ a ease off the throttle and reduce your speed
- ❑ b let go of the handlebars and let it correct itself
- ❑ c brake hard and hold the brake on
- ❑ d increase your speed as quickly as possible

14.18

When riding with a sidecar attached for the first time you should

Mark two answers

- ❑ a keep your speed down
- ❑ b be able to stop more quickly
- ❑ c accelerate quickly round bends
- ❑ d approach corners more carefully

14.19

When may a learner motorcyclist carry a pillion passenger?

Mark one answer

- ❑ a If the passenger holds a full licence
- ❑ b Not at any time
- ❑ c If the rider is undergoing training
- ❑ d If the passenger is over 21

14.20

When carrying extra weight on a motorcycle, you may need to make adjustments to the

Mark three answers

- ❑ a headlight
- ❑ b gears
- ❑ c suspension
- ❑ d tyres
- ❑ e footrests

14.21

To obtain the full category 'A' licence through the accelerated or direct access scheme, your motorcycle must be
Mark one answer
- ❏ a solo with maximum power 25kw (33 bhp)
- ❏ b solo with maximum power of 11kw (14.6 bhp)
- ❏ c fitted with a sidecar and have minimum power of 35kw (46.6 bhp)
- ❏ d solo with minimum power of 35 kw (46.6 bhp)

14.22

Any load that is carried on a luggage rack MUST be
Mark one answer
- ❏ a securely fastened when riding
- ❏ b carried only when strictly necessary
- ❏ c visible when you are riding
- ❏ d covered with plastic sheeting

14.23

Pillion passengers should
Mark one answer
- ❏ a have a provisional motorcycle licence
- ❏ b be lighter than the rider
- ❏ c always wear a helmet
- ❏ d signal for the rider

14.24

Pillion passengers should
Mark one answer
- ❏ a give the rider directions
- ❏ b lean with the rider when going round bends
- ❏ c check the road behind for the rider
- ❏ d give arm signals for the rider

14.25

When you are going around a corner your pillion passenger should
Mark one answer
- ❏ a give arm signals for you
- ❏ b check behind for other vehicles
- ❏ c lean with you on bends
- ❏ d lean to one side to see ahead

Answers

14.14 a A good stabiliser can make the combination easier to handle, however, it does not relieve you of the responsibility of correct loading.

14.15 a The noseweight can be measured by using a gauge available from caravan accessory stockists.

14.16 a

14.17 a

14.18 a, d You will need to adapt your riding technique when riding a bike with a sidecar, particularly on bends and when turning. The combination must be steered because you cannot lean the machine over.

14.19 b

14.20 a, c, d

14.21 d

14.22 a

14.23 c

14.24 b

14.25 c

14.26

Which of these may need to be adjusted when carrying a pillion passenger?

Mark one answer

- a Indicators
- b Exhaust
- c Fairing
- d Headlight

14.27

You are towing a trailer with your motorcycle. You should remember that your

Mark one answer

- a stopping distance may increase
- b fuel consumption will improve
- c tyre grip will increase
- d stability will improve

14.28

Heavy loads in a motorcycle top box may

Mark one answer

- a improve stability
- b cause low-speed wobble
- c cause a puncture
- d improve braking

14.29

You are entering a bend. Your side stand is not fully raised. This could

Mark one answer

- a cause an accident
- b improve your balance
- c alter the motorcycle's centre of gravity
- d make the motorcycle more stable

14.30

Overloading your motorcycle can seriously affect the

Mark two answers

- a gearbox
- b steering
- c handling
- d battery life
- e journey time

14.31

Who is responsible for making sure that a motorcycle is not overloaded?

Mark one answer

- a The rider of the motorcycle
- b The owner of the items being carried
- c The licensing authority
- d The owner of the motorcycle

14.32

Before fitting a sidecar to a motorcycle you should

Mark one answer

- a have the wheels balanced
- b have the engine tuned
- c pass the extended bike test
- d check that the motorcycle is suitable

14.33

You are using throwover saddlebags.
Why is it important to make sure they are
evenly loaded?

Mark one answer

❑ a They will be uncomfortable for you
to sit on
❑ b They will slow your motorcycle down
❑ c They could make your motorcycle
unstable
❑ d They will be uncomfortable for a pillion
passenger to sit on

14.34

You are carrying a bulky tank bag.
What could this affect?

Mark one answer

❑ a Your ability to steer
❑ b Your ability to accelerate
❑ c Your view ahead
❑ d Your insurance premium

14.35

To carry a pillion passenger you must

Mark one answer

❑ a hold a full car licence
❑ b hold a full motorcycle licence
❑ c be over the age of 21
❑ d be over the age of 25

14.36

When carrying a heavy load on your
luggage rack, you may need to adjust your

Mark one answer

❑ a carburettor
❑ b fuel tap
❑ c seating position
❑ d tyre pressures

14.37

You are carrying a pillion passenger. When
following other traffic, which of the following
should you do?

Mark one answer

❑ a Keep to your normal following distance
❑ b Get your passenger to keep checking
behind
❑ c Keep further back than you normally
would
❑ d Get your passenger to signal for you

14.38

You should only carry a child as a pillion
passenger when

Mark one answer

❑ a they are over 14 years old
❑ b they are over 16 years old
❑ c they can reach the floor from the seat
❑ d they can reach the handholds and
footrests

Answers

14.26　d
14.27　a
14.28　b
14.29　a Riding with the side stand down
could cause an accident
particularly when cornering
because the side stand could hit
the ground.
14.30　b, c
14.31　a
14.32　d
14.33　c
14.34　a
14.35　b
14.36　d
14.37　c
14.38　d

14.39

You have fitted a sidecar to your motorcycle.
You should make sure that the sidecar

Mark one answer

☐ a has a registration plate
☐ b is correctly aligned
☐ c has a waterproof cover
☐ d has a solid cover

14.40

You are riding a motorcycle and sidecar.
The extra weight

Mark one answer

☐ a will allow you to corner more quickly
☐ b will allow you to brake later for hazards
☐ c may increase your stopping distance
☐ d will improve your fuel consumption

14.41

You are carrying a pillion passenger. To allow
for the extra weight which of the following is
most likely to need adjustment?

Mark one answer

☐ a Preload on the front forks
☐ b Preload on the rear shock absorber(s)
☐ c The balance of the rear wheel
☐ d The front and rear wheel alignment

14.42

You want to tow a trailer with your motorcycle.
Which one applies?

Mark one answer

☐ a The motorcycle should be attached to
a sidecar
☐ b The trailer should weigh more than the
motorcycle
☐ c The trailer should be fitted with brakes
☐ d The trailer should NOT be more than
1 metre (3 feet 3 inches) wide

14.43

A trailer on a motorcycle must be no wider
than

Mark one answer

☐ a 0.5 metres (1 foot 8 inches)
☐ b 1 metre (3 feet 3 inches)
☐ c 1.5 metres (4 feet 11inches)
☐ d 2 metres (6 feet 6 inches)

14.44

You have a sidecar fitted to your motorcycle.
What effect will it have?

Mark one answer

☐ a Reduce stability
☐ b Make steering lighter
☐ c Increase stopping distance
☐ d Increase fuel economy

14.45

Which THREE must a learner motorcyclist
under 21 NOT do?

Mark three answers

☐ a Ride a motorcycle with an engine
capacity greater than 125 cc
☐ b Pull a trailer
☐ c Carry a pillion passenger
☐ d Ride faster than 30 mph
☐ e Use the right-hand lane on dual
carriageways

14.46

Carrying a heavy load in your top box may

Mark one answer
- ❑ a cause high speed-weave
- ❑ b cause a puncture
- ❑ c use less fuel
- ❑ d improve stability

14.47

You want to tow a trailer behind your motorcycle. You should
Mark two answers
- ❑ a display a 'long vehicle' sign
- ❑ b fit a larger battery
- ❑ c have a full motorcycle licence
- ❑ d ensure that your engine is more than 125 cc
- ❑ e ensure that your motorcycle has shaft drive

14.48

To carry a pillion passenger your motorcycle should be fitted with
Mark two answers
- ❑ a rear footrests
- ❑ b an engine of 250 cc or over
- ❑ c a top box
- ❑ d a grab handle
- ❑ e a proper pillion seat

14.49

Your motorcycle is fitted with a top box. It is unwise to carry a heavy load in the top box because it may
Mark three answers
- ❑ a reduce stability
- ❑ b improve stability
- ❑ c make turning easier
- ❑ d cause high-speed weave
- ❑ e cause low-speed wobble
- ❑ f increase fuel economy

Answers

14.39	b
14.40	c
14.41	b
14.42	d Also, the laden weight of the trailer must not exceed 150kg or two-thirds of the weight of the motorcycle, whichever is less.
14.43	b
14.44	c The sidecar is extra weight and is likely to increase your overall stopping distance.
14.45	a, b, c
14.46	a
14.47	c, d
14.48	a, e
14.49	a, d, e